KINGSHIP AND THE PSALMS

STUDIES IN BIBLICAL THEOLOGY

A series of monographs designed to provide the best work in biblical scholarship both in this country and abroad

Advisory Editors:

STUDIES IN BIBLICAL THEOLOGY

Second Series . 32

KINGSHIP
AND THE PSALMS

J. H. EATON

ALEC R. ALLENSON INC.
635 EAST OGDEN AVENUE
NAPERVILLE, ILL.

© *SCM Press Ltd*
ISBN 0-8401-3082-1

Published by Alec R. Allenson Inc.
Naperville, Ill.
Printed in Great Britain

In memory of
F. M. LEMOINE O.P.
† 1975
École Biblique, Jerusalem

Thou art in my heart;
there is none other that knows thee
save thy son Akhenaten.

Egyptian hymn

Thou shalt guide me with thy counsel
and after that receive me with glory.
God is the strength of my heart
and my portion for ever.

Psalm 73.24, 26

O what great troubles and adversities
    hast thou showed me,
and yet didst thou turn and refresh me,
yea, and broughtest me from the deep of the earth again.

Psalm 71.20

CONTENTS

Preface   ix

Abbreviations   xi

I   HOW MANY PSALMS ARE ROYAL?
    GENERAL ARGUMENTS
    1   The aim of the enquiry   1
    2   The weakness of Gunkel's position   2
    3   The weakness of institutional non-royal theories   5
    4   The growth of royal interpretations   11
    5   General arguments for extensive royal interpretation   20

II PARTICULAR PSALMS
    1   Psalms with clearly royal content   27
        Pss. 3; 4; 7; 9–10; 17; 22; 23; 27; 28; 35; 40; 41; 57;
        59; 61; 62; 63; 66; 69; 70; 71; 75; 89; 91; 92; 94; 108
        (cf. 44, 60, 74, 80, 83, 84); 118; 138; 140; 143
    2   Less clear cases   64
        Pss. 5; 11; 16; 31; 36; 42–3; 51; 52; 54; 55; 56; 73;
        77; 86; 102; 109; 116; 120; 121; 139; 141; 142.
    3   Psalms not to be used   85

III THE ROYAL RITES
    1   Rites of new year and enthronement outside Israel
        (a) Mesopotamia   87
        (b) Egypt   96
        (c) Hittites   100
        (d) Canaanites   101
    2   The Israelite autumn festival as clarified by
        Mowinckel
        (a) The chief annual festival   102
        (b) The celebration of Yahweh's kingship   105
        (c) The dramatic character of the celebration   108
        (d) The involvement of the Davidic kingship   109
    3   The interpretation of Gunkel's 'Royal Psalms'   111
        Pss. 2; 18; 20; 21; 45; 72; 89; 101; 110; 132; 144
    4   The setting of the king's psalms
        (a) The setting of Gunkel's 'Royal Psalms'   129
        (b) The setting of the other royal psalms   130
        (c) Conclusions for the royal rites   131

IV THE IDEAL OF THE KING'S OFFICE IN THE
     PSALMS

   1 Davidic rule lies within God's kingdom   135
   2 The enemies of God as personal enemies of the king   137
   3 The laws of the kingdom are God's   141
   4 The king is drawn into God's aura   142
   5 The king as God's son   146
   6 The king as God's servant   149
   7 The king as God's covenant-partner   150
   8 The king assisted by the personified covenant-
        graces   152
   9 The king aided by God's word   154
  10 The king aided by God's name   155
  11 The king aided by God's spirit   156
  12 God's assurances to his king   157
  13 God gives his king abundant life   160
  14 The king's life benefits the people   165
  15 God's gifts balanced by demands on his king   168
  16 The king's warm response to God's grace   169
  17 The king's designations for God as his personal
        saviour   170
  18 The king as God's chief cultic minister   172
  19 The king's work of atonement   177
  20 The king as admonisher of mankind   181
  21 The king as God's witness to the world   182
  22 The role of witness as a plea in royal prayers   185
  23 The king's witness is inspired   187
  24 Sacrifice in relation to the king's witness   187
  25 The subject of the king's witness   188
  26 Characteristic elements of the king's witness   192
  27 The king's grace of answered prayer   195

V CONCLUSION   198

   Notes   202

   List of works cited   213

   Select indexes   221

PREFACE

I have cited modern works in as brief a form as practicable, often with author's name only; the details appear in the lists of works cited and of abbreviations. Such citations, far from exhaustive, are usually made to specify evidence or to illustrate various lines of interpretation. More elaborate bibliography is given by de Fraine, Bernhardt, and above all Lipiński (*Royauté*).

The verse-numeration of the Hebrew psalms, unlike modern versions, includes the titles. To trace my psalm-references to the English Bible, therefore, readers should in most cases deduct 1 from the (Hebrew) verse-number which I give. The Select Indexes merely supplement the detailed Contents and cross-references; the scholars included relate to the history of the subject.

I am much indebted to Professors G. W. Anderson and James Barr, who read my draft and made valuable suggestions; also to my Birmingham colleagues Professor W. G. Lambert and Mr. John Ray, who have been ever ready with help in their fields of Assyriology and Egyptology respectively. To Professor A. R. Johnson I am grateful not only for his inspiring books, but also for many helpful letters. My clear-minded colleague Frances Young helped me unravel at least one tangle. Jean Cunningham of SCM Press has done her onerous part with her customary skill and kindness. My good friend Herbert Adams, assisted by his wife Barbara, worked into the small hours over the Christmas season checking many details in the proofs, like an inspired rugby full-back bringing down many a cunning foe just short of the line.

I pray that the truth may be served and not hindered by this work, which after its fashion is turned towards the greatest mystery of religion, towards the representative figure that carries all the world's agony and hope.

Department of Theology
University of Birmingham

JOHN EATON

ABBREVIATIONS

ANEP	Pritchard, *The Ancient Near East in Pictures*
ANET	Pritchard, *Ancient Near Eastern Texts*
ANVO	Avhandlinger utgitt av Det Norske Videnskaps-Akademi i Oslo
ASTI	*Annual of the Swedish Theological Institute*, Leiden
BDB	Brown, Driver, Briggs, *Hebrew Lexicon*
BJRL	*Bulletin of the John Rylands Library*, Manchester
BKAT	Biblischer Kommentar. AT, Neukirchen
BZ	*Biblische Zeitschrift*, Freiburg i. Br., Paderborn
BZAW	Beihefte zur *ZAW*
CR	*Compte rendu de la 3. rencontre assyriologique*
DSK	Bentzen, *Det sakrale kongedømme*
EI	*Eretz Israel*, Jerusalem
ET	English translation
EVV	English version
FRLANT	Forschungen zur Religion und Literatur des Alten und Neuen Testaments, Göttingen
G	Greek version (LXX)
GK	Gesenius, Kautzsch, *Hebrew Grammar*
GT	Mowinckel, *Det Gamle Testamente* IV.1
HAT	Handbuch zum AT, Tübingen
HKAT	Handkommentar zum AT, Göttingen
HR	Bleeker, *Historia Religionum* I
HTC	Mowinckel, *He that Cometh*
J	Jerome
JAOS	*Journal of the American Oriental Society*, Baltimore
JNYF	Snaith, *The Jewish New Year Festival*
JSS	*Journal of Semitic Studies*, Manchester
JTS	*Journal of Theological Studies*, Oxford
KAT	Kommentar zum Alten Testament, Leipzig
KJ	King James English Version, 1611

KM	Bentzen, *King and Messiah*
MR	Hooke (ed.), *Myth and Ritual*
MRK	Hooke (ed.), *Myth, Ritual and Kingship*
Mss.	Hebrew manuscripts
MT	Massoretic text
NEB	New English Bible, 1970
OTL	Old Testament Library, London
OTMS	Rowley (ed.), *The OT and Modern Study*
OTS	*Oudtestamentische Studiën*, Leiden
PEQ	*Palestine Exploration Quarterly*, London
PIW	Mowinckel, *The Psalms in Israel's Worship*
Ps. st.	Mowinckel, *Psalmenstudien*
11Q Ps.	Qumran Psalms Scroll, ed. Sanders
RA	*Revue d'Assyriologie*
RSV	Revised Standard Version (1952), ed. of 1965
S	Syriac version
SAHG	Falkenstein, von Soden, *Sumerische und akkadische Hymnen und Gebete*
SBT	Studies in Biblical Theology, London
SBU	Engnell (ed.), *Svenskt Bibliskt Uppslagsverk*
SEÅ	*Svensk Exegetisk Årsbok*, Lund
SK	Widengren, *Sakrales Königtum*
SKAI	Johnson, *Sacral Kingship in Ancient Israel*
T	Targum
TBC	Torch Bible Commentaries, London
TRP	Thomas, *Text of the Revised Psalter*
TWAT	Botterweck, *Theol. Wörterbuch zum AT*
UUÅ	Uppsala Universitets Årsskrift
V	Vulgate
Vss.	The chief ancient versions
VT	*Vetus Testamentum*, Leiden
ZA	*Zeitschrift für Assyriologie*, Berlin
ZAW	*Zeitschrift für die alttestamentliche Wissenschaft*, Giessen, Berlin

I

HOW MANY PSALMS ARE ROYAL?
GENERAL ARGUMENTS

1. *The aim of the enquiry*

Kingship is one of the most important and fascinating subjects in the field of biblical studies. It is also one of the most controversial. Differences arise not only in the interpretation of the source-materials, but also in deciding what materials are relevant. This is particularly true of the psalms.

Before the rise of modern criticism, most of the psalms were, in a sense, taken to have a royal connection. King David was thought to be their author, referring partly to himself and partly to the future messiah. But as criticism developed in the nineteenth century, it seemed necessary to date most psalms later than David, later indeed than the end of his dynasty in 586 BC. The person who speaks in the psalms was then thought to be a collective, a personification of the nation or of a pious group within it. Such a collective interpretation was even applied to psalms which now seem unquestionably royal, such as 2 and 110, though these were taken by others to refer to the Maccabean rulers or to foreign emperors or to the messiah.

A decisive change came with the work of Hermann Gunkel, considered in detail below. He argued that ten psalms pertained to the kings of the Davidic dynasty. As for the other sixty and more psalms in which an individual is prominent, the collectivist interpretation was to be rejected; though indebted to royal and other cultic prototypes, explained Gunkel, most were the lyrical

out-pourings of commoners, a spiritualizing development, lib-
erated from institutional settings.

To this day many scholars agree with Gunkel's estimate of the
number of royal psalms. Like him they treat the mass of psalms
which feature an individual as the prayers and praises of commoners, though they are more willing to grant an institutional
connection for some of these. A few prominent scholars, however,
mostly in Scandinavia, have considered that the bulk of psalms
concerning an individual are royal; it is envisaged that in some
cases the speaker will have been a person taking the king's place,
even a governor or high priest after the end of the monarchy.

Such differences of view as to the extent of the royal psalms will
obviously make for substantial differences in the reconstruction of
the ideal of the royal office. Just as Gunkel's identification of ten
psalms as royal led to a drastic reappraisal, so the identification of
a much greater mass of texts as royal could be expected to lead to
further important conclusions.

And hence the basic purpose of this book. The argument will
be that in fact the view that only some ten psalms are royal is mis-
taken and hinders our understanding of the king's office. It will be
argued that many of the other psalms concerning an individual
are royal and provide a valuable source for the royal ideal. With
the extra help they give, I shall attack the basic problem of the
royal rites in the new-year festival, at the same time examining
each of Gunkel's royal psalms. I shall then expound all the elements of the royal ideal which emerge from the larger identification
of royal psalms and from the clarified rites.

2. *The weakness of Gunkel's position*

In his article 'Die Königspsalmen' (1914) Gunkel performed the
valuable service of relating nine psalms to the Davidic monarchy
and drove from the field the various theories involving a later
dating. Psalms 21 and 72, he thought, were for the royal anniversary (coronation or birthday); 132 for anniversary of the royal
sanctuary and palace; 45 for a royal wedding; 20 before war and
18 after war; and 2, 101 and 110 for the king's enthronement. He
showed that there was sufficient resemblance to royal texts of
Egypt and Mesopotamia to establish his interpretation. These
psalms reflected the ideal of the royal office rather than particular

characters. But as regards other psalms which mention the king (28; 61; 63; 84; I Sam. 2) he gave his opinion that these were originally psalms of a purely private, non-royal character to which a royal reference had been added in order to adapt them for a king's use.

His views remain the same in his later work, the great commentary (1926) and its companion *Einleitung in die Psalmen* (completed by Begrich, 1933). With the nine royal psalms just mentioned he reckons also 144.1–11 and, in a remoter sense, 89. The numerous other psalms concerning an individual are, he thinks, the utterances of private persons, though containing many elements strictly only explicable of a king; such psalms, he explains, have been adapted from an extensive royal psalmody now unfortunately perished (*Einl.*, pp. 147–9).

Why this extensive royal material had less chance of preservation in the psalmody of the royal temple than did the outpourings of the various persecuted invalids, exiles etc. whom we meet in Gunkel's commentary is not explained. In view of the importance of the king's prayers (below, p. 195) we must think it incredible that the Jerusalem temple should have bequeathed us, according to Gunkel, only one example, Psalm 144 (*Einl.*, pp. 155, 145; cf. Ps. 132.1). What a contrast to the extant prayers and laments of the Mesopotamian kings which, Gunkel notes, are 'extraordinarily numerous' (*Einl.*, p. 161)! Is it not more likely that many of Gunkel's 'laments of the individual',[1] recognized by him to contain elements explicable only of a king and to be broadly formed in cultic style, are in fact the missing prayers of the Davidic kings?

Gunkel's account of the 'laments of the individual' (*Einl.*, pp. 172–265) is tortuous. He sees this class as corresponding to those he calls 'thanksgivings of the individual'. But whereas he sees the latter as belonging to the cult, the former are said to have become divorced from it. The sufferer, he argues (*Einl.*, pp. 283f.), pours out his griefs in the privacy of his room, while his thanksgiving must be public testimony. So he requires us to think of a psalter made up of classes which generally had a cultic setting and function, except that one of the most important, the 'laments of the individual', has mostly only cultic prototypes. In the case of this one class, he supposes, there is admittedly use of cultic forms and royal elements, but the actual psalms were composed away from the cult; and yet, he has to add, some were later taken and adapted for the use of the king or national spokesman, and all eventually were gathered into the official temple psalter. He thinks this theory is necessitated by occasional allusions to absence from the temple, by the relative sparseness of cultic references, and by the personal spirituality which sometimes disparages sacrifices. But we may object that such features are not incompatible with a cultic setting. The cult might operate away from the temple during military campaigns, or at outlying stations on processional routes. A warm personal tone is actually appropriate in the royal cult (below, pp. 169f.). Reflections on the relative merits of sacrifice could be relevant in cultic songs (e.g. Ps. 50). A scholar of comparable importance, S. Mowinckel, long opposed Gunkel on these psalms, and other scholars generally more in line with Gunkel have parted company from him here, proposing cultic interpretations (pp. 5f.). It would be more convincing if this class of psalms could be explained more directly and in conformity with the rest of Gunkel's work. And this is possible when they are recognized as prevailingly royal.

But he gives the impression of never seriously considering this possibility. Let us take two examples from his commentary. His first opportunity to raise the question is with Psalm 3. In its compressed brevity, he says, it is the very pattern of its type, the 'lament of the individual'. He finds the decisive point for his interpretation in the theme of safe sleep (v. 6); from this he concludes that the psalmist is a private person, not a leader, general or high priest. He enlarges on this with general impressions drawn from other psalms of this class: the speaker will be suffering some personal misfortune, such as an illness, on account of which he is being treated as an outcast; his heart burns with the sense of injustice even more than with his pain. Such an interpretation, however, has no basis in the actual text before us. The theme of safe sleep is in itself equivocal; the safety of a ruler is not less a matter of anxiety than that of a private citizen. (Thus a Pharaoh warns his son and successor: 'Even when thou sleepest, guard thy heart thyself, because no man has adherents on the day of distress', *ANET*, p. 418.) The rest of Gunkel's interpretation is surmise.

The data which the text does offer, and which constitute the bulk of the psalm, are given no weight at all. The repeated description of large opposing armies (vv. 2, 3, 7) is said to be only a metaphor, inherited from older royal psalms; so presumably is the theme of Yahweh as the speaker's protector in battle, the one who gives him glory and supremacy (v. 4). Gunkel is not aware of any connection between kingship and the theme of answered prayer (v. 5, see below, pp. 195f.). The concluding battle-cry 'Victory is Yahweh's!' and the blessing on Yahweh's people or 'army' (v. 9) are given no significance, being, he thinks, perhaps later additions. He also feels that v. 8 contrasts starkly with the preceding material concerning the personal life of the psalmist and therefore seems to be an addition. By such means does Gunkel escape the obvious!

As a second example let us take Psalm 63. In order to interpret this also as a psalm of 'private' spiritual experience, he asserts that the mention of the king in v. 12ab was a later insertion between v. 11 and v. 12c. He does not argue this from the switch to the third person ('But the king shall rejoice') since he knows that this is normal, as he later explains on Psalm 89.52. He simply assumes that the sentence is out of keeping with the personal piety of the rest of the psalm. The possibility of a true unity throughout the psalm and related to the mentioned king is not even discussed. The awkward fact, however, is that the rest of the psalm does contain elements best explained of the king. Among these may be mentioned God's grasping his right hand (below, pp. 143f., 157), residence in the shadow of God's wings (p. 143), and the fate requested for enemies, who are to be cut down by the sword and left in the field for the foxes – surely a battle scene. Verse 12 is thus entirely in place as a clear identification of the speaker as king (see further p. 50).

In short, it is apparent that Gunkel does not approach the question with an open mind. His desire to classify and then treat members of the class alike leads him to avoid the obvious in a particular text. And in his basic notions, used to interpret the whole class, he misjudges the religious aspect of Israelite kingship, failing to understand the spiritual warmth with which the king's relation to God was expressed.

3. *The weakness of institutional non-royal theories*

While Gunkel's limitation of the number of royal psalms has remained widely accepted, some of his followers have deviated from him in one respect. They are less inclined to see in the 'laments of the individual' cult-free compositions merely influenced by earlier cultic poetry. They have proposed various cultic circumstances where psalms of this class might have been composed and used. In this respect, they have rightly found Gunkel's position untenable. Ignoring the claims of a royal interpretation, however, they have failed to solve the problem. Some discussion of their efforts will help to advance my argument.

H. Schmidt, in *Das Gebet der Angeklagten* (1928), proposed for some twenty of the laments a setting in the juridical processes of the sanctuary. Such a psalm would then be the prayer of one whose case could not be settled by the lay courts, and who is being held in custody at the temple pending a verdict of God revealed through the priests. Since some of the psalms in question seem to reflect sickness, he further supposes that in some cases a man has come under suspicion because he is sick. Schmidt was able to point to several prose texts which are evidence of sacral trials in difficult cases: I Kings 8.31f.; Deut. 17.8f.; 21.1-8; Ex. 22.6f.; Num. 5.11f. These are rather diverse and none of them present the situation he requires – the singing of a psalm by an individual held in custody for examination. His attempts to adduce references in the psalms to such detention are of no value. Psalm 107.10f., for example, refers only to an imprisonment that was punishment of wrongdoers; again, there is no reason to interpret Psalm 118 in terms of Schmidt's thesis at all. In fact he fails to find any evidence to connect psalmody with sacral trials. Gunkel (*Einl.*, p. 252) rightly objects to Schmidt's theory that it is not firmly grounded either in the prose texts or the psalms.

It has been further objected that the psalmists in question often seem to speak of being in a friendly shelter, an asylum, rather than in prison.[2] Their expectation is not just defensive, looking for their own exoneration, but rather offensive, looking for God to strike down their enemies.[3] Moreover, Schmidt's treatment of particular psalms is sometimes arbitrary. Psalm 118 has already been mentioned. Psalm 31 would not fit his theory if he did not remove the ending; nor Psalm 27 if he did not remove the beginning. In Psalms 7; 9; 54; 56; 59, he has to emend or treat as secondary the embarrassing reference to the enemies as nations. In Psalm 35 he arbitrarily assumes that the prayer for judgment must be taken strictly of a legal process, while that for God's

intervention in battle is metaphorical. Finally, one may feel that
Schmidt's idea that several of the psalmists were subjected to
ritual trials in the temple because they were invalids and hence
suspects is flimsy, not to say grotesque.

Another notable and indeed more far-reaching theory is that of
L. Delekat, *Asylie und Schutzorakel* (1967). His theory embraces
most of the 'laments of the individual'. The cultic setting he
proposes arises from the institution of asylum. The laments are
mostly prayers of impoverished individuals, he thinks, appealing
for divine protection in the asylum of the Jerusalem temple. They
are awaiting the decision of God through the priests, while their
pursuers wait outside to pounce on them if they are rejected by
God and expelled. He reconstructs the details of their situation
from allusions in the psalms. Mostly they are found to be day-
labourers afflicted by debt or accusation of crime. The concluding
passages which change to a tone of thanksgiving were added by
the same individual later in acknowledgment of a favourable
decision. Such a verdict had enabled the fugitive to leave with a
safe-conduct or to remain as a cultic servant. Delekat does not
consider these laments and acknowledgments as originally psalms
for singing, but as inscriptions deposited in the sanctuary on
memorial stones or scrolls.

This theory is open to grave objections. It seems unwarranted
thus to deny a living usage in worship to one large class of psalms
while the other classes clearly had one; the classes cannot be
separated so sharply. But even more questionable is Delekat's
interpretation of particular psalms, which borders on the absurd.
In Psalm 69, for example, we are asked to envisage a hapless
fellow imprisoned in a cistern. It begins to rain. As the cistern fills,
he prays, 'Save me, O God, for the waters come up to my neck'.
What is more, he is ill, and thinks he must have been poisoned
('They gave me poison for food'). His crime is to have been over-
generous in bequeathing his goods to the temple ('Zeal for thy
house has consumed me'). The aim of his apparent generosity had
been to elude the debt-collectors, but the consequence had been to
enrage his creditors and family. Fortunately he was allowed up
from the cistern in the nick of time to plead in the temple. There
he deposited his prayer-inscription and then received a protective
oracle.

Or again, take Psalm 22. Delekat supposes that, while the

fugitive waited in the sanctuary for the divine decision, the
practice was to deny him food or water. He would then be too
weak to resist if the decision was to eject him, and so violence in
the holy place would be avoided. So the psalmist waits day after
day, and naturally becomes quite emaciated ('I can count all my
bones') and thirsty ('My tongue cleaves to the roof of my mouth').
Outside wait the pursuers, ready for him with swords and hunting
dogs ('Deliver my soul from the sword, my life from the power
of the dog').

In Psalm 65 Delekat finds a party of workers who have gone on
strike. They have chosen the moment of maximum effect, just
before harvest, and then wisely placed themselves in the asylum
of the temple. Delekat's evidence of strikes in Ptolemaic Egypt
hardly succeeds in making this a convincing explanation of Psalm
65. No more convincing is his picture of Psalm 118 as the song of
such a wretch who became a cultic gate-keeper and was careful
to bless the entering pilgrims profusely ('Blessed be he that
cometh . . .') with an eye to generous rewards from the festal food.

Delekat's theory has been criticized recently by W. Beyerlin
(*Die Rettung der Bedrängten*, 1970). The heart of these psalms, he
says (pp. 44f.) is not the theme of Yahweh's protection, but his
judgment, which will fall also upon the enemies. Asylum is thus
not the dominating concern of these psalms. In any case, Beyerlin
continues, provisions for asylum in Israel were designed to curtail
indiscriminate blood-revenge, not to hinder the punishment of
actual offenders, which indeed would contradict the ethical
standards of the holy place. It is not legitimate for Delekat to
reconstruct procedures of asylum on the basis of the psalms, since
their connection with asylum must be proved first. Most of the
psalmists in question do not in any case show interest in remaining
in the temple for a lengthy period, and the hypothesis that an
oracle might provide a safe-conduct is quite unfounded. Generally
the psalmists complain of being falsely accused, says Beyerlin;
their need is for judgment, not for the resignation of asylum.

Rejecting the theories of Schmidt and Delekat, he puts forward
one of his own, which could, however, be described as a refinement
of Schmidt's. The prose texts which tell of ordeal trials or the like
are again used to illustrate the original setting of a group of psalms
of conflict and judgment. Beyerlin, however, does not think that
an imprisonment is involved and his selection of psalms is more

restricted: 3; 4; 5; 7; 11; 17; 23; 26; 27; 57; 63. Their varied character is said to be due to their belonging to various stages of the ritual, some before the decisive moment (e.g. Ps. 3), some just after it (e.g. Ps. 23). But the basic difficulties which beset the theory in its earlier form persist. There is nothing in the texts about cultic trials to suggest that the proceedings were interspersed with psalms. There is nothing in the psalms which specially requires this particular setting, nor is there any tradition about their use to point to it. The psalms which he has explained in this way are diverse in relation to one another and hardly stand out as a group from numerous other psalms of conflict and supplication. Could the authors and performers have been laymen? The matter is not clarified. Beyerlin's exposition of these psalms in turn tends to ignore the obvious. In a long treatment of Psalm 3, for example, he gives no reason why the repeated references to enemy armies could not possibly mean what they say. Again we find the exegete eluding the bulk of his data in order to force the psalm into a setting which nothing in the psalm requires or even suggests.

At this point it is relevant to criticize the treatment of the problem in two of the most important of recent commentaries, those of H. J. Kraus and A. Weiser. In his introduction, Kraus has reiterated Gunkel's principle that the psalms of a particular class must have in common an origin in a definite occasion of worship, or at least have grown from that occasion (Kraus, *Psalmen,* 1960, p. xxxviii). Yet in his treatment of the 'laments of the individual' (pp. xlvf.), he says we meet sick, accused and guilt-laden people, three groups which are difficult to distinguish absolutely from each other. He thinks therefore that one should not divide them into sub-classes. And yet clearly different cultic settings are involved: for the sick, he suggests prayers by proxy; for those in need of expiation or cleansing, special purificatory rites; and for the accused, the situation is much as suggested by Schmidt. Surely there is some inconsistency here. Such rites of the 'accused' would have a very special character and therefore, according to the aforementioned principle, psalms of the 'accused' should constitute a distinct class. Gunkel at least was consistent here in not acknowledging Schmidt's 'psalms of the accused'.

Two examples of Kraus's exegesis may be given. On the setting of Psalm 3 he can say nothing positive. He is not persuaded by Schmidt that it is a 'prayer of the accused', although he accepts that in v. 4 the raising of the head may be a metaphor derived from a rite of acquittal. He shows considerable sensitivity to royal features, which he thinks are more than figures of speech ('nicht nur Bilder und Vergleiche'). But he will not consider that this could be a royal psalm, his reasons apparently being that the hostile forces bear upon an individual and speak scornfully – considerations which are in fact of no weight (see below, p. 140). So Kraus feels he must hold to the interpretation given by Gunkel, though with some reservations. He explains that the speaker has 'transferred himself into a royal situation', he approaches God 'through the medium of royal words', he rediscovers his own fate in the world of the king who stands under God's special promise of salvation. This explanation, however, does little to clarify the situation.

Kraus is happy to define Psalm 7 with Schmidt as a 'prayer of the accused', the setting being clarified by I Kings 8.31f. Even so, Gunkel is said to be right in hearing the echo of royal words; the praying person enters the sphere of words and conceptions of the king, the master of the temple ceremonies, blessed by God's special dispensation of salvation. But no consideration is given as to whether a simple royal interpretation might be possible.

Weiser is content to understand Psalm 3 as a king's prayer and Psalm 7 as a 'prayer of the accused', but in these and many other cases he argues for a setting in 'the cult of the covenant'. He thinks that, as Hannah in I Samuel 1–2 brings her personal need to the central autumnal festival and utters a psalm of national dimensions, so individuals of all kinds, kings and commoners, and even those in the special situation of 'the accused', offered psalms on the occasion of the great festival, reflecting both their personal needs and the festal themes.

We must doubt whether the case of Hannah can bear such a weight. She is not shown as using a psalm in her supplications. Nor will the redactor of these chapters have regarded her as just another simple woman; she was the mother of Israel's great leader, whether Samuel or originally Saul.[4] If there was no reason to suppose that the ordeal-trials were interspersed with psalm-singing, still less can we assume that they took place in the annual festival. While Weiser is willing to take some of the 'laments of the individual' as royal (e.g. Ps. 3), in other likely cases he does not even consider the possibility. In Psalm 63, for example, the worshipper is thought of as a private person who has seen the festal revelation of God and in the presence of king and community has his case adjudicated; his enemies are to be executed and exposed for jackals; and yet, Weiser continues, it was not so much a question of calumnies against himself but of their denial of fundamental religious truths; in v. 12 he thinks the worshipper is interceding for the king to show his concern for the good of the community. This cannot be regarded as the most direct interpretation.

In short, both these commentators seem to have got into rather a tangle. They have rightly felt obliged to modify the 'cult-free' account which Gunkel gave of this class, but have not reached a satisfactory position.

4. *The growth of royal interpretations*

Throughout the period in which the exegesis described above has dominated the field, studies with a keener appreciation for the royal character of many psalms have continued to appear.

S. Mowinckel early felt the need to interpret the kingship of the psalms as a central part of Israel's life and religion. The royal material was not just a grandiose style borrowed with court etiquette from the great foreign empires. The Israelite kingship was a sincere religious conception and the king and his psalms belonged to the centre of the great festivals. This is the main theme of his little book *Kongesalmerne* (1916). The 'divinity' of kings, he explains, takes the form in Israel of endowment by Yahweh's spirit. The Israelite king mediates between God and man since in addition he is representative of the community. As God's 'son' and intimate, he can fulfil a priestly office. He is eminent as warrior, judge and ruler, pious man, bearer of success and blessing. The psalms are regarded as compositions of cultic circles specializing in music and the like. As royal texts Mowinckel adduces those specified by Gunkel, but, significantly, a number of others too: from Gunkel's 'laments of the individual' Psalms 28; 61 and 63 (he suggests many more from this class could be added); from Gunkel's 'laments of the people' Psalms 44; 60; 80 and 83; and, further, Psalms 66; 84; 68 (where vv. 23f. are taken as an oracle to the king), 118, and I Samuel 2.1–10. He makes comparisons with Mesopotamian and Egyptian texts and also considers the relation of the royal psalms to the messianic oracles in the prophets.

This book was thus of great value as a preliminary study, pointing to the main areas in which Gunkel's work on the royal psalms needed development and correction. There remained much detail to be quarried, and at least one large issue to be identified. This issue was brought out clearly in the work of A. R. Johnson (discussed below, pp. 109f.) and concerned the role of the king in the main ritual of the autumnal festival. Were the situations depicted in psalms like 18; 20; 89; 118 real battles, or were they rites portraying the king's fight on God's behalf against evil, a sacred drama of humiliation and restoration? Mowinckel thought chiefly along the former lines, Johnson along the latter. We must return to this question at a later stage.

A few years later, Mowinckel had occasion to interpret the main class of 'laments of the individual'. This was in his famous *Psalmenstudien* I (1921), where he saw the setting as cultic but not royal. They were texts provided by the temple for use of individuals in rites pertaining to sickness and injuries attributable to sinister thoughts, curses, spells and the like, of personal enemies.

> The 'I' who speaks in these psalms is hence in general not a living individual of flesh and blood, but a type of the pious man who is in need, provided with the features which he was supposed to have according to the ideal of the official religion . . . It is therefore entirely mistaken to seek the personal circumstances of the author, his personal case, who his enemies are and what they may have done to him (p. 138).

About a dozen years later, Mowinckel changed this view. Looking back near the end of his life, this is how (in the Foreword to the reprint of *Ps. st.*, 1961) he describes his shift of position:

> I had to subject my interpretation of the 'laments of the individual' in *Psalmenstudien* I to a fundamental revision. . . . The error was that I still held on to Gunkel's purely mechanical distinction between I-psalms and We-psalms, and consequently interpreted the I-psalms as a whole as psalms of sickness. Through H. Birkeland's *Die Feinde des Individuums* (1933) I let myself be taught that there are many I-laments (among them especially the so-called Psalms of Confidence, in which the need still stands before the eyes of the speaker only as a threatening danger) in which the 'I' is not just an 'Everyman', but

the king of the people, and the enemies are accordingly of a national, political kind, though characterized by expressions which originally denote sorcerers and demons . . .

The book which thus persuaded Mowinckel is an extensive, thorough and clear-headed argument that the enemies in Gunkel's 'psalms of the individual', as in his national and royal psalms, are foreign peoples, as De Wette had argued long before, and the speaker correspondingly is Israel's leader, usually the king. Its subsequent lack of influence on the followers of Gunkel may be due to the sheer width of the rift between the respective positions, perhaps also to Birkeland's insufficient appreciation of the variations in the situation of the praying king and in the nature of his enemies; the subtle richness of the royal ideology and rituals are given little attention, and almost all situations are reduced to a military confrontation with foreign nations or to an accusation to a foreign overlord about breach of political covenant. The book remains, however, a valuable demonstration of the weakness of Gunkel's position and an exceptionally well-organized argument to the effect that the speaker is generally a king who prays with the needs, duties and privileges of a king. It is therefore worthwhile to trace the line of his argument.

Birkeland begins by claiming that his approach reconciles the parties to an old controversy. He is referring on the one hand to those who believed the psalmist was really a collective figure, a personification of the pious party in post-exilic times, a view championed by R. Smend in 1888, and on the other to those who had insisted that this was an artificial interpretation and that the real individuality of the psalmist must be upheld, a view championed by E. Balla in 1912. Gunkel had awarded the victory to Balla, who had based his argument on Gunkel's work (*Einl.*, p. 173). Yet the collectivist interpretation, favoured in various degrees by so many discerning critics, could surely not have been without foundation. Birkeland argues well that the collectivists have seized on numerous features which cannot be explained in terms of a common individual, but make sense in terms of the king. The king can pray both as national representative and as an individual; in solidarity with his people and in distinction from them. So Smend and Balla can be reconciled.

But the central question for Birkeland is the character of the enemies in the psalms, and he insists that the argument must move across the divisions of Gunkel's classifications. He begins with the terminology and imagery of the enemies in the communal laments and thanksgivings (Pss. 44; 60; 74; 79; 80; 83; 124; 125) and finds the enemies here clearly to be other nations. Notable traits included their harmful, scornful speaking, their plotting, their godlessness, their appearing as voracious beasts and as bird-trappers.

He carries the examination into the acknowledged royal psalms where similar national foes appear as the worshipper's personal enemies (18; 20; 21; 89; 144). Passing to 28; 61; 63, I Samuel 2, which all contain designations of the king, he argues against Gunkel for the integrity of these psalms on the grounds that they concern the king and foreign foes. Then he treats 12; 14; 58; 82, and finds the scope to be national and the enemies again foreign nations.

He now turns to the rest of the 'laments of the individual' and finds that their enemies are substantially the same as in the national and royal psalms already treated. A few references to personal experience – desertion by old friends, solitariness – are compared to utterances of political leaders in foreign texts. So the psalmist here is normally the king, though in some cases an army leader or post-exilic ruler may be considered.

Thus in almost all the psalms of conflict he finds the enemies to be foreign armies, kings or peoples. In many cases it is a question of a threatened, not an accomplished, assault. The term 'lament', says Birkeland, should only be used when the blow has already fallen; otherwise we should speak of *Schutzpsalmen*, 'psalms of protection'.

As to whether it is too bold to regard so many psalms as royal, he quotes opinions of Mowinckel and A. Jeremias that the royal psalmody will have been the original core of the Jerusalem tradition. He cites Gunkel's identification of royal elements in the 'psalms of the individual': kings and nations are the audience or the opposition; the plea for salvation in terms of world judgment; warfare; the psalmist triumphs like a bull; divine paternity. To these features Birkeland adds the lavish character of the worshipper's sacrifices and various formulae and phrases: God's 'delight' rests on the psalmist; God acts 'for his name's sake'; God's 'servant'; 'my God', 'my King', 'God of my salvation' and the like.

Birkeland has been criticized for overlooking the process of 'democratization', whereby features originally applicable to the king came to be appropriated by ordinary worshippers. However, Birkeland is fully aware of this question and his position is that the primary sense of the texts should not be put aside without adequate justification. Gunkel did not furnish evidence that the psalms in question contain only stylistic imitations of royal psalms and were not in their wholeness royal psalms.

Less secure is Birkeland's argument that the enemies of the king are more likely to be external than internal, in accordance, as he supposes, with the acknowledged royal psalms; he allows exceptions only when there are positive indications to this effect. But a full appreciation of the role of God's anointed would rather lead to a blurring of the distinction between Israelite and foreign trouble-makers.[5] In some of the very texts on which Birkeland founds this argument, namely Psalms 18 and 144, the king faces enemies of the living order, evil death-powers manifest in Sheol, Belial and the Great Waters, who assault all good society on earth, harming natural and political life. The range of imagery used of such enemies can readily be applied to any danger or hurt to the life and domain of God's anointed. Exegesis in terms of foreign armies needs support from the particular context as much as would any other interpretation.

Birkeland then reinforces his arguments by studying all the psalms of conflict in turn, in an order which again provides a cumulative demonstration: first, psalms in which 'I' and 'we' alternate (66; 118; 94; 36; 77; 75; 123; 130; 131); then 'psalms of the individual' which specify the enemies as other nations (59; 56; 9–10; 7; 42–3; 54); then those where battle is explicit or the enemies are called 'nations' (3; 27; 35; 31; 120; 109; 69; 22; 140; 71; 55.; 11). These are the clearest cases. He then adduces 'psalms of the individual' which, in the light of the preceding expositions, can readily be seen as of national and royal scope (57; 138; 5; 23; 17; 62; 52; 64; 92). Then he examines those where the cause of mischief seems to be actual foreign rule (37; 49; 73), probably early post-exilic. And so to psalms of law-piety (119; 19B; 25; 86; 116; 143; 32), which include prayers of a high priest against external and internal foes. In his next group he finds the enemies to be quite unspecified (141; 142; 26; 139; 40.14–18; 70; 13; 34; 39; 51). Finally he examines those which could be psalms of sickness (41; 38; 30; 6; 102; 88), though most of these could be related primarily to war against nations; in fact only 41 and 38 seem to him to be undoubtedly psalms of sickness where the king has to reckon with internal foes.

These expositions are followed by further general arguments. The theme of false witness, while not justifying the theory of H. Schmidt (see above, p. 6) is said to be more than metaphorical, since it is accompanied by fairly specific claims of innocence. Birkeland's explanation, doing justice also to the elements of a royal, national and military nature, is that the king is refuting accusations made against him by his enemies to his foreign over-lord, accusations of the type which we know often occasioned punitive campaigns. Parallels are adduced from the Amarna letters. Next, a study of the expressions 'poor', 'needy' (*'ānī, 'ebyōn*) argues that these could be applied to the king or people before God, an admission of need and helplessness to move him to intervene. In a concluding discussion of Babylonian-Assyrian psalms, Birkeland claims that the relevant evidence supports his explanation of the Israelite 'psalms of the individual' better than the anti-sorcery theory of the early Mowinckel. He shows how 'individual' the Mesopotamian laments over public distress can appear.

In 1955 Birkeland was able in *The Evildoers in the Book of Psalms* to restate his position and reply to his critics; he scarcely yields any ground, and indeed takes his claims a little further. The enemies in the so-called 'psalms of sickness' (6; 30; 38; 41; 102) are now said to be foreigners; even 101 and 26 refer to the virtue of avoiding foreign associates. He summarizes his position thus:

> The evildoers in the Book of Psalms are gentiles in all cases when a definite collective body or its representatives are meant. Israelite groups are included as far as co-operation with foreigners is concerned. Evildoers in a general sense do occur, but even so the application to gentiles seems probable (p. 93).

Accordingly, the speaker is the national leader, usually the king.

As already mentioned, Mowinckel accepted Birkeland's main argument. He applied it extensively in the ample prefaces and notes that accompany his Norwegian translation of the OT of 1955 (*GT*), a work unfortunately little known abroad.

Another important scholar whose opinions on our topic show a significant evolution is A. Bentzen. No one who has read his large Danish commentary (1939) can deny his wisdom and expert knowledge in the field. In his early work he was attracted by the theme of asylum (as in *Jahves Gaest*, 1926) and found H. Schmidt's work congenial to his own. In his commentary, therefore, he did not extensively follow Birkeland, but explained many psalms in relation to private individuals seeking from the temple asylum or clearance from accusations. The psalms he identified as royal or probably so, in addition to Gunkel's, were 8; 9–10; 28; 61; 63; 66; 75; 89; 138. In 1945, however, he published *Det sakrale konge-dømme*, a re-assessment of his position in the light of recent work on kingship, especially that done by I. Engnell (below). Whereas Birkeland's overall pattern of 'king versus foreign enemies' had not convinced him, he was now impressed by the extent to which the king's ritual warfare in the autumnal festival (Pss. 2, 110) might be represented in the 'psalms of the individual'. He re-surveys the whole Psalter from this point of view. With an eye on Engnell, he is anxious to stress uncertainties and to maintain the possibility of non-royal psalmists in some cases; Schmidt's theory of the 'accused' may occasionally be right (as perhaps in Pss. 5; 7; 26; 35; 109; 120; 142), and the possibility of the 'democratization' of royal materials must be kept in mind. As a result of his survey, the number of psalms which, with varying degrees of confidence, he thinks may be royal has risen to about fifty. Fairly definite changes from his commentary to a royal interpretation are notable in the cases of Psalms 3; 27; 55; 57; 62; 69; 91; 92; 94; 140; 141. The same point of view underlies his *Messias – Moses – Menschensohn* (1948), which appeared in English soon after his death as *King and Messiah* (1955). Here he thinks of most of the individual laments, at least in their formal origin, as derived from the royal ritual of combat.[6] As examples he mentions Psalms 3; 11; 12; 13; 14; 22; 27; 28; 42–3; 52; 54; 55; 57; 58; 59 (*KM*, p. 25). Even where psalms are not direct expressions of royal ritual and may be 'democratized', they are still important for our knowledge of the enthronement festival of Yahweh and his anointed (p. 31).

This reconsideration, as we have said, was a response to new emphases in the contemporary study of kingship. In particular, mention must be made of the provocative work of I. Engnell. In the last pages of his *Studies in Divine Kingship* (1943), he turns from foreign kingship to anticipate his treatment of Israelite kingship,

which was in fact never to be accomplished. He notes his intention
to examine the king's priestly role in prayer, blessing, sacrifices,
dances, divination, dream-visions etc. In the Enthronement
Festival he would study the king's cultic silence and wailing, his
collective responsibility as expiator, his positive and negative
confession of sins, his 'passion' and 'death'; then the more positive
side, – the king as bearer of peace, justice, wisdom, fertility. He
would make a detailed investigation of the psalms as royal
documents, taking as starting-point a purely cultic interpretation
and the assumption that they are almost exclusively pre-exilic. His
view is that the Davidic heading (*leᵈāwīd*) is a rubric inherited from
Jebusite times, signifying 'a psalm for the king', and he intended
to support with detailed studies the conception of the relevant
psalms as royal psalms.

    A fuller statement of his position on the psalms is given in his
articles in the Swedish encyclopaedia *SBU* (1962–3).[7] Here he is
more careful to qualify his views, though he clearly regards the
Psalter in the main as a royal corpus. He finds the titles to be a
valuable indication in this direction, though each psalm requires
careful weighing (II, cols. 618f.). Among seventy-three psalms
headed *leᵈāwīd*, some thirty can be shown to be royal, and another
thirty are probably so. The heading *lamᵉnaṣṣēᵃḥ* he takes as a
North Israelite parallel to *leᵈāwīd* and signifying 'pertaining to the
leader (the king)'. In several other titles he finds possible references to royal passion rites. In connection with such rites he
specially mentions Psalms 18; 22; 49; 88; 116; 118 (II, col. 1335).
He describes Psalm 22 as one of the most central royal psalms,
being almost a paradigm in its representation of the characteristic
motifs (II, col. 656). He thinks Psalm 73 is indubitably a royal
lament (I, col. 1488).

    The basic situation of the suffering and assaulted psalmist is best
understood, he thinks, as in the drama of the annual festival. The
foes are thus originally symbolic, embodying cosmic evil. In some
psalms the cultic stereotypes are applied to actual needs; they
should not be interpreted literally. He gives an outline of how he
understands the king's passion in the festival: a combat against the
evil forces and a symbolic death in atonement for his people's sins,
followed by a rising to life and glory. He stresses that this rite
evidenced in the passion psalms is the predecessor of the Isaianic
Suffering Servant (I, cols. 1487f.). The psalms in question,

however, are not systematically cited, apart from the briefest analysis of Psalm 22 (II, col. 656).

Some of his theories find more diffident expression in the work of H. Ringgren, particularly *The Messiah in the OT* (1956), where much reference is made also to the writings of G. Widengren. In a short chapter he looks over the psalms especially mentioned by Engnell in connection with the king's passion (Pss. 18; 22; 49; 88; 116; 118), and he adds Psalm 71 and Isaiah 38; from these he details eight common motifs covering the psalmist's suffering, salvation and testimony. His conclusion is that this pattern can well be imagined, but not proved, to reflect 'a ritual according to which the king has suffered symbolical death and thus has been humiliated for one night and in the morning returned to life and proclaimed his salvation to the people gathered for the Festival' (p. 64). What is certain, he says, and in itself significant for the interpretation of the Isaianic Servant Songs, is 'that there has existed in Israel a pattern of (innocent) suffering, death and restoration, and that psalms built on this pattern on some occasions have been laid in the mouth of a king' (p. 64).

In the same book (pp. 54–5) Ringgren summarizes an article in Czech, which interprets Psalm 22 as a royal cultic passion psalm. The writer, M. Bič, appeared as an advocate of extensive royal interpretation in another article (*Numen* Sup. 4). Here he propounds the bold view that Psalms 1–41 are an ancient liturgical sequence, a drama in which the king is the leading person. The reasoning does not seem sufficiently close or compelling in view of the difficulties in the way of such a theory. Nevertheless, the article serves to remind us that the order of the psalms may sometimes be of importance in the study of original liturgical usage.

In the largely philological commentary of M. Dahood (1966–70) many of the 'psalms of the individual' are recognized as royal, chiefly on grounds of phraseology; vol. III, p. xxxviii lists as royal: Psalms 3; 22; 27; 41; 54; 57; 59; 61; 63; 86; 91; 92; 127; 130; 138; 143.

Finally here, I venture to refer to my small commentary of 1967. Aware of the many conflicting explanations of the person of 'the psalmist', of which only a sample has been discussed above, I set out to ponder each psalm with an open mind. Contradictory witnesses such as Kraus and Mowinckel were constantly at my side. The result was that I found a royal interpretation to be the most satisfactory in about the same number of cases as had Mowinckel in *GT*. But what gave me the impetus to write the present book was that in many cases the text seemed to spring to life as a totality only when seen from this point of view. Moreover, such cases began to combine to give me a more rounded picture of the royal office than I had won from Gunkel's royal psalms. The time seemed ripe to present a detailed treatment of the subject, which, as the foregoing survey indicates, has not been treated with due thoroughness since the pioneering book of Birkeland four decades ago.

5. *General arguments for extensive royal interpretation*

In considering whether a psalm is royal, one must see arguments about particular features against a background of general considerations. Some of the considerations which favour extensive royal interpretation have been touched on above. The following list will summarize and add to them.

(i) The heading *leᵈāwid* stands over seventy-three psalms (eighty-four in the Greek) and is by far the most frequent of the headings.[8] In spite of problems of detail, this can reasonably be taken as an indication of the large place which royal psalmody has in the collection.

Whether the expression is of pre-Israelite origin, *dwd* denoting the royal office,[9] or whether it originated as a reference to David, extending later to his dynasty,[10] a royal link remains. Similarly, it will make little difference whether we explain the heading as a reference to the series in which the psalm was kept, or to its subject, or to its usage;[11] the link with the royal house remains. The fairly ancient view of David as an author of psalms[12] is not in opposition to such explanations. It is not difficult to allow that the idea of royal authorship had some currency from the beginning alongside the practical purposes of the heading and in the long run became the dominant understanding. (In similar manner the Greek rendering fluctuates between 'for' and 'of' David.) The lack of the heading where it might have been expected (e.g. Pss. 2; 44; 45; 89; 132) may be due to the taking of a psalm from an earlier sequence where one notice had served for a group of pieces (most of the psalms lacking the heading occur in blocks, e.g. 42–50; 71–85; 87–100; 146–150, and all but four of 111–137). No doubt some variations of practice here would exist between different circles and periods. What must be admitted, in view of all the uncertainties, is that the superscription in itself cannot provide firm ground for the interpretation of a psalm.

(ii) The biblical belief that David was a composer and performer of psalmody has just been mentioned. But the tradition goes further than this. It sees the temple's music as a whole as taking its rise from the king. The inspired musical service was said to have been assigned to the various guilds by David and his officers; all was done under the king's command, *'al y*ᵉ*dē hammelek* (I Chron. 25.1–8; 15.16f.). The instruments of the 4,000 priestly musicians were said to be made or invented by David (23.5; II Chron. 29.26f, Neh. 12.36; Amos 6.5). It is not clear how far psalms of the kind headed 'song' (*šīr*) were represented in Solomon's reputedly vast output of 'songs' (I Kings 5.12 [EVV 4.32]), though it is likely that, with the building of the temple and the flowering of kindred arts, the Psalter owes much to his reign (cf. the titles of Pss. 72 and 127). King Hezekiah, to whom is attributed a psalm in Isaiah 38, is also represented as renewing the Davidic appointments of psalmody. He directs the sacrifices and accompanying praises, where the instruments of David and the compositions of David and his assistant Asaph are prominent (II Chron. 29.25–30). Around 190 BC Ben Sirach expresses the tradition poetically; David, author and performer himself, was responsible for providing shifts of singers in the temple to offer praises in the festivals and in a daily round (Ecclus. 47.8–10). In the last years of the temple, the view that the Psalter stems largely from King David remains general. Josephus says: 'David, being now free from wars and dangers . . . composed songs and hymns to God in varied metres' (*Antiquities* VII. 305–6). In the New Testament the psalms are generally cited as David's (Pss. 2; 16; 32; 69; 109; 110) or 'David' (Heb. 4.7). In the Talmud (Briggs, p. liv) it is said that David wrote the psalms with the aid of Adam, Melchizedek, Abraham, Moses, Heman, Jeduthun, Asaph and the sons of Korah, i.e. figures of royal dimensions or of royal appointment. A psalm-scroll from the first century AD credits David with the composition of 3,600 psalms and hundreds of songs for offerings (Sanders, p. 136).

When modern scholarship held most of the psalms to be post-exilic, traditions about the Davidic origin were treated as worthless. This difficulty of late dating has largely gone, and the probability must be faced that the view most evident in the Chronicler will have had a genuine basis. The signs are that the Chronicler was heir to traditions of the ancient musical and other guilds of the temple and that in these traditions the king's religious responsibilities were well and fairly represented. The dynastic founder is accordingly shown as pre-eminent in cultic psalmody, extending his work of praise through guilds which he directs. And so in the last years of the temple, when its old traditions were still undisturbed, the Psalter is ascribed largely to the composition of the first Jerusalem king of Israel. This ancient view of a Psalter stemming from the king can be harmonized fairly well with the extensive royal exegesis here advocated, and it throws on to the defensive those, like Gunkel and Kraus, who would limit the royal psalms to six or seven per cent of the collection.

(iii) Directly reinforcing the preceding argument is the picture of royal responsibility in religion which has emerged from modern studies of kingship. That the psalmic prayers and praises of kings should form the main part of the corpus of classical psalmody of the royal temple is wholly to be expected.

(iv) Many and various have been the suggestions as to who were the original subjects of the 'psalms of the individual' and what their circumstances. But the only 'situation' which is certainly attested is that of the king; it is certain that he is the subject in a number of psalms, and the dispute is only about how many. This cannot be said of the other suggested usages. It is not certain that any single piece in the Psalter is of an 'accused', whether in prison, in asylum, or just on trial. It is not certain that any piece is a dedicatory inscription of a persecuted peasant, nor that any is the song of a commoner taking part in the covenant festival, nor that any was composed outside the cult. For these and other theories no doubt some clues can be argued. But such evidence is at best indirect. Of all the proposed 'situations', only that of the king is known for certain to exist in the Psalter.

(v) Coupled with the preceding point is the general homogeneity of the psalms. Notwithstanding the scope for classification and the pleasing freshness of so many psalms, there is a prevailing similarity which is in accord with an origin within a restricted range of royal and national cultus. Even the so-called wisdom psalms hardly step out of line. By contrast, texts from other nations which

are known to be, for example, dedicatory inscriptions or formulae
for private citizens in sickness have distinguishing characteristics.[13]
The later Jewish psalmody composed away from the official cultus
likewise diverges considerably in form and style.[14] It is difficult to
accept, say with Beyerlin or Kraus, that among similar psalms
some, by hair-splitting arguments, can be said to belong to the
specialized situation of the ordeal trials and the others elsewhere.
It would be remarkable if the numerous and various private
individuals imagined by some commentators had not left clearer
traces of their identity and situation, while the theory that they
used 'formulae' composed for the use of any pilgrim does not do
justice to the quality of the psalms.

(vi) More particularly, there is some force in the reasoning of
Birkeland (above, p. 14), who emphasizes the continuity between
Gunkel's national psalms, royal psalms, and 'psalms of the individual', especially with regard to the portrayal of enemies. The
separation of these classes, which is still maintained by Kraus,
seems particularly forced in the case of those pieces classed as
'laments of the individual' which contain designations of the king
(Pss. 28; 61; 63; cf. I Sam. 2); these make excellent sense as prayer
for one cause throughout, namely the king's, and there is no adequate justification for supposing that the designation of the king
is a later insertion or a sudden change of theme.

(vii) The special problems presented by psalms where 'I' and 'we'
alternate can be resolved by taking account of the representative
character of the king. What is remarkable in such psalms as 9–10;
22; 44; 60; 66; 75; 102 is on the one hand the unity of the cause of
the 'I' and the 'we', and on the other hand the vivid reality of the
individual, who is more than a colourless choir-leader or a personification. This is the tension between Smend and Balla (above,
p. 13), and the possibility of its resolution in the royal person was
seen long ago by A. Jeremias (see Birkeland, p. 117) and by
Mowinckel (*Ps. St.* II, pp. 300f.).

(viii) Throughout the 'psalms of the individual' there occur motifs
or expressions which are royal or at least specially appropriate for
the king. About twenty-four such elements can be counted.

    Gunkel (*Einl.*, pp. 147f.) identifies the following. All nations
attend to the psalmist's thanksgiving (Pss. 18.50; 57.10; 138.1, 4;
119.46). His deliverance has vast repercussions (22.28f.). He
invokes a world-judgment to rectify his cause (7.7, 9; 56.8; 59.6;

59.9; cf. 43.1). He depicts himself as victorious over the nations through God's intervention (118.10–12; 9). He confronts armies (3.7; 27.3; 55.22; 56.2f.; 59; 62.4; 109.3; 120.7; 140.3, 8). He is like a bull raising horns in triumph (92.11; I Sam. 2.1). He is God's son (2.7; 27.10; cf. below, p. 146).

Birkeland (p. 122) adds here other elements, most of which presuppose that the psalmist has a specially close relationship to the national God, as follows. His offerings are on a lavish scale (27.6; 61.9; 66.15f.; cf. I Kings 3.4). Yahweh's 'pleasure' rests on him (18.20; 22.9; 41.12; cf. below, p. 146). Yahweh's honour is bound up with the psalmist's fate ('for thy name's sake', 23.3; 25.11; 31.4; 109.21; 143.11). The psalmist is designated Yahweh's servant (19.12, 14; 27.9; 31.17; 35.27; 69.18; 86.2, 4, 16; 109.28; 143.2; 119 often). He calls God 'my God', 'God of my salvation', 'my King' etc. (below, p. 170). He resides in God's house (23.6; 27.4; 41.13; 61.8; below, p. 143). He speaks of 'my people' (59.12; cf. 144.2; 78.1).

To these items from Gunkel and Birkeland we may add considerably. The speaker vows continual psalmody (see below, p. 173). He stands out before the vast festal congregation (22.23, 26; 40.10f.). His head is raised on high (p. 158). His glory receives special mention (p. 145). He is blessed with superabundant life (p. 160). His designations of God as his helper are often related to warfare (p. 172). He describes God in terms which seem designed to match the king's own work (p. 171). He is called with some emphasis *ṣaddîq*, 'the righteous one', *ḥāsîd*, 'the faithful one' or 'covenant partner' (p. 151). Enemies, military and national in character, aim at him personally rather than at his country and people (p. 137). God extends his hand to deliver, support or take the hand of the psalmist (18.36; 41.13; 63.9; 73.23; 80.18; cf. Isa. 41.10; 45.1). Likewise, the psalmist is at God's right hand, or God is at his (110.1, 5; 139.10; 16.8?). He is recipient of God's counsel (16.7; 73.24; cf. 20.5; Isa. 11.2; Ps. 32.8?). And last but not least, his prayers are availing (p. 195).

(ix) Although there is no doubt that royal motifs can come to be used of ordinary people, such 'democratization' should not be taken for granted in the Psalter. In view of all that is here said about the royal basis of the Psalter, it is reasonable to regard royal items as evidence of royal psalms unless in a particular case there is adequate reason to the contrary.

(x) In many cases the royal interpretation is especially to be preferred because it allows the psalm as it stands to be seen as a consistent and meaningful whole. Other interpretations spoil this
unity as much by assuming the irrelevant use of royal elements
(references to enemy nations, world-judgment etc.) as by reckon-
ing with later additions and redactions. In almost every psalm
examined in the next chapter, the royal interpretation leads to
some gain in cohesion, while in some the improvement is very
marked, e.g. Psalms 9–10; 22; 28; 40; 41; 61; 63; 66; 89; 118, etc.

(xi) As argued on p. 3, the narrow identification of royal psalms
leaves an astonishing gap. There would be scarcely any royal petitions or intercessions. On Gunkel's exegesis we could count
144.5–8 and perhaps 132.1 (he loses 101.2b through emendation!).
For a collection stemming from the royal temple, this is incredible.
A great feature of the king's office was that God invited his
prayers and made them efficacious (pp. 195ff.). With all the personal
and communal burdens which weighed upon the kings, they
would not have so neglected their grace of prayer. Nor is it likely
that all their psalms of supplication were lost, while those of all
and sundry were carefully treasured in the official corpus.

(xii) That the king should be portrayed in glory in some texts and
yet speak in others with little or no reference to his exalted rank
is to be expected. The heightening of his majesty has its appropriate context in enthronement rites, but when he approaches God
in supplication his splendour is subdued or cast off altogether.
Even in Psalm 101, which probably belongs to the great rites and
turns upon the strong exercise of the king's authority, the king
uses no royal designation for himself as he humbly beseeches God
to come to him. His prayers in war ascribe all power of action to
God alone (pp. 138f.).

A comparable reticence can be observed in the royal style of
neighbouring countries. The Sumerian ruler was called *lugal* in
relation to his inferiors, but in relation to his god he calls himself
his *ensi*, vicar or vassal; the Assyrian kings long preferred to call
themselves the equivalent of *ensi*, *iššakku* – so for example Eriba
Adad, who uses *šar*, 'king', only when calling his son 'son of the
king' (Labat, pp. 2f.). There are also variations in willingness to
glorify a king's military prowess (Albright, p. 151). It is said that
the designations of the Pharaoh in the Old Kingdom were varied
with strict consistency according to whether reference was made

primarily to his particular and human person, *ḥm*, or to the divine office which he represented, *njśwt* (Goedicke). A similar duality has been found in Mesopotamian kingship (below, p. 134).

Such, then, are the general considerations which, like Joshua's twelve stones, should stand before us as a perpetual memorial while we work through the relevant psalms one by one in the next chapter.

II

PARTICULAR PSALMS

It is now time to study one by one those psalms which should, in my view, be added to Gunkel's royal psalms for a reconstruction of the royal ideal in the Psalter. Their relationship to each other and to ritual situations will be discussed in the next chapter, where some questions about Gunkel's group will also be treated. In the present chapter the aim is simply to argue that the texts in question are royal.[1]

While one must beware of a circular argument, it will obviously be convenient to make forward references to pages in chapter IV especially, where material on specific themes is gathered and presented as a whole. The texts will be considered in three divisions: first, those where the internal evidence for a royal interpretation seems abundant; second, those where such evidence is not so clear, but sufficient in the light of the general considerations; third, and more briefly, texts which call for some comment but which are best not used in the subsequent reconstruction of the royal ideal. In the interests of brevity it will be assumed that the reader kindly keeps a copy of the psalms at hand.

1. *Psalms with clearly royal content*

Psalm 3

It is not too much to say that this psalm expresses clearly and directly the situation of an embattled king. His enemies are many, in fact an 'army'; for this military sense of *'am* (v. 7) Gunkel compares Numbers 20.20 and Psalms 18.44. These forces have

been 'deployed' (*šātū* v. 7, cf. Isa. 22.7) to encircle him. The
Israelite army, the '*am* of Yahweh, is alluded to in v. 9, where the
exclamation 'Victory is Yahweh's' sounds like a battle-cry. Otherwise, however, the psalmist himself appears as the enemy's opposition and target. This feature is in accord with royal style, as is also
the characterization of the enemies as the 'wicked' and as voracious beasts (p. 140). It is also usual for the enemies of the nation
and king to be depicted as speaking harmful words, as for
example in Psalms 44; 74; 79; 89 (Birkeland, pp. 23f., 61, 72f.). In
the present case they propagate the damaging charge that their
opponents will not be saved by God (or 'his God', G). This
would be especially relevant in the case of Yahweh's anointed; the
time to assail him was when God abandoned him, nullifying
former guarantees of divine protection (p. 140).

The psalmist holds on to God's promises, however, and his
references to them fit the king's position extremely well. Yahweh
is a shield about him (p. 158), giving him glory (p. 145) and lifting
high his head (p. 158); he only has to raise his voice in prayer and
Yahweh sends help from his sanctuary (p. 196). He is supported
by Yahweh (cf. p. 157 and Pss. 51.14; 54.6) and so can sleep in
safety, trustfully relinquishing his own watchfulness against
secret enemies. Such an allusion to sleep is certainly not inappropriate for a king (p. 4). Indeed it may be this feature which
suggested the situation of David to the interpreter who expanded
the psalm's title (cf. II Sam. 17, Briggs). We may wonder if a rite
of 'incubation' lies behind the passage; by sleeping in a holy place,
the Israelite, like the Assyro-Babylonian kings (Labat, pp. 255f.),
will have sometimes sought a reassuring encounter with God in
dream or oracle on the eve of battle.[2] In any case, the passage does
suggest that the psalm belongs to a ceremony of morning prayer.
Mowinckel (*GT*) thinks of the psalm as offered by the king with
morning sacrifice on a field-altar while campaigning away from
Jerusalem (cf. v. 5). But a setting in ritual warfare, perhaps a continuation of Psalm 2, is not out of the question (cf. Weiser).

With a royal interpretation, every part of the psalm fits perfectly
into place, – a contrast with other interpretations (pp. 4f., 9f.). The
king laments over the strength of the opposing army and the
accusations that he has lost God's favour. He counters with
testimony to the special graces God has extended to him, and so
prepares also for the climax of the psalm, where he launches his

powerful prayer. Here he summons the arising of Yahweh (p. 174), 'my God' (p. 170), envisaging with prophetic confidence (p. 175) that Yahweh will smite the bestial jaws of his foe. Victory is in Yahweh's hand! So he cries and invokes a blessing on Yahweh's host.

Whatever may be said of the expansion in the title, 'when he fled because of Absalom his son', it does nothing for the theory of democratization (p. 15). Rather, the interpretation seems to rest on a thoughtful comparison with the situation of King David, derided as forsaken by God (II Sam. 16.7–8), threatened at night (II Sam. 17.1f.), heavily outnumbered (II Sam. 15.13; 17.11).

Psalm 4

There are striking similarities with Psalm 3, especially in what is said about effective prayer, earlier experience of grace, sleep, the 'many who say . . .', glory and derision. While one cannot affirm with Kirkpatrick that the circumstances are the same, or with Budde that the two psalms should be joined together, at least their interpretations should not diverge too widely.

In fact Psalm 4 requires a royal interpretation hardly less clearly than Psalm 3. The strong admonition delivered to the 'sons of men' is comparable to the warning which the king utters to 'the kings and judges of the earth' in Psalm 2 (p. 181). The speaker is again demanding respect both for himself and for Yahweh, the two loyalties almost merging. With a string of seven imperatives he enjoins recognition of his own glory (p. 145) and submission and worship before Yahweh. If he is Yahweh's anointed, one can understand the wide sweep of his address to mankind and why he needs to assert his own glory against those who prefer 'vanity and lies'; to judge from the following exhortations, *rīq* and *kāzāb* here involve adherence to false gods; his opponents, like those in Psalm 2, are turning against the true God and his representative. He warns them of his power in prayer, one of the king's graces (p. 195), and the parallel clause, v. 4a, will also be a warning of his intimacy with Yahweh: Yahweh has given him high distinction as his covenant-partner (p. 151).

In v. 7 the multitudes seem to be complaining of dearth; the light of God's face 'has fled from over us', that light known in the high moment of the festival, token of God's favour to come in fields and flocks (cf. my note in *Theology* 67). Such 'good' had not materialized. Corn and wine were scarce (cf. v. 8 ; G and S add 'oil'). But how does this theme relate to the preceding? Here the royal interpretation makes for coherence. If a satisfactory king meant fertility in his kingdom (p. 166), dearth might well contribute to criticisms of the king. (For such blame falling on the Assyrian king, cf. Labat, pp. 323f. The idea was persistent, for Caliph Walid II says of his predecessor, the extortionate Hisham, 'The shrewd and evilbringing one is dead, the rain is already falling : we have ascended to the throne after him, the trees are now blossoming' – Widengren, *Muhammed*, p. 201.) Perhaps dearth would also encourage recourse to religious practices of Canaanite type, a turning to Baal, and so the psalmist's call for religious loyalty would be all the more in place.

Mowinckel (*GT*) suggests that v. 9 may indicate preparations for the sleep of incubation, and, as mentioned above on Psalm 3, the suggestion is not unreasonable. The verse at least points to an occasion of evening prayer.

In this psalm, then, we see a king who prays for gracious help to 'the God of my righteousness', the God who is specially pledged to uphold him in right and salvation. A large part of his psalm, however, he directs at his opponents, who are imagined rather comprehensively as in the great royal rites (Ps. 2). One cannot declare them with Mowinckel (*GT*) to be foreigners; they are just the formalized opposition to Yahweh and his anointed, and are summoned back to this dual allegiance. The circumstances become more definite in vv. 7f. The king's subjects are discontented because of dearth, and this must contribute greatly to the weight of opposition against him. Rather as in Psalm 3, he indicates the lamentable circumstance only to counter with testimony to his joy and trust in God his protector. Here he leaves his appeal implicit in his testimony. The depth of his piety matches the king's great saying in 63.4a. Especially in its passages of exhortation, the psalm is further comparable with Psalm 62, which abounds in royal phrases (p. 49).

Psalm 7

The psalmist summons God to 'arise' in judgment over the nations (vv. 7f.) and so resolve the crisis he is facing. The royal character of this passage is admitted by Gunkel and Kraus. Only Yahweh's anointed could appropriately invoke the world-dominating epiphany to bring his personal salvation. But this royal element should not be insulated from the rest of the psalm, where in fact there are indications of threatening war (vv. 11 and 13f.) and of the psalmist's military capacity (vv. 5, 11) and 'glory' (v. 6; p. 144). There is nothing to clash with this interpretation. True, the enemy is likened to a lion (p. 140) while the psalmist pitifully seeks shelter in God; but such self-depreciation in intercession is normal for the king (p. 180).

Since the royal psalms frequently acknowledge God's requirements of righteousness (p. 141), it is natural that when the king is accused by his enemies of the sin of breaking covenant he should face the charge with the utmost seriousness. Accordingly, he clears himself with an oath before Yahweh: 'If I dealt evilly with my covenant-fellow or plundered my enemy without cause, may the enemy pursue and overtake my soul and trample my life on the ground and lay my glory in the dust.' Here the language still points to a king, who has treaty relations and may undertake plundering raids. The point still applies if we take *ḥlṣ* as NEB: '. . . or set free an enemy who attacked me without cause', an implausible rendering. There is thus no justification for forcing through an interpretation of the psalm as pertaining to an accused commoner (pp. 6, 10) on the strength of this oath.

The heading designates the psalm as a *šiggāyōn* (*leʰdāwīd*), an apparently ancient term which some have connected with Akkadian *šegu*, Sumerian *eršaḥunga* ('lament', 'song for the comforting of the heart'),[3] and which occurs in Habakkuk 3 above a psalm relating to the salvation of king and people in a time of national distress. The expansion, 'which (David) sang to Yahweh concerning the words of Cush the Benjaminite' is obscure. Some equate 'Cush' with Saul (so the Targum) or Shimei (cf. I Kings 2.44 with Ps. 7.16). Others think of a tradition otherwise unrecorded (Kirkpatrick).

The psalm emerges now as a vigorous unity. A king prays for salvation in the face of a formidable adversary and assailed by accusations that he has broken covenant. He swears his innocence and invokes for his aid Yahweh's great epiphany, the assertion of his kingship over the nations. His prayer passes into strong declaration that the fomenter of trouble will suffer it himself. Here the king with prophetic power sets up an image of the enemy in words and crushes it with doom (p. 197). He ends with a promise to testify of Yahweh's righteousness (p. 182) and to celebrate the name of Yahweh Elyon (p. 156).

Psalms 9–10

These belong together (as in some Mss., G, S, V), since one acrostic scheme runs throughout. The enemies and oppressors are nations (*gōyīm* occurs six times) and afflict the community, especially the poor. In the royal manner, the psalmist speaks of these enemies as 'mine' (p. 137) and the theme of his personal salvation is woven into the national concern (p. 191). Much use is made of the festal themes of God's kingship, and the lamentation for the defenceless is meant to provoke God's kingly action (p. 135). We can recognize Yahweh's anointed, as he draws on the tradition of his own part in the kingship liturgies: he was saved from affliction, restored from the gates of Sheol (9.14), and made victorious over all his foes, to stand forth as the preacher of God's kingship and as witness to his mighty works (p. 182). Characteristic also is the abrasive interplay of testimony and lament (p. 185).

The heading might be connected with the rites of the king on the lines of G, 'concerning the secrets of the son',[4] and Engnell, thinking of a royal passion, renders 'over the death of the son' (*SBU* II, col. 635). This must remain very uncertain. Comparison with the situation of Habakkuk suggests that the psalm may relate to sufferings caused by the Assyrian or Babylonian conquests, a historical affliction being viewed in relation to the liturgical gospel.

The king comes forward with his masterpiece of intercession. With measured power he traverses the alphabet and skilfully contrasts the proclamations of worship with the actual sorry state of God's kingdom. He begins in his role as celebrator of the name of Yahweh Elyon, and as the one promised victory by the God who is triumphant King of all. He hymns this God who is enthroned in Zion, defender of the weak, never forsaking those who trust in him. But soon his praise begins to be interspersed with supplications, which in royal style combine the personal and national and culminate in the great call for Yahweh's arising (p. 174): 'Have mercy on me, Yahweh, see my suffering caused by my enemies, O thou that raisest me from the gates of death . . . Arise, Yahweh, let not man triumph! Let the nations be judged before thy face . . .'

In the second phase (Ps. 10), lament predominates and the bitter contrast is pressed. For all that the king has proclaimed of the divine Judge, his protection is little in evidence. It may be that foreign domination is portrayed primarily as social oppression by a poetic convention, or it may be that the foreign intrusions really did involve such social evil. At all events, the theme is well calculated to appeal to God as King, as well as corresponding to the psalmist's royal responsibility.[5] His prayer mounts in urgency: 'Arise, Yahweh . . . break the arm of the wicked!' In his concluding appeal to God's kingship the note of testimony returns. Surely Yahweh the eternal King must free his land from oppressor nations, and save the poor, the orphan and the widow!

Psalm 17
While there is textual uncertainty about the plural suffixes in v. 11a ('In our goings now they have surrounded us'), the verse as a whole indicates military enemies who are making dispositions to penetrate the land: 'they have set their eyes to spread into the land'. That the reference is to national invasion or similar massive influx is supported by the only other occurrence of *nāṭā b-*, Num. 21.22. As often in the depiction of such enemies, singular and plural interchange (Birkeland, pp. 112f.): in v. 12 a tearing lion (cf. v. 4), in v. 7 men who rise in rebellion against God and threaten his loyal people, in vv. 9f. the arrogantly speaking wicked, armies which 'beleaguer' and 'devastate' (*nqp*, *šd*).

The psalmist who stands against them is notable for his favoured intimacy with Yahweh. Like Israel in Deuteronomy 32.10 and Zechariah 2.12 (EVV 2.8), he is God's darling, dear as the tiny figure reflected in the eye, and like the Pharaoh he nestles under the wings of his patron deity (v. 8, p. 143). As danger mounts, he seeks to be strengthened by the visitation of God, apparently in incubation (v. 15, p. 175).[6]

We may render the title 'a royal supplication', and the points just treated bear out this character. The king is apparently threatened by a punitive expedition on the grounds of some accusation. He is at all events anxious to stress his being in the right, and in preparing for his sleep in the sanctuary he expresses his readiness to be examined by God. He is confident that God will find his cause just. He claims, as a good ruler, to have 'guarded the paths of the disrupter' (v. 4b, cf. p. 141). He has followed closely in the tracks of Yahweh (cf. p. 174). He stresses the fact of his prayer (v. 6, cf. v. 1), alluding perhaps to God's promise to hear his king

(p. 197). He asks as an intimate and favourite for God's help
against the threatened invasion. The climax is the powerful
'Arise!' (p. 174). May Yahweh attack the enemy with his divine
sword! After the obscure v. 14, he concludes with confidence that
in his forthcoming sleep he will see God's favourable face and
form and so awake replenished in grace and glory, equal to the
task ahead.

Psalm 22

Such is the scope of the concluding hymn (vv. 23–32) that it can
hardly be interpreted of the salvation of anyone but the sacral
king, God's 'son', focus of the cause of God's kingdom and the
health of all the world. In similar fashion Delitzsch concluded that
the singer could be none but the 'theocratic king', while Gunkel
thought that 'originally such songs of thanksgiving were sung by
kings, in whose mouths the lofty words sound more intelligible'.
When such a passage is encountered in a collection concerning
which the twelve points on pp. 20ff., can be made, it is difficult to see
how a royal interpretation can be fairly set aside.

In several respects the lament (vv. 2–22) points to the same conclusion. The special relationship with God claimed in the threefold 'my God' (vv. 2f., p. 171) is brought out still more strongly
in the depiction of God as the psalmist's birth-helper and adoptive
father (vv. 10f.); having Yahweh as 'my God' (*'ēlī*) from the womb
is here, as shown by the context, similar to an expression of sonship (cf. 89.27, p. 147). The taunting by the enemies likewise
reflects the fact that the psalmist had claimed such a status, involving the protecting favour and choice of God, such as was declared
in royal ordination (p. 146). In keeping with this is the psalmist's
treatment of his situation on a national scale: Yahweh enthroned
as the Holy One and the Splendour of Israel, Saviour of the
nation's ancestors (vv. 4f.). Significant also is his description of
his abasement (vv. 7f.) in language reminiscent of the fourth
Servant Song (Isa. 52.13–53.12), a passage which at the least
begins and ends with royal colour. The enemies have an archetypal character, encircling death-powers which assume the form
of terrible beasts. Their character is wholly appropriate in view of
the concluding gospel; for the failure of this very foe against
God's son is good news of life for all.

Birkeland, pp. 216–28, argues at length that the king is facing

particular foreign enemies, 'nations' (v. 29), while Mowinckel
(*GT*) similarly thinks of a case like that of Hezekiah in 701 BC.
Such situations could no doubt be presented as irruptions of the
death-powers, but in this psalm it seems to be the archetypal
rather than the particular which holds the stage. There is much to
be said for Engnell's characterization of the psalm as paradigmatic
(above, p. 18). It is an absolute expression of the horrors faced by
God's son in the realm of death, and an equally absolute expression of the good news of his restored life. There is a roundness
about the treatment of both phases which suggests liturgical scenes
rather than a historical crisis, of which there is really no trace. A
ritual enactment of royal abasement and exaltation would most
directly explain the actuality of the two parts. As Ridderbos sees
(*BZAW* 117, p. 101), the lament is not a retrospect, nor is the
hymn anticipatory. The lament rises as from one in the grip of
death, while the following hymn goes out as from a festal celebration of salvation.

The heading 'over the hind of the dawn' suggests an ancient
rite where the hind was used in sacrifices.[7] Otherwise, we can
interpret with G 'over (the rite of) the help of dawn'; in view of
v. 20 (*'eyālūtī*) the reference would be to the turning point from
darkness to salvation, linked with the sunrise (so Engnell, *SBU* II,
col. 634). In this case there might be some link with the fact that
the king in Psalm 110 is greeted as new-born from the womb of
dawn (p. 147).

In the first scene, the king begins his prayer from the depths
with strong appeal to his bond with God and the promises God
gave with it (cf. 89.27): 'My God, my God . . . my God'. His for-
sakenness is the contradiction of his election, his unanswered
supplication the contradiction of his prayer-privilege (p. 195). In
a sharp contrast he sets on the one hand Yahweh the supreme
King, Splendour of Israel (cf. Deut. 10.21), saviour of Israel's
patriarchs, and on the other hand himself, horribly abased, reviled
like the great atoning figure in Isaiah 53. Here (vv. 4–7) is implicit
the king's role as representative of his people, which will come to
light in the second scene.

He tells how the mockers taunt him with Yahweh's election
promises (v. 9) and presses his relationship even further, vividly
recounting how Yahweh had accepted him at birth as his son.
None other can help. He is all alone as the monsters of death

encircle him (p. 140). He tells of the disintegration of his body, as in symbol he falls into Sheol, 'the dust of death'. He can survey his own corpse, his very skeleton. The demonic foes have fastened him like a hunter's victim (?, v. 17).[8] The dead man can see his garments shared out (war-spoil? Cf. Birkeland, p. 222), for we are on the plane of ritual poetry and symbol. And he can still utter a last plea that his soul be saved from the animals of hell. With this the turning point is reached.

In the second scene (vv. 23–32), the king sings a hymn of testimony. He is at the centre of the *qāhāl rāb*, the great festal assembly ('die Vollversammlung der Gemeinde zur Zeit der grossen Jahresfeste', Kraus). Votive sacrifices are offered and a communion-feast is held; the restored king pronounces the blessing as the tokens of eternal life are shared (vv. 26f.). To the festal brotherhood he witnesses of Yahweh's grace and power, recounting his name (p. 156). (The 'brothers' in v. 23 could of course be fellow dignitaries, but the people as a whole can be thus addressed by their king, as in I Sam. 30.23 and II Sam. 19.13.) He then summons all the seed of Israel, all worshippers of Yahweh to celebration and awe in that Yahweh has not rejected the suffering of the sufferer; here was no 'hiding of face' (Isa. 53.3); his cry was answered (vv. 24f.). The act of salvation (v. 32) sets forward God's universal kingship (v. 29). Not Israel only, but all the ends of the world, all the families of the nations must worship Yahweh (v. 28). In Sheol even, there is an awakening to worship (v. 30).[9] Future generations too will continue the testimony and worship. Presumably this 'seed' (v. 31) is the outcome of the king's restoration, the dynastic children in whom his life flows on for ever (cf. Isa. 53.10). A translation of this passage is attempted on p. 167. The existence of such 'passion rites' is argued from other texts on pp. 179f.

Psalm 23

It is notable that this psalm consists only of trustful testimony, a motif which elsewhere is combined with others (Gunkel). This suggests that it originated as part of a sequence and in fact, as Delitzsch observed, it is a fitting sequel to Psalm 22. God is again prominent as King, defender and provider of life; again, from the realm of death the psalmist is restored and eats and resides in God's house, to the greater glory of God's name.

The designation of God as 'my shepherd' suggests that the speaker is representative of Israel, God's flock. Against frequent portrayal of God as the nation's shepherd, there is only one partial parallel involving an individual; Jacob in Gen. 48.15 speaks of 'the God who shepherds me'. The context there shows that the father of the nation is speaking with all the weight of the cult-founder, the intimate of God. And certainly in Psalm 23 the boldness of the expression with the personal pronoun is typical of royal prayers (p. 170), while the allusion it contains to God's kingly character, developed especially in v. 4, is again a favourite tendency of the royal style (p. 171). We may thus say that the traditional feeling that the psalm is indeed appropriate for David the shepherd-king is not baseless; only it is the office of the king rather than a real personal history which is decisive.

'For his name's sake' points in the same direction. Where God was known to be committed, as he was by covenant to Israel and to his king, his honour was at stake in the eyes of the watching world (Birkeland, pp. 123f.). The king's association with Yahweh's name is prominent in the psalms (p. 155). Also appropriate for the king is the assumption of enmity around him as part of the scheme of things. Verse 5 alludes to a demonstrative act of God which warns the enemies that he has extended his protection and favour over his vassal king; he has entertained him in the gaze of his enemies, rather as Pharaoh is to make gifts to vassal kings 'while our enemies look on'. This parallel with the Amarna tablets (Knudtzon, Nr. 100.33–35) is cited by Gunkel and further expounded by Kraus.

Also suitable for the king is the picture of his being personally conducted by Yahweh the Shepherd-King, who goes at his side with the emblems and weapons of his sovereignty, keeping at bay the forces of death. (For 'comfort' in this connection, v. 4, cf. 71.21, following restoration from the 'depths of the earth'.)[10] It is striking also how the psalmist is God's personal guest, the two figures appearing to dine alone.[11] If the anointing in v. 5 is ostensibly that of a guest, allusion to the royal anointing is probably also intended, in view of the point of this verse discussed above. Three themes suit the king in v. 6: the attendance on the king of the personified covenant-graces 'goodness' and 'fidelity' (p. 153); the residence (or 'enthronement', *šibtī*?) in Yahweh's house (p. 143); and his 'length of days' or unending life (p. 161).

It is significant that in tone and in some details the psalm re-sembles Psalm 61, which has explicit mention of the king. There also we find the experience of the realm of death, God's leading of the king to safety, defence in the face of the enemy, his residence with God, his eternal life, his protection by the covenant-graces 'fidelity' and 'truth', his testimony to God's name, and votive sacrifices which could involve a communion meal. Comparison can also be made with 27.1–6, a trusting testimony where royal and military expressions abound.

Dahood relates Psalm 23's theme of pleasant pasturage to a heavenly abode, a transcendental eternal life as in the Elysian fields. He is led to this by numerous associations, not least with Ugaritic phraseology. While this may seem to be going far beyond what the interpretation of this psalm requires, it is likely that much conventional exegesis has gone too far the other way, diminishing the depth of meaning.[12] The study of the royal rites, which we shall consider especially in chapter III, helps to clarify the ideology of the psalm. The king's passage through the 'valley of the shadow of death' is like the symbolic experience of death in Psalm 22 (cf. 44.20). Against the compound term 'shadow of death' there need be no morphological objection, as D. Winton Thomas has shown (*JSS*, 1962). And since 'shadow' is not in itself a sinister thing for the Israelite, the qualification 'of death' in its full sense as the ultimate horror and foe of mankind is in place; that is, it is not just a superlative ('very deep shadow'), as Thomas sug-gested. The king was brought in symbol to that dreadful chasm where death's 'shadow' or dominion was spread. But Yahweh proved stronger than the grim shepherd of the dead (49.15). He brought back the ebbing soul of his king. He bestows on him a higher life beyond the reach of death. He leads him in a procession of 'righteousness' or salvation. The king lives for ever in God's house, feeding on the rich repast God shares with him there.

These pregnant concepts from a ritual setting have a poetic quality, and their application in the practical theology of those times may have been far from direct. But texts like Psalms 22 and 23 show that in some way the mysteries of death and life were treated in the royal rites at the centre of the community, and were treated with hope and promise.

Psalm 27

The psalmist's abundant designations of God accord with the royal style (p. 172): 'my light' (also p. 171), 'my salvation', 'stronghold of my life', 'my succour', 'God of my salvation'. So also does his relation to God as adopted son (v. 10, p. 148)[13] and servant (v. 9, p. 149). His enemies are armies which manoeuvre and storm against him, their individual adversary – a royal trait (p. 140).[14] We hear of his residence or enthronement (*šibtī*) in Yahweh's house (p. 143), where he divines and 'sees the beauty of Yahweh' (pp. 170, 175); the latter phrase may imply access to the Holy of Holies (Birkeland, pp. 184f.). Verse 6 is also fitting for the king: his head raised high by God above the encircling foes, his victory-sacrifices accompanied by the *tᵉrū'ā*, festal trumpets and acclamations (cf. Num. 10.10; Birkeland, p. 183), and his song of witness. In Birkeland's words, it seems difficult to deny that this is a royal psalm.

The king prefaces his prayer with a testimony of trust (vv. 1–6) as in Psalms 9–10, 40 and 89. In style and tone this testimony resembles Psalm 23 (Gunkel). Speaking of Yahweh in the third person throughout, as if to a congregation, he tells of the safety and victory which Yahweh affords him as part of a standing relationship. However terrible the armies that bear down upon him, he trusts that Yahweh will exalt him in victory above them all. He has prayed to be able to continue in the joy of life beside Yahweh, and here he stresses his intimacy with him: no greater joy can he conceive than dwelling in the house of Yahweh all his days, seeing the beauty of Yahweh's face, discovering his will by divination; exalted on the rock of Zion, he is hidden in the covering of Yahweh's tent (p. 143). After victory he will offer outstanding sacrifices and testimony.

After this preparation, which should make it difficult for the deity to reject him, he launches into his prayer (vv. 7f.), calling attention to the loudness of his voice (cf. p. 193). He pleads for the continuation of his privileges as Yahweh's servant, seeing Yahweh's face, having his fellowship; may he now not be forsaken, may that face not be hidden. (A translation of v. 8 is offered on p. 176.) Yahweh's fatherly love to him is more than that of human parents. His earlier reference to divination (v. 4) makes it likely that in v. 11 also he thinks of guidance by a revelation to him (p. 142). The 'level way' of v. 11 is also 'the way of equity' where

he enjoys God's saving justice; there Yahweh will lead him in view
of his enemies.[15] May he not be given into the throat of the beast-
like enemies (v. 12a, cf. v. 2)! They hurl against him many harmful
words, puffing out violence, making false accusations. This last
feature is quite understandable in political, perhaps inter-state
relationships (Birkeland, pp. 312–17). He has confidence that he
will again have the vision of Yahweh's 'goodness' or beauty in the
sphere of life. The final word of comfort (v. 14) may be addressed
to him by a priest or choir. Like Joshua when commissioned and
on the threshold of his campaign, he must 'be strong and of a
good courage'.[16] Or this may be his encouragement to Israel, in a
long tradition of leadership – Moses (Deut. 31.6), Joshua (Josh.
10.25), Joab (II Sam. 10.12), David (I Chron. 22.13; 28.20), Hezekiah (II Chron. 32.7). Either way, the association is with warfare.

Psalm 28

There is good reason to maintain that Yahweh's 'anointed' in v. 8
is a designation of the psalmist, since this expression of confidence
in the king's salvation comes in a passage where the psalmist has
already been speaking in the royal style of his own deliverance and
saving bond with Yahweh. There is no change of reference likely
as we read: 'Yahweh is my power (p. 171) and my shield . . . To
Yahweh belongs power[17] and he is the stronghold of salvation for
his anointed.'

In the rest of the psalm there is ample evidence of the psalmist's
character as king. At the outset, he designates God 'my rock'
(p. 172), while he concludes by interceding for the people to
experience Yahweh as their Shepherd-King (pp. 136, 171). The
threat to his person is in the end treated as a threat to the community. What danger he faces is hard to say, though the concluding verses suggest that a military struggle is involved (Birkeland,
pp. 39f.). Mowinckel (*GT* and *PIW* I, p. 74) prefers to think of a
king's illness, for which the curse-spells of enemies are held
responsible.

The king begins his psalm against the threat of death with the
usual stress on his relationship to Yahweh and calling attention to
his loud crying for help (p. 197); he makes supplicatory gestures
towards the inmost sanctuary (p. 174). He faces treachery (v. 3b),
perhaps of external allies, and calls strongly for the divine retribution, the prophetic tone becoming marked in v. 5 (p. 197). From

v. 6 there is confidence of having been heard. The change would fit a ritual progress, some sign of acceptance having been given. He blesses God (p. 193); Yahweh is true to the bond he has made with his anointed, the king's trust is not in vain; he will surely be mightily helped and so exult and sing testimonies again. And he ends with intercession for Yahweh's blessing on his people; not himself, but Yahweh is the true shepherd who must carry them in his bosom.

Psalm 35

The most obvious royal feature is the way in which at the very outset the psalmist boldly invokes for his personal salvation the intervention of the divine champion of the holy wars. With the urgent 'Arise!', he summons Yahweh to take up shield and weapons and join battle with the hosts who storm against him. If he hears the favourable oracle, confirming that God is still his salvation (v. 3b),[18] he will be confident that the enemy will be routed, driven like chaff before Yahweh's angel. Then, as commonly in royal and national hymns, he will sing of the incomparability of Yahweh (p. 193), happy to present himself as one with no strength of his own, the poor sufferer who owed all to Yahweh (v. 10, p. 180). There is a resemblance to Psalm 22 as in pathetic tones he depicts his soul as assaulted by lions (v. 17), then vows to give praise in the great congregation, the festal assembly (v. 18). In v. 23 he summons the arising of Yahweh as his champion (p. 170), 'my God and my lord' (p. 170). He anticipates that those who delight in his cause will say of his deliverance 'Yahweh grow(s) great, who delights in the prosperity of his servant', language reminiscent of national deliverance and the royal covenant.[19] The community's involvement here may be compared with the communal danger in v. 20: the psalmist's enemies fashion evil against the peaceful people of the earth or land.

In other parts of the psalm he makes further allusions to his relations with adversaries. They have been thought appropriate for a private citizen, and his psalm must in that case be an example of the democratization of royal motifs. But Birkeland (pp. 188–94) has shown that this remoter choice of interpretation is not necessary. In vv. 16, 21 and 25 the descriptions of the enemy as gloating, grinding teeth, avid to swallow, can well fit a national foe, as shown by Lam. 2.16; in vv. 7f. description of the enemies as using

hunting nets is found elsewhere of royal or national enemies
(7.16; 9.16; 57.7; 124; Ezek. 19.8; Hab. 1.15). In vv. 12f. the
psalmist complains that his gestures of friendship have not been
reciprocated; in particular he has mourned for them in their sickness. Such acts of sympathy, however, could happen between
leaders (cf. II Kings 20.12f.), who would act precisely *as though*
they were brothers (v. 14). A vassal king in particular would be
careful to show such concern. Several expressions may refer to the
use of curse-spells in war (cf. Num. 22f.). Finally, the 'violent witnesses' (v. 11, cf. 1a, 23f.), even if the reference is to actual
charges, can obviously still be political; the inter-state atmosphere
was thick with charges and counter-charges (cf. Birkeland, pp.
312–17).

Psalm 40

Engnell has described this as a royal lament, in which the 'anti-
sacrifice' passage (vv. 7–9) is hyperbole, an example of the Hebrew
habit of expressing relativities absolutely; he suggests that this and
kindred passages (51.18f.; 69.31f.) would be at home in the royal
rites of the annual festival at the point where ethical requirements
were stressed (*SBU* II, cols. 649f.). N. Ridderbos has also treated
the psalm as royal and related the document of v. 8 to an enthronement ceremony, a possibility already envisaged by Kaiser (*Der
königliche Knecht*, p. 37). I had independently reached similar
conclusions,[20] which are in marked contrast to the fragmentation
and late dating commonly practised on this psalm.

The psalm's structure, where thanksgiving is followed by
lament, resembles Psalms 9–10, 27 and 89. The pattern lent itself
readily to royal laments, no doubt because of the distinction of the
king as object of God's grace (cf. 71.7, p. 185) and as God's
witness; a telling contrast could be made between the surpassing
promises given to the king and the awful suffering which now fell
to his lot, all the more so because he was prominent in preaching
God's fidelity (p. 185). In fact vv. 2–11 could not be considered as
an independent psalm; their character as a preparatory plea
becomes all the clearer in vv. 10f. The lamenting supplication
(vv. 12–18) fits on perfectly, v. 12 echoing the thoughts of vv. 10f.
Psalm 70 corresponds substantially to vv. 14–18, but has a frag-
mentary character, lacking the opening verb 'Be pleased'. It might
derive from Psalm 40, rather than *vice versa*; thus for Delitzsch it

is a fragment of Psalm 40, 'losgerissen und elohimisch umgesetzt'. At all events, Psalm 40 is clearly a deliberately organized whole and should be expounded as such.[21]

While the community is involved in this act of praise and prayer (vv. 4, 6, cf. 10, 11, 17), the psalmist stands out as more than just a cultic spokesman. As usual in royal psalms, the enemies, who are contrasted with the loyal adherents of God, aim at the psalmist personally to destroy him (vv. 15f., p. 137). He has a great role as witness to the festal assembly (vv. 10f., p. 184); in conjunction with testimony to the mighty works of God, he can tell of his own salvation in a scheme like that of Psalm 18, the deliverance from the Pit (vv. 2f.). His experience is a model for all (v. 5, p. 190) and is expressed in a 'new song', such as elsewhere belongs to the great festal salvation (v. 4; 33.3; 96.1; 98.1; 144.9; 149.1; cf. Isa. 42.10; Rev. 5.9). It is not unusual for a suppliant king to stress his humility or neediness (v. 18, p. 180). When he is saved, Yahweh's people will say, 'Yahweh grows great' (p. 41). He ends with typical royal use of epithets for God which reflect God's covenant promises, 'my succour, my deliverer, my God' (p. 172; $m^epal^e\underline{t}i$ elsewhere only in the royal texts 18.3, 49; 144.2, with the parallels 70.6 and II Sam. 22.2).

The context of the important vv. 7–9 indicates that they are part of the preparatory plea. The other items in the plea can well be interpreted of the faithful performance of the king's cultic role, – how he suffered and was restored in the symbolic festal enactment of salvation (pp. 129f.), and how he then preached the gospel to the festal congregation (v. 10a, p. 185). It is likely that vv. 7–9 also relate to these ceremonies. The oft-emended v. 8a will then fit in well with reference to liturgical response and processional entry, while v. 8b can very well refer to a scroll presented at the king's installation.[22] Such a document, comparable to the Pharaoh's protocol, embodies the royal covenant. In it God declared this man his chosen one, his son, and added to the promises the requirements of obedience, which come to the fore in our psalm. The king could thus aptly say that here it was written 'concerning' him, or (cf. Dahood) 'as an obligation upon' him (*'ālay*); it may indeed have been fastened *on him* like a phylactery (cf. II Kings 11.12, *SKAI* p. 24). The point of the passage would thus be that in the enthronement ritual or its re-enactments he had received this document and responded in ceremonies which demonstrated his ready obedience, and it was there taught that this self-offering was more valuable to God than the substitutionary animals sacrificed in the festival (p. 180). That God had 'dug open' his ears (v. 7) may stress his special grace of hearing and so carrying out Yahweh's commands, rather as Mesopotamian rulers often claim that the gods have given them a wide or open ear and hence heavenly wisdom.[23] Or it may indicate that this teaching was given him through an oracle. Similar teaching is appropriately represented in I Samuel 15.22f. as conveyed in verse-style by the prophet to the king. In Egypt also such teaching is imparted by the king to his successor: 'More acceptable is the character of one upright of heart than the ox of the evildoer' (*ANET*, p. 417).

Along these lines the psalm as a whole makes good sense; indeed it emerges as one of the most significant for our study. The festal rites have recently been celebrated, and the king alludes to them, and especially to his part in them, to sharpen a supplication about some particular attack from his enemies. The whole of vv. 2–11 are by way of preparation. A moving plea is here established by pointing to the past grace of God and to the king's basic fidelity (in spite of faults, v. 13), as symbolized in the recent festal rites. The king thus refers to his escape from Sheol (vv. 2–4) and his subsequent thanksgiving and teaching (vv. 5f.). Then he recalls how at his enthronement he signalled his readiness to obey (vv. 7–9). Finally he speaks of how he amply fulfilled his duty as God's witness and evangelist before the great assembly (vv. 10f., pp. 185, 191f.).

From this preparation his supplication unfolds naturally: surely God will not withhold from him the grace of which he has so witnessed (v. 12)! No doubt many faults can be found in him, the consequences of which now overwhelm him (v. 13). But may Yahweh hurry to his aid! May his enemies turn and flee and be covered with the shame of defeat, along with all who gloat over his present discomfiture. So Yahweh's worshippers will hail the victory and acclaim the unfolding of God's greatness. And the king ends with stress on his need and with appeal to his special bond with the divine saviour, 'my lord, my succour, my deliverer, my God'.

Psalm 41

Some take this as a thanksgiving for healing, which in vv. 5–11 quotes the prayer that had been made in sickness (Gunkel, etc.). Delitzsch and others, however, think that the psalm is rather an actual prayer in sickness, in view of the large proportion constituted by vv. 5–11. The latter view is followed here, but the dispute does not affect the question whether the psalm is royal.

Indications that the speaker is a king can be found in the machinations of enemies around him during his sickness; in his determination, by Yahweh's aid, to punish them on his recovery (v. 11); and in his being grasped or upheld by Yahweh (p. 157) and stationed in his presence for ever (p. 143), v. 13. On this view, furthermore, the beginning of the psalm ceases to be difficult, as I suggested in *JTS*, 1968. Both the phraseology and the isolated nature of the thought have been found difficult and often emended. If the psalmist is a king, however, it will be an example of how care of the poor can be cited as the essence of the king's calling (p. 33 n. 5). The language fits into place, and we can render, 'Blessed be he that rules wisely on behalf of the weak.'[24]

The ailing king thus begins his psalm by quoting a divine promise to a righteous ruler; in particular he will be sustained in sickness and tenderly nursed by God himself. The application of this promise is now claimed, though the king acknowledges that he must in some way have displeased God: 'So now I say (cf. 82.6; II Sam. 19.29; Jer. 10.19), O Yahweh be gracious to me, heal my soul, though I have sinned against thee.' His lament centres not on his ailment but on the opportunity it gives to his enemies, those perpetual accompaniments of a king's life. Respectful visitors to the sickbed secretly plot his overthrow. A trusted associate who ate at his table (probably as a courtier, cf. II Sam. 9.7; I Kings 18.19) has broken covenant and moved against him. He prays Yahweh to restore him that he may requite these wicked men. He looks to the time when Yahweh will have confirmed the continuance of the 'delight' in which his election was grounded (p. 146), through the discomfiture of his enemies (v. 12). Then, whole again and grasped by God's hand, he will be stationed in the divine presence for ever.

Gunkel cites an Egyptian parallel describing treachery against a king by his table-vassal; the preceding lines are also not irrelevant to our v. 2. King Amen-em-het says to his successor: 'I gave to the destitute and brought up the orphan. I caused him who was nothing to reach (his goal), like him who was (somebody). (But) it was he who ate my food that raised troops (against me) and he to whom I had given my hands that created terror thereby' (*ANET*, p. 418, cf. Dan. 11.26f.).

Psalm 57

In his opening prayer the psalmist speaks as one especially close to God: he shelters under God's wings (p. 143) and appeals to the Most High as the God pledged to accomplish victory for him, *lā'ēl gōmēr 'ālay*. The meaning here is filled out in v. 4: God sends from heaven, as for the king in 18.7 and 144.7; he makes sport of his enemy (if God is subject of *ḥērēp*, so NEB, cf. 2.4); he sends the covenant-angels Fidelity and Truth (p. 153). Meanwhile the psalmist laments that he is among enemies like monsters, voracious lions with teeth and tongues of deadly power (p. 140); like a fire they consume (*lōhᵃṭîm*) the sons of men, – and the description reflects the king's responsibility for mankind as a whole. He summons God to arise (p. 174) in glorious epiphany over all the earth, and this again fits the world-wide scale of the king's struggle in the festal conceptions (Ps. 2 etc.). The enemies are portrayed as attacking him personally (p. 137), hunting his soul with a net (p. 140). He declares their doom with prophetic force: they will fall in their own pit (p. 197).

Birkeland, p. 246, thinks 'I will lie down' (v. 5) indicates that the king is preparing for incubation (cf. above, p. 28), vv. 8f. being an anticipatory thanksgiving. Perhaps we should rather think of two scenes, vv. 2–7 being a night prayer, followed by 8–12 in connection with the sunrise. In vv. 8f. he is confident of salvation and already celebrates it. He summons into wakefulness his own 'glory' (p. 145), the cultic instruments, and the angel of dawn, *šaḥar*, who was a deity among the Canaanites (cf. Dahood). The reference to his glory perhaps implies that he now discards a garb of ritual affliction. With an expansiveness which Gunkel characterizes as royal, he witnesses among the nations (p. 183), praising the infinite fidelity and truth of God 'my lord' (pp. 153, 171). His final call for God's epiphany over all the world suggests that he still looks for the realization of the salvation which he has been celebrating in faith.

From first to last, the psalm thus appears to be a clear example of royal psalmody. The superscription 'Do not destroy' occurs also over Psalms 58, 59 and 75, which all seem to have national or

royal reference. Comparing Isaiah 65.8, Mowinckel suggests that
it denoted a rite of supplication for the nation on the strength of a
righteous nucleus.[25] A further heading, *miktām*, found also over
Psalms 16 and 56–60, seems to indicate rites of atonement.[26] The
expansion 'when he fled into the cave because of Saul' may be
based on v. 7 – the hunter suddenly at the mercy of his prey;
again, in its fashion, it shows the leaning of tradition to royal
interpretation.

Psalm 59
The psalmist personally bears the brunt of an international
struggle; his prayers use royal phrases and invoke world-
judgment. A royal interpretation is thus entirely in place. The
elaborate title points also to a context of national and royal rites
(pp. 46f.).

The king appeals to God to save him and set him on high
(cf. 20.2; 91.14) above those who have exalted themselves against
him (cf. 17.7). His epithets for God show both his bond and his
military role: my God, my high fortress, refuge, my power, God
of my fidelity (p. 172). The enemies are described throughout the
psalm in lurid fashion, the terms being generally such as can
describe national enemies (Birkeland, pp. 145–50). At night they
are able to close in around the city, jackal-like, demonic. Their
aggression is no doubt made under some pretext, but he protests
to God that he has done nothing to justify their attack (cf. p. 31).
For his deliverance he calls on God to 'awake' (p. 174) and, as
Yahweh Sebaoth, God of Israel, to judge all the nations. Like the
king in 2.4, he pictures how God laughs at the vain ambitions of
the nations (v. 9). God's wrathful intervention will demonstrate
that he, God, is 'ruler from within Jacob to the ends of the earth'
(v. 14). And so the king promises to sing praise (p. 185), centring
his testimony on God's fidelity and on the proved relationship
with himself (vv. 17f., p. 188). This fidelity is sent as an angel to
assist God's king (p. 153), and we should probably vocalize v. 11
to give 'As for my God, his fidelity will come to meet me' (cf.
21.4 which refers to the king).

Psalm 61
A common pattern in supplicatory psalms is that the psalmist
passes to confidence in his prospect of relief and finally promises

thanksgiving. It would therefore be natural in this psalm also to assume that the king whose preservation becomes a matter of confidence in vv. 7f. is none other than the psalmist who has been asking for help and who ends with a vow of thanksgiving. The switch to self-reference in the third person ('the king' v. 7), similar to that in Psalms 28 and 63, is done to stress a privilege peculiar to the king, here his gift of abundant life (p. 160). Other examples may be found in 2.2, 6f.; 18.51; 89.51–2; Jeremiah 38.5; King Yeḥawmilk of Byblos refers to himself in the first person, changes to the third, then back to the first (*ANET*, p. 502; Dahood). The rather formal wording in our psalm at this point is probably intended to echo the people's prayer for the king, alluded to in v. 6 as 'the desire of those who fear thy name' (the root *yrš* being equivalent to '*rš*, Thomas, *TRP*; Dahood). That the psalmist is indeed the king is further indicated by his exaltation and his finding a fortress in God (vv. 3f., pp. 158, 172) his everlasting sojourn in God's tent, sheltering under God's wings (v. 5, p. 143) and his vow of daily sacrifices with music for ever (v. 9, p. 173).

It is a king, then, who asks God to hear his supplication. That he prays 'from the end of the earth' may suggest that he is on a distant campaign; a similar phrase is used by Pharaoh Ramses II of prayer at the battle of Kadesh (Gunkel). But more likely the phrase denotes the entrance of Sheol (Bentzen, Dahood), where the heart 'faints' (cf. Jonah 2.8). Already the language can be taken as trusting testimony – 'whenever I call . . . thou dost lead me'; certainly vv. 4f. has this character. Verse 3 would thus be a longer equivalent of 9.14b 'thou that exaltest me from the gates of death'. His being led by God from Sheol's mouth to a high rock is suggestive of his enthronement on Zion after processional ascent. The use of 'shelter' and 'tower of glorious strength' in v. 4 is equivalent to the king's personal designations of God (p. 172); on Zion the king is in that presence of God which constitutes '*ōz*, divine power, a fortress against the chaos-enemy (8.3, with the same absolute use of 'enemy').

And so in v. 5 he refers to his eternal sojourn in God's tent and his nestling under God's wings (p. 143). In vv. 6f. he is confident that his prayer and vows have been favourably received, along with the community's prayer for his unending life (p. 166). He will be enthroned for ever before God, guarded by the angelic

graces Fidelity and Truth, and so be able to celebrate God's name
(p. 156) and offer sacrifices daily and everlastingly (p. 24, 173).

The psalm is a notable example of how, in virtue of the rich
promises given to him, the king can make equally rich testimony
of trust (cf. Pss. 3; 4; 23; 27; 62).

Psalm 62

The psalmist accumulates epithets for God in relation to himself
in the royal style (p. 172): my rock (twice), my salvation (twice),
my high fortress (twice), rock of my power, my lord. Similar in
implications are the phrases 'from him my salvation', 'from him
my hope', 'on God my victory and my glory', 'my shelter in God'.
The last phrase has its counterpart in v. 9, 'God is a shelter for us',
and it is a feature of the psalm that the danger threatens the people
('*am*, v. 9) as well as the psalmist in particular. The expressions
already quoted point to enemies that can assume a military aspect.
Their aggressiveness is portrayed as a storming assault in v. 4,
though the exact meaning is uncertain (p. 182). In v. 5 they hold
counsel to thrust from his eminence him who is the target of their
enmity; they use the weapon of deceit. From vv. 10f. we gather
that their power and rich resources overawe the king's people, so
that he must exhort them with traditional wisdom to trust only in
God as the true source of power and judgment.

His address to his opponents (v. 4) may be compared with other
royal admonitions (p. 181); similarly his exhortations to the people
(vv. 9f.), commending trust in God. The disparagement of human
strength is a feature of royal witness (p. 192), as also is the conveying of an oracle (p. 181) and the praise of God's fidelity (p. 153).

The heading '*al y^edūtūn* may refer to the ritual context, perhaps
a ceremony of confession (cf. I Kings 8.33–5).[27] A national rite of
this kind, in face of a looming danger, is probably reflected in v. 9.
Pouring out water as in I Samuel 7.6 may have dramatized the
'pouring out' of heart (or soul, I Sam. 1.15; cf. Lam. 2.19).

Birkeland, pp. 257–60, argues that the enemies are national and
foreign and best thought of as the forces of an imperial overlord,
intent on replacing the vassal Judean king. A similar line is taken
by Mowinckel (*GT*). One could cite Habakkuk 1–2 for the use of
traditional ethical categories with reference to imperial oppression.
However, it is difficult to penetrate the traditional phrases of our
psalm, and the trouble could rather centre on disloyalty within the

Kingship and the Psalms

people. There is an affinity with Psalm 4, in that the king's admonitions cover those who are in direct opposition as well as those in need of encouragement; there are other resemblances: 'lies' in 4.3 and 62.5, 10, 'sons of men' in 4.3 and 62.10, 'how long' in 4.3 and 62.4, 'my glory' in 4.3 and 62.8, 'be still' in 4.5 and 62.6, etc. The appeal of the psalm to God is implicit in trustful testimony and declaration rather than in direct supplication; this tendency of royal psalms has been noted on p. 49.

Psalm 63

'The connection is unintelligible unless the king (v.12) is identified with the psalmist whose enemies are destroyed.' Thus, long ago, Kirkpatrick expressed the simple truth. An interpretation like that of Kraus is not natural. He thinks of a commoner seeking asylum and wisely slipping in a deferential prayer for the king as master of the sanctuary. But v. 12 follows the common pattern of anticipated thanksgiving for deliverance from the enemies previously described, in this case in v. 11. And in fact there is ample indication in the rest of the psalm that it concerns the king's cause throughout. Especially we note the battle-scene of v. 11 and the privileged language of vv. 8f. For the switch at v. 12 to self-reference in the third person see p. 48. The interpretations of Gunkel and Weiser have been discussed on pp. 5 and 10f.

The king's first words, 'Thou art my God', fit his personal covenant (p. 151). The sequence in vv. 2–9 is difficult to establish exactly. It seems that he approaches God in weakness and need, seeking to be replenished by a vision in the sanctuary (p. 175). Preparation for incubation seems likely from v. 7. He hopes to see the 'power and glory' of revelation, the divine majesty from which his own kingship derives (p. 144). So he will be sure of victory and so will be able to renew the perpetual royal witness and proclamation of God's name (vv. 4–6, p. 156). The customary royal witness to God's fidelity (p. 153) surpasses itself in v. 4. Confidently he speaks of God as his succour and of his safety in the shade of God's wings (p. 143); he closely accompanies this God, who leads him (v. 9a, p. 174) and grasps him with his right hand (p. 157). The enemies aim at him personally (v. 10a, p. 137); their overthrow is to be like that of an army, slain by the sword, left on the field for foxes (v. 11), a cause of rejoicing for all the loyal community (v. 12b). 'Speakers of falsehood' (v. 12b) are not out of place on this interpretation; enmity towards king or nation often includes this feature (cf. 144.8, 11; Birkeland, pp. 24f., 42, 66f.).

The expansion in the 'Davidic' heading seems to be based on the imagery of drought in v. 2.

Psalm 66

The thanksgiving of the community for its relief (vv. 1–12) flows into that of an individual for his personal deliverance (vv. 13–20). The composition as a whole can thus be seen as another example of how the national cause appears as 'personal' for the king. That this unified interpretation is correct seems confirmed by the huge scale of the individual's sacrifices (v. 15). There are further features which at the least are agreeable to this conclusion: he testifies to the whole assembly, 'all the fearers of God' (v. 16; cf. 22.24, 26; 40.10f.), addresses God as 'my lord' (p. 171), emphasizes the fact of answered prayer (p. 197), blesses God (p. 193), and is accompanied by God's fidelity (p. 153). The great sweep of thought is somewhat reminiscent of Psalm 22; it passes from a whole world praising the God exalted over the nations to the testimony of one soul's deliverance. For the common cause of king and world we may also compare Psalms 9–10.

In the communal hymn, there is reference to salvation in the manner of the exodus, but newly experienced; such praise arose from the re-living of tradition in the festivals. But especially in vv. 8–12 there may be allusion to recent national deliverance. Out of this flows the king's thanksgiving, presenting the experience as the deliverance of his own soul in response to his own vows and prayers. He makes solemn entry into the temple to fulfil his vows of lavish sacrifices and to testify to the whole assembly. Like the king in 18.21f., he underlines the lesson for all: Yahweh faithfully hears him who keeps faith (p. 190). He concludes in the same personal terms. The whole issue, for which earlier all the nations were called to praise Yahweh, is finally summarized as the answering of his prayer and the abiding of the divine fidelity with him.

Psalm 69

A lamenting prayer (vv. 2–30) is followed by a hymn of thanksgiving (31–37); structure and contents have some similarity with Psalm 22. Many traits show the psalmist as the typical and

representative sufferer, bearing the community's cause in his
person. He first presents himself as sinking in the floods of the
underworld (cf. Pss. 18 and 40), calling with his last strength for
'my God' (p. 170). His enemies are innumerable. God, who knows
all his sins, must know he has given them no cause for their
assault (cf. Pss. 7 and 35). In vv. 7f. it is expressly 'Adonay
Yahweh Sebaoth, the God of Israel' whose worshippers are
oppressed by shame over the plight of the psalmist, who suffers
for the sake of this God. He looks for the answering of his prayers
through God's abundant fidelity and saving truth (p. 152) in the
'time of favour' (v. 14), a phrase suggestive of the dawn of a
general salvation (cf. Isa. 49.8; 58.5; 61.2).

In the thanksgiving, the communal aspect emerges strongly.
There is now confidence of salvation; the worshipping society,
humble before God (cf. 18.28), rejoice together over his deliverance and are addressed with blessing (v. 33), as in the communion
meal of Psalm 22. He envisages universal hymnody, the salvation
of Zion, and the 'building' or strengthening of the cities of Judah.
The new gift of life will be manifest in a succession of generations
granted to God's servants (cf. 22.31f.).

In the style of a king, the psalmist combines such communal
associations with the strong delineation of his own persona. He is
God's servant, normally before God's face (v. 18); belonging to
God, in that he should now be 'redeemed' (v. 19). The numerous
enemies aim at him personally. He suffers on God's account
(v. 8; cf. 44.23). He opposes those who mock God (v. 10). The
temple is especially his care, and zeal for it has consumed him
(p. 175). He counts on God's salvation to raise him from his utter
abasement and set him on high (v. 30, p. 158). His enemies,
attacking on some false pretext, require him to return what he has
not plundered (v. 5, 'this I am required to restore', *'āz* demonstrative as in Phoenician). He counters them with an elaborate and
terrible curse, an exercise to which the king's office gave special
force (p. 197).

A substantial part of his lamentation, however, is so 'individual'
as almost to conflict with the communal references. But as
Birkeland, pp. 90–4, points out, the princes of the Amarna letters
and even the Pharaoh himself portray themselves as isolated,
helpless, betrayed (*ANET*, p. 418b). When the king entered into
the role of the representative penitent, he became the bearer of all

the typical sorrows, including the sense of alienation; in similar manner the Assyrian king took on the character of the 'poor man' (Labat, p. 108). In fact, betrayal by brothers and covenant-fellows was common enough on the political stage (cf. Pss. 35 and 41).

The simplest interpretation of vv. 31f. is that the psalmist underlines the importance of his testimony: it is more acceptable to God than the best of animal sacrifices. The tendency to such comparisons seems to be ancient and would be especially appropriate where sacrifice was offered (p. 187). It is not necessary to assume that the psalm is 'anti-cultic' or that the cultus was in abeyance. Nor is it necessary to follow Birkeland, who regards vv. 35–7 as an exilic addition (comparing Isa. 44.26; 61.4; Amos 9.14; Ezek. 36.10) to a pre-exilic royal psalm (he thinks the temple stands, v. 10). The passage chimes in well with the 'time of favour' of v. 14, and there is nothing inapplicable to the period of the monarchy. Devastation and uprooting of population was already known, and allowance must also be made for a tradition of language describing ritual desolation and restoration.[28]

The heading is found elsewhere over what are certainly royal or national psalms, 45; 60; 80. It is best understood as Mowinckel suggests (*Ps.st.* IV, pp. 29–33; *PIW* II, p. 214), as 'over the rite of the lilies', their budding being observed as a sign of God's acceptance (cf. Num. 17.21f. [EVV 17.6f.]). Such a sign would be in place at the transition to thanksgiving in v. 31. Mowinckel (*GT*) follows Birkeland in supposing that the psalmist is a king (or equivalent leader) who has suffered defeat; he has had to pay reparations from his treasures (v. 5) and many of his people have been taken prisoner (v. 34). While one cannot be sure of such details, comparison with Psalm 22 does suggest that Psalm 69 refers to a historical crisis but draws on the tradition of the ritual texts exemplified by Psalm 22.

Psalm 70

This is substantially the same as 40.14–18. As argued on p. 43, this passage is in the royal style. Even considered on its own, it can best be regarded as the prayer of a king. There is a new element in the heading, *lᵉhazkir* (also over Ps. 38). This may indicate a liturgical act to prompt Yahweh to take note of the supplicant's need; there may have been some resemblance to the *'azkārā* ceremonies of sacrifice (Lev. 2.2; 5.12; Num. 5.18; *Ps.st.* IV, pp. 15f.; *PIW* I, p. 3; II, p. 212).

Psalm 71

The psalmist pleads with God on the strength of a relationship very much in the royal tradition: 'Thou hast appointed for my salvation, yea thou art my rock and my refuge . . . my God . . . my hope' (vv. 3f., p. 170). It is the relationship of the son to the father, who aided his birth and accepted him then (vv. 5f., p. 147), and who taught him as he grew (v. 17, p. 148). One so protected in the divine love is attacked when the enemies see evidence that God changes to forsaking him (v. 11, p. 140). Especially in old age a king might be accused of losing the divine approval and so being 'forsaken' (vv. 9, 18; cf. I Kings 1 and *ANET*, p. 149a). Then the enemies, ever watchful for an opportunity against his soul, hold counsel together against him (v. 10). But God who raises his king from Sheol and 'comforts' him (cf. 23.4) will again expand his 'greatness'; that $g^e dull\bar{a}t\bar{i}$ (v. 21) here denotes royal power is likely both from the context and from usage in Esther 1.4; 6.3; 10.2 (cf. II Sam. 7.21; Ps. 145.3; I Chron. 29.11). Also appropriate for a king is his standing over against the masses as a marvellous sign of God's dealings (v. 7); the context makes it probable that he so appears as the recipient of God's faithful love and salvation, God being his 'glorious shelter' (p. 186, similarly Briggs, and Birkeland, p. 233).

The psalm now appears to be a striking example of how the king could build a powerful plea on his function as God's witness (p. 185). He begins by stressing how he is depending on God's righteous fulfilment of all his former assurances. May God now prove to be the rock of safety as promised for his king, and rescue him from the wicked and bitter enemies. His office has meant that he has been the great exemplar of grace, the recipient of God's supreme favour and so the witness to his glory. Let not God reject him now that he grows old and weak and his enemies conspire against him. Let God consider how, when saved, his king will be able to add to his former witnessing. He will 'enter' (v. 16) in the great ceremonies to preach of the powerful and faithful acts of God, fulfilling the ministry in which God has instructed him from youth.

To rising generations (or 'to the congregation', v. 18, p. 187) he will preach of the incomparability of Yahweh (p. 193). His own story will be central to the testimony (p. 188), a story of sufferings in the realm of death, and restoration to life, exaltation and grandeur. So with the music of the temple he will make confession of the loyal 'truth' of the God covenanted both with him and with the nation, 'my God' and 'the Holy One of Israel' (v. 22), who will have redeemed his soul and laid the shame of defeat on his enemies.

There is no heading in the Hebrew, but *l^e dāwīd* is represented in G (which also proposes a connection with the Rechabites and the first exiles). Commentators note verbal similarities with Psalms 22; 31; 35; 40. The plural suffixes of the consonantal text in v. 20 ('thou hast shown us . . . thou hast revived us') could indicate either the representative character of the king or, if not original, the development of a collective use of the psalm; the former is to be preferred with Birkeland, p. 231, as the harder reading.

Psalm 75

The division proposed by Mowinckel (*GT*) and Gunkel is the most likely: v. 2 hymnic introduction in 'we' style, vv. 3f. God speaks (followed by *selā*), vv. 5–11 speech by a leader in 'I' style. Kraus accepts this analysis, but thinks the text in v. 11 must have originally been '*he* will hew off all the horns of the wicked', 'I' being impossible in the context. Gunkel's explanation of this 'I' is that the speaker is raised by his enthusiasm to imagine himself co-operating in the divine judgment. It is not a question of 'co-operating', however. The speaker takes on himself individually the execution of the divine judgment. This is the work of God's king, as for example in 101.8: 'In the mornings I will destroy all the wicked of the earth, cutting off from the city of Yahweh all workers of iniquity'. It is also appropriate for the king to warn those who would exalt themselves to grandeur, and to use the figure of horns (vv. 6, 11), ornaments of the royal helmet.[29] His admonition here to such rebels is comparable to that in the royal texts Psalm 2 and I Samuel 2.3f.

The psalm begins by acknowledging God's nearness. The festal community has praised God, invoked his name and recited his great deeds, and so is now filled with the sense of his cultic presence. The oracle is now conveyed (vv. 3f.), God declaring his determination to correct the world with justice at the due hour (*mōʿēd*, a festal day?). It is possible that the speaker throughout has so far been the king, speaking first for the community, then for God. It is his duty to execute God's righteousness in society, and particularly in curbing the mighty men of ambition. And so from vv. 5f. he warns them that power and authority are of God (p. 181), whom he depicts with visionary inspiration (p. 175) as preparing a heady cup of doom for the wicked of the earth. He speaks of his own part as unceasing celebrator of Jacob's God (p. 183) and fierce executor of his vengeance. His last phrase concerning the exalting of 'the horns of the righteous one' could allude to himself as the rightful bearer of kingship (p. 151).

The disagreements of commentators about the analysis of the psalm can be seen as due to the very closeness of the king's identification with God's judgment. Verse 11 has already been discussed in this connection. In v. 5 the king's tone is so authoritative that it is not surprising that Delitzsch, Bentzen and the early Mowinckel (*Ps.st.* III, pp. 47f.) saw here the continuation of the oracle. It may even be wondered if the 'I' of vv. 2f. is not the king himself; comparison could be made with Psalm 101, where the king's hymnic introduction is followed by his main speech. The oracular interpretation is to be preferred, however, in view of the preceding reference to God's nearness.

Although Gunkel himself does not consider a royal interpretation of this psalm, it is interesting that the two foreign parallels he adduces do illustrate the assertion of divine order through a king: Darius I tells how the deity made him king to put the earth back in its place (Weissbach, p. 89), while the god Amon announces that he made the Pharaoh and so restored right to its place, steadied the earth and brought joy to heaven on his account (Erman, p. 59).

For the heading 'Do not destroy', see p. 46.

Psalm 89

This is explicitly royal (vv. 51f. and possibly v. 19), treats at length of the Davidic covenant and of the king's humiliation, and is generally in the grandest royal style. Kraus and Weiser have no hesitation in accepting it as a royal psalm. Why then did Gunkel not place it unreservedly in his royal group?

The main reason was that he understood vv. 39–46 to describe the cessation of the dynasty from 586 BC. The combination of 'forms' (hymn, lament, etc.) also inclined him to a late date, when older elements might be mixed; the conflicting moods and circumstances seemed also to point to such compilation. He noted there was no reference to return from exile and concluded that the psalm as a whole dates from about the fifth century BC. The composition, he thought, had incorporated a North Israelite hymn from about the time of Jeroboam II and complete in itself (vv. 2f., 6–19), along with a poetic version of the oracle to David (vv. 20–38). Verses 4f. were newly composed to assist the adaptation of these pre-exilic materials, which were now made the prelude to a general lament over the fallen dynasty (vv. 39–52). Gunkel met the difficulty that the 'anointed' himself seems to be the speaker (vv. 51f.) by supposing that the completed psalm was presented in public worship by the senior member of the surviving family of David, regarded by the faithful as the rightful king.

Even on this view the psalm is a rich treasure-house of royal psalmody and can serve our purpose in ch. IV. Whether we can improve on the rather artificial interpretation of Gunkel and explain the psalm as a unity from the time of the kings will be best considered in ch. III (p. 121).

Psalm 91

Elaborate oracular promises here bestow invulnerability, triumph, glory and surpassing life. The individual on whom such promises are lavished could hardly be any but the king. It may be claimed that the details amply confirm this judgment.

Verses 14–16 are purely oracular, while the preceding promises have the nature of sacral blessing-words or assurances; whether the recipient himself speaks briefly in vv. 2, 9a is dubious.[30] Similar bestowals of glorious blessings occur in royal Psalms 21 and 45.

Expressions in v. 1 suit the king well: the one 'sitting (enthroned) in the covering of the Most High' (p. 143); in Amos 1.5 such a royal 'sitter' is described in parallelism as 'one who holds the sceptre' (see further Dahood here and on 2.4). In the very shadow, the personal emanation, of the Almighty he nestles; this last word, *yitlōnān*, used of eagles nesting high on the rock in Job 39.28, is used here of the king on Zion's rock, likewise secure under the feathers and wings of his parent deity (cf. v. 4, p. 143). Equally appropriate for the king is the characterization as 'the one who says to Yahweh, My shelter and my refuge, my God in whom I trust' (p. 172).

For the king, the air is ever thick with deadly darts, whether of plague (often a danger on campaigns), hostile curse or weapons. But God confers safety on him day and night, though armies fall in ten-thousands at his side (cf. II Sam. 18.3). The covenant angel Truth protects him as a shield (v. 4, p. 153). Because of his constant confession of trust ('Yahweh is my shelter', etc., v. 9), he needs but to look and he will see that Yahweh has routed his enemies, 'the wicked'. Perhaps it is his military 'tent' (v. 10) which is kept free of plague (Dahood).

Yahweh appoints his messengers to guard him constantly (v. 11, p. 153). Their bearing him on their palms to protect his feet from rough ground suggests the notion of a royal palanquin such as was used at the coronation of Assyrian kings (Labat, pp. 83f.); we may also compare representations of the Egyptian king being carried on a sedan throne (Erman, p. 69; *MR*, fig. 5), and also the bearing of God's throne-dais by sphinx-like attendants in Ezekiel's vision. Verse 13 seems to show him as victor over the chaos-powers, his foot trampling on serpents, lion and dragon (p. 144); the coupling of *tannīn* and *peten* in this sense is paralleled in Ugaritic mythology, as noted by Dahood. Gunkel also sees the connection with the mythology of the divine champion treading on the defeated monsters and cites various examples.

In v. 14 the king's passionate love of Yahweh is expressed boldly (*bī ḥāšaq* only here of love for God, p. 169). Yahweh promises to 'set him on high' (p. 158), because of his cultic loyalty ('he knows my name'). His prayers will be answered (p. 195). In affliction God will be at his side to deliver him and make him glorious. He will be sated with abundant life and divine salvation; 'length of days' is probably equivalent to 'life unending' (p. 161; cf. 21.5 and Dahood there and on 23.6).

There is no heading in the Hebrew, but *lᵉdāwīd* is represented in G. The Targum supposes that David addresses the psalm to Solomon, while a tradition of royal-messianic interpretation is also evident in the temptation stories (Matt. 4.6; Luke 4.10–11).

Psalm 92

That the psalmist is king is indicated by the way his victory (vv. 11f.) is joined to Yahweh's own triumph (esp. vv. 9f.).

He begins his psalm in typical royal role, celebrating with cultic music the name of Yahweh Elyon (p. 156) and his fidelity and faithfulness (p. 153). Verses 5f. have the appearance of a response to God's festal enthronement. The representation of God's supremacy as Creator and Ruler has filled the king with joy, for in God's defeat of the evil forces of the world is his own salvation. God's foes and the king's are one. And so, directly after the declaration of the doom of Yahweh's enemies (v. 10 resembling Ugaritic affirmations about Baal's enemies, so Kraus, Dahood), he exults that through Yahweh his own 'horn' is raised high like that of a savage bull, and he is moist[31] with the oil that means vitality and he sees the doom of those who rise against him. The figure of the horn is obviously appropriate of royal triumph (cf. 89.25; 132.17; I Sam. 2.10; and p. 55). The anointing, here associated with God-given power, could well allude to the king's sacral anointing, indicating its renewal in connection with the festal celebration of God's kingdom.

The thought of the life-power transferred from the tree[32] has its counterpart in v. 13, where 'the righteous one' (p. 151) is compared to the kings among trees (cf. Delitzsch), the palm and the cedar of Lebanon, mighty in lively growth. In vv. 14f. the thought is applied to a plurality and related to the temple, indicating the participation of the community in the triumph of God and the king. The theme of the royal vitality was particularly a communal interest (p. 165). 'Our God' (v. 14) matches this shift, while 'my rock' (v. 16) suits the royal covenant (p. 172) and task of witnessing to Yahweh's righteousness.

The heading 'for the day of the sabbath' indicates a usage in the regular public cult; the note may derive from the later centuries of the temple, when a psalm was prescribed for each of the daily morning sacrifices. G has a Davidic heading.

Psalm 94

After appealing for God's world judgment, lamenting the affliction of the nation, and issuing admonishments, the psalmist, in the royal manner, treats the situation as a confrontation between himself and the wicked (vv. 16f.). He relates himself to God in the royal style (p. 170): 'Yahweh is help to me (v. 17a), 'thy fidelity supports me' (v. 18), 'Yahweh is become my high fortress and my God the rock of my shelter' (v. 22). Within this 'personal' passage he

weaves further lament about the communal distress (vv. 20f.), which
may be caused by an enemy kingdom, 'the throne of destruction'.

With a royal interpretation, all the elements can be seen as
appropriate. The king summons God's great arising (p. 174). He
appeals sharply to God's kingly responsibility for the widow and
suchlike (p. 135). He addresses the trouble-makers,[33] who are in-
sensitive to God; he warns, teaches and witnesses, bringing comfort also to the faithful (p. 181). In this last respect, v. 12 can be
seen as a use of *'ašᵉrē* ('Happy . . .') to give the lesson of the royal
rites general application (p. 194). Confidence is then expressed in
terms of God's faithful help for his king and of the king's sublime
joy in God (v. 19, p. 169). The national concern emerges again in
the final 'Yahweh our God'.

G has a Davidic heading. The psalm was used at the feast of
booths according to the Talmud *Bab. Sukka* 53a.

Psalm 108 (with 44, 60, 74, 80, 83, 84)

This picturesque psalm, combining parts found in Psalms 57 and
60, deserves to be considered in its own right. Vivid testimony
precedes bitter lament, in keeping with the king's role as witness
(p. 185). The king can thus present himself as supremely committed to the praise of Yahweh, having stood out before all heaven
and earth as witness to Yahweh's fidelity (vv. 2–5, cf. on 57.8–12,
p. 46); surely this must move Yahweh not to discard him now!
In vv. 6f. he calls for the world-dominating theophany to relieve
God's people. In vv. 8–10 he cites the oracle in which God had
proclaimed his mastery of Canaan and adjacent territories; the
details suggest the territorial basis of David's kingdom. In v. 11 he
speaks as though leading a campaign against Edom. The conclusion, in 'we' style, expostulates with God for allowing the army to
suffer a reverse, but passes to confidence that God will give victory, for 'vain is salvation from man' (p. 192). The heading includes
lᵉdāwid.

In this form, the materials thus combine to show the king as the
great celebrator of Yahweh's praise to all the world and also as the
leader of Yahweh's martial hosts. We observe first the usual prominent royal ego, but notice then how this gives way to the collective national voice, in accordance with a tradition which we may
suppose survived from the wars of the tribal league, 'Yahweh's
people'.[34]

It is this latter tradition which characterizes Psalm 60, where
vv. 7–14 (=108.7–14) are preceded by a lament in 'we' style.
Verse 11 may still be taken of the king as leader of the army, but
otherwise the collective voice prevails. The balance is similar in
Psalm 44. The 'I' is heard only in vv. 7, 16 and perhaps 5; as
leader of the nation in cult and war, he is presumably the king. In
Psalm 80 the lamenting supplication is in the 'we' style throughout, but the king has his place as the object of the plea in v. 18.
Similar examples of supplications where the collective voice pre-
ponderates, but where the royal ego briefly emerges, may be 83
('My God' v. 14) and 74 ('my King' v. 12; the leader here may be
exilic).

In Psalm 84 there is prayer for the king in v. 10, where we do
best to construe with Gunkel 'Look upon our shield, O God;
regard the face of thine anointed'. The 'I' who presents this psalm
in a festal context is thus some other cultic soloist, who voices the
sentiments of the gathered pilgrims. This interpretation seems
easier than that of Mowinckel (*GT*), who thinks the 'I' is the king
himself.[35]

Psalm 118

The psalmist speaks in splendid royal style (vv. 5–21, 28), as
Gunkel himself recognizes, while the hymnic framework points to
a major national festival. There is thus good reason to add this
psalm to the grand royal texts of Gunkel's list, as Johnson did,
calling it 'an obvious companion piece to Ps. 18' (*SKAI*, p. 123).
Gunkel's own curious interpretation as a psalm borrowing old
royal elements for a purely private occasion is without justification. In fact he offers none, apart from supposing that the phrase
'fearers of Yahweh' means 'proselytes' and requires a post-exilic
date. If the psalm were post-exilic, however, a fair exegesis would
still have to reckon with a national leader in a major festival. But
proselytes are as old as Yahwism (Gunkel himself notes Ex. 18.10;
I Kings 8.41f.; II Kings 5) and in any case, 'fearers of Yahweh'
may simply embrace all worshippers; this is the view of Birkeland,
p. 134, while Johnson, p. 124, describes the expression as 'a simple
description of the devout Israelite'.

The psalm opens with the summons for praise, the theme being
Yahweh's fidelity (p. 153). The festal assembly, grouped in orderly
array, is indicated by the address to 'Israel . . . the house of Aaron

. . . the fearers of Yahweh'. The king now begins his testimony (v. 5), and here and throughout it is plain that his experience is the core of the national celebration. He gives prominence to the fact that Yahweh answered his prayer (p. 194) and that Yahweh was committed to his cause and so conquered his enemies. Yahweh is better than all human allies (p. 192); Gunkel aptly compares Ishtar's oracle to King Esarhaddon, 'Do not trust men; turn your eyes to me' (*ANET*, p. 450), and also the sole reliance of Ramses II on Amon at the battle of Kadesh. By invocation of Yahweh's name, the king was able to beat off 'all nations' (p. 155). He acclaims Yahweh with epithets expressing the saving relation (v. 14, p. 170). The 'tents of the righteous' ring with the shouts of praise and victory; the expression seems to combine the thought of the military camp and festal booths. Yahweh's hand has won a great victory. The king has escaped death and will testify (v. 17, p. 182). He was sorely proved by Yahweh's discipline, but saved at the last.

He now enters the sanctuary gates, symbolizing his being accepted by Yahweh; he is demonstrated 'righteous' (p. 151). After apparent rejection, he is glorified as the main stone in the structure of God's society. It is all the marvellous plan of Yahweh, fulfilled on this appointed day of festival. In view of the earlier description of victory by the name of Yahweh (vv. 10f.), the traditional rendering, 'Blessed be he who comes in (by) the name of Yahweh', seems best (rather than 'Blessed with the name of Y. be he who comes'); the king is thus seen again in his special association with that name (p. 155). We may compare David, who 'comes in the name of Yahweh' against Goliath (I Sam. 17.45), and Christ who has 'come in the name of' his Father (John 5.43). The procession moves into the sanctuary, and command is given for rituals about the altar; the *ḥag* is most likely the dancing procession of the annual festival, *heḥāg*. Expressions of relationship mark the royal testimony: 'My God art thou and I will confess thee; my God, I will exalt thee' (p. 170). In conclusion, the congregation are again called to celebrate Yahweh's fidelity.

Jewish tradition linking the psalm with the Feast of Tabernacles (Mishna *Sukka* 3.9; 4.5) is supported by the theme of festal light (v. 27, cf. the torch processions of Tabernacles),[36] the *ḥag* of v. 27, the 'day' of v. 24, and the 'Hosanna' of v. 25 which is associated with autumn prayers for rain (Petuchowski). How the psalm fitted into the pre-exilic autumnal festival will be considered in chapter III.

Psalm 138

This is in the grand manner. The psalmist celebrates Yahweh to an audience of gods (v. 1) and of all the kings of the earth (v. 4). His testimony aims at the conversion of these kings, who will be moved by what is told them of Yahweh's words (fulfilled promises?) and by the great glory which Yahweh has gained from the psalmist's deliverance. Gunkel recognizes the royal character of these elements and quotes parallels of foreign kings. He even goes so far as to say that a royal interpretation of the psalm is near to hand. But he rejects it on the grounds that v. 2 shows that the psalmist has no right to enter the temple, but can only bow down towards it. To this we may reply that the psalm may have first been used at cultic service on campaign; or better, that 'thy holy temple (*hēkāl*)' simply refers to the building (of which the largest room was strictly the *hēkāl*) as seen from the open court where much of the cult took place (cf. 5.4–8). Thanksgivings were usually accompanied by sacrifices and would be likely to take place in the court by the great altar.

The psalm, headed *le dāwīd*, well suits the king's role as Yahweh's witness before the world (p. 182), especially exalting his fidelity, truth and word (pp. 152, 154), calling attention to answered prayer (p.   ). The king is made exultant, his soul filled with glorious strength (v. 3b, p. 194). He was accepted because of his lowliness (v. 6, p. 144). Yahweh's promise of protection has been proved; whenever his king walks in the midst of affliction, Yahweh restores his life. He stretches out his right hand to save him from his enemies (cf. 18.17, 36; 20.17, p. 157). He is pledged to his aid; he will accomplish all for him, maintaining covenant-love for ever (v. 8).

In many Mss. and S the psalm ends: 'Do not abandon the work of thy hands'; with this we may compare the common epithet of Mesopotamian kings, who designate themselves 'the creation of (the hands of)' a god (Seux, pp. 61–4; Labat, pp. 53f.).

Psalm 140

The psalmist individually confronts men who prepare war against him (*milḥāmōt* v. 3, *nešeq* v. 8). Their evil words will be their

scheming, false charges, propaganda or curse-spells, as often in
psalms relating to warfare (Birkeland, pp. 62, 74–6). As elsewhere,
such enemies are compared to crafty hunters (Birkeland, p. 86,
and below, p. 140). As leader in prayer and in warfare and as bearing the hostility individually, he is likely to be the king. Confirmation can be found in vv. 7f.: in keeping with the royal privileges,
he is the one who says to Yahweh, 'My God art thou, hear, O
Yahweh, the sound of my supplications; Yahweh my lord is the
power of my salvation; thou hast sheltered my head on the day of
battle.' Here we note the privilege of prayer (p. 195), the epithets
for God as personal saviour (pp. 170f.), and trust in promised protection (p. 158). He looks for God to rout his enemies with hot coals,
a conception reminiscent of the king's deliverance in 18.13f. King
and people are 'poor', acknowledging no resources but the grace
of God (v. 13, p. 180) who will decide justly on their behalf. The
community will celebrate the deliverance, sitting in God's presence
at the sacrificial feast (v. 14).

The heading includes *l^edāwīd*.

Psalm 143

Because he is God's servant, the psalmist can expect God to
annihilate his enemies (v. 12, cf. v. 2); the connection is certainly
suggestive of the royal 'servant' (pp. 149f.). He claims a covenant-
bond in appealing to God's faithfulness, righteousness (vv. 1, 11)
and fidelity (vv. 8, 12, pp. 152f.). God will conduct him by means of
his angelic spirit (v. 10, p. 157). The exceptional relationship which
all this implies is further reflected in the expression 'for thy name's
sake restore my life' (p. 37). He would be instructed by God to
carry out his will (v. 10, cf. v. 8, pp. 142, 148); he affirms 'thou art
my God' (p. 170). His frailty is that of mankind (v. 2; cf. 89.48f.;
40.13). What he suffers from his enemies is presented pathetically
to God as a thrusting into Sheol by the supreme enemy, presumably Death (v. 3); for his revival he invokes the classic traditions
of God's ancient salvation, the primeval work for cosmos and
people (v. 5). All in all, there is sufficient reason to see the singer
of this *l^edāwīd* psalm as the king.

2. Less clear cases

The psalms in this section are less clear for the present discussion, but, in the wake of the preceding section and of the considerations listed in chapter I, the probability that they are royal emerges as strong.

Psalm 5

As Gunkel admits, this does not fit into his idea of spiritual, non-cultic 'individual laments'. The psalmist seems to be offering sacrifice in the court of the temple at dawn, ready to divine a signal of God's favour (v. 4); thereupon he will make entry into Yahweh's house (v. 8). His distress is caused by arrogant and raging men (v. 6), violent in word and deed, and he states that in their counsels they rebel against God (v. 11); this fits well the situation of the king who shares Yahweh's sovereignty (Ps. 2). His use of 'my King and my God' (v. 3, elsewhere in the national psalms 44.5; 68.25; 74.12; 84.4, pp. 139, 170) points the same way, as also does the force of his prayer against the wicked (p. 197). God's people will rejoice 'for ever' over his deliverance (v. 12), which suggests a situation of great national concern. His prayer that Yahweh should personally conduct him (v. 9) may reflect royal processions (p. 174).

That he faces a king, kings or would-be kings is likely not only from their description as *hōlᵉlîm*, 'upstarts' (cf. 75.5f.), and rebels against God. Verses 5f. suggest that they aspire to the privileges of God's ruler – to have God's legitimizing favour (p. 146), to reside with him and be stationed before his eyes (p. 143). But the psalmist trusts that it is he, not they, who will be confirmed in the royal covenant: he will enter God's house in the multitude of his covenant love (v. 8); he will be led by God's hand in 'righteousness'. He is confident that he will be confirmed as 'the righteous one' (p. 151), crowned with the divine pleasure (v. 13).

The heading includes *lᵉdāwīd* and may specify an accompaniment of flutes.

Psalm 11

Its formal resemblances are with psalms included in the preceding section (cf. Gunkel): testimony of trust before a group, Psalms 23 and 27; admonition to faint-hearted friends and to foes (2), 4, 62. The psalm keeps the form of such address throughout and has a distinct tone of authority.

There are indications that the crisis affects the community. The

foundations of order are threatened with destruction (v. 3); the
wicked aim the weapons of death at 'those who are true of heart';
according to the consonantal text, the counsel of flight given to
the psalmist is in the plural: 'Flee, birds, to your mountain' (v. 1);
warning is given of Yahweh's universal surveillance and judgment (vv. 4f.). The threat of God's volcanic fire suggests an intervention like that to save the king in 18.13f. (also 140.11).

Like Psalm 4, the psalm can well be understood as the utterance
of the king facing hostility and despair. Yahweh's *ṣaddīq* (p. 151)
is not without recourse. He relies on the heavenly King (v. 4),
who, despite appearances, dominates the world with searching eye
and powerful judgments. Sennacherib's annals describe how the
Babylonian king fled from him like a bird (Labat, p. 35) and how
the besieged Hezekiah was shut up like a bird (*ANET*, p. 288); it
seems likely that Psalm 11, headed *leḏāwīd* and opening with the
figure of the fleeing bird, also relates to an invasion, as Birkeland
and Mowinckel (*GT*) believe. If we can translate the difficult end
of v. 7 'the true-hearted shall see his face' (Delitzsch), the allusion
could be to the hope of a vision by incubation, giving the king
strength before battle (cf. on 3; 4; 17; 63).

Psalm 16

In asking for God's protection, the psalmist avows his devotion
to Yahweh to the exclusion of all other cults. He speaks as one in
special covenant with Yahweh: 'I have said to Yahweh, Thou art
my lord' (p. 171),[37] and as one who would lead in the cult, pouring
out drink-offerings and invoking the deity's name (v. 4, p. 155).
Verses 5f. have been explained as reflecting the circumstance that
the priesthood lived from the offerings (Num. 18.20; Deut. 10.9;
Josh. 13.14, cf. Kraus after von Rad). But it is not a question of
differentiation between Israelite priests and laity; an explanation
is needed which would be more appropriate to the preceding
renunciation of other gods (translated p. 163). From Jer. 10.16 and
Deut. 32.9 we should rather think of the cultic bond which dif-
ferentiates Israel from other nations: when the peoples were allotted their lands and patron deities, Yahweh became the choice
portion and lot of Israel and *vice versa*. The king, as representative
of Israel, naturally adopts this concept. Moreover, just as Israel is
distinct from the nations, so he is distinct from other kings in
being personally in unique covenant with Yahweh (p. 150).[38] The

emphasis would especially assist his prayer if the danger came from foreign rulers claiming the aid of other cults.

It is common for the king to 'bless' Yahweh (v. 7, p. 193) and in the present case the reason would be appropriate for the king: Yahweh has given him counsel, instructing him by night (p. 175). The reference may be to a dream-vision during incubation (cf. Solomon, I Kings 3.5f.). His inner organs are there made receptive to God's will (cf. 40.9, p. 180). In v. 8 the concluding words are textually uncertain, but the thought is clearly that of continual nearness to Yahweh (p. 143). Appropriate also for the king would be his reference to his flourishing 'glory' (v. 9, p. 145) and his description of himself as Yahweh's covenant-fellow, *ḥāsīd* (p. 151). What is particularly notable, however, is that as Yahweh's *ḥāsīd* he hopes not to be given over to Sheol, but to enjoy rich life in God's presence for ever. Older commentators regarded the language here as surpassing what an individual Israelite could say of himself and they referred it to Israel as a whole (e.g. Baethgen). The phraseology of Ugaritic texts has strengthened the view that the reference is to much more than a temporary individual deliverance (cf. Dahood). It seems easier to explain such expectations of a marvellous gift of life if the psalm is indeed royal; it is suggested below, p. 162, that the abundant life bestowed on Yahweh's king could involve a hope of continuing in some form eternally near him; threat of a shameful overthrow and rejection in this life would be felt as a threat also to that eternal prospect.

The heading includes *leḏāwīd*; *miktām* (also over Pss. 56–60) may indicate ceremonies of atonement (p. 47). The New Testament represents a royal-messianic line of interpretation with a reference to immortality (Acts 2.24f.; 13.34f.). Kirkpatrick notes similarity with Psalm 17, included in our preceding section, and he connects both with David. Birkeland, p. 162, says that it seems to be quite clear that the psalm is royal. Mowinckel (*GT*) likewise thinks of a king or equivalent leader who is threatened by foreign powers and who prays to ward off the danger in a propitiatory ceremony on a specially appointed day of intercession.

Psalm 31

A rich and elaborate psalm. The pattern 'lament – thanksgiving' (cf. Pss. 22 and 69) is here traversed twice: thus the prayer from affliction gives way to praise for salvation first in vv.8f., and then more decisively in vv. 20–25. There is a strong presentation of the psalmist in individual and privileged relation to God. The royal designations for God (p. 172) can be found in vv. 3f.: 'Be to me a rock of refuge, a castle . . . for thou art my crag and my strong-hold, and for the sake of thy name (p. 37) thou shalt lead me and guide me (p. 174), for thou art my refuge . . . (v. 15) I say, Thou art my God.' The covenant graces (p. 153) are prominent: fidelity (vv. 8, 17, 22), truth (v. 6), righteousness (v. 2), goodness (v. 20). God's 'servant' who stands in the light of God's face can well be the king (v. 17, p. 150). The enemies fit the king (p. 137): they are 'the wicked' (v. 18), but also 'my adversaries' (v. 12); they are 'many' (v. 14); they hold counsel together against him (v. 14); they are like cunning hunters (v. 5). They besiege him in his city (v. 22), which perhaps reflects a real event. 'Terror on every side' (v. 14) is an expression usually connected with warfare (Birke-land, p. 196).

In his thanksgiving he blesses God (p. 193), especially for a miracle of fidelity (p. 152). He seems to be surrounded by a con-gregation of Israel and addresses 'all his covenanted ones . . . all who hope in Yahweh' (vv. 24f.). He encourages them in terms which the old leaders of God's armies used: 'Be strong and let your heart take courage' (p. 40, Birkeland, pp. 187f.).

The psalmist depicts himself pathetically (vv. 10f., p. 80) as worn out, taunted, shunned by friends and passers-by, forgotten like one long dead, a broken vessel. Here we should probably allow for traits of the archetypal sufferer. Some are associated with King Jehoiachin in Jeremiah 22.28, 'a despised broken pot, a vessel no one cares for' (also Jer. 48.38 of Moab). Such traits would be heaped upon the king when he afflicted himself before God in penitential rites and attire.

The circumstances of the psalm will be somewhat as concluded by Birkeland, pp. 194–201, and Mowinckel (*GT*), who think of a king presenting special supplications in face of the enemy's initial success in advancing to the city. Their success has covered him with shame, but he probably exaggerates his plight in seeking to move Yahweh. A sign is given in the service to signify God's favour, and the king concludes with confidence and with the sum-mons to Yahweh's soldiers to acquit themselves valiantly. The heading includes *leḏāwiḏ*.

Psalm 36
In the title, *leᵈāwīd* is preceded by 'for the servant of Yahweh', as
elsewhere only over royal Psalm 18. There is a blend of community and individual: 'we' occurs in v. 10, v. 11 prays for the
faithful as a whole, and echoes of the autumn festival are heard
especially in vv. 6–10, 13; but in v. 12 the threat of aggression is
as though against the individual psalmist, who may speak also of
his personal inspiration in v. 2 (text uncertain). As Birkeland,
p. 140, argues, the deliverance of the plurality and of the individual
is one whole.

We can understand the psalm as a festal prayer of the king,
ostensibly against the wicked in general. In an act of protection
for himself and his society, he portrays the type of the elusive
trouble-maker (vv. 2–5), thus setting up an image for condemna-
tion and demolition (p. 197). Before proceeding to invoke doom
upon it, however, he interposes testimony to God's faithful care
of the living order. As often in the festal liturgies of Jerusalem,
the terms for God's covenant love are here applied to his rich provision for all his creation. Even so, it would be especially appropriate for the king, as responsible for all the earth, to tell of divine
salvation for mankind and animal life, and to see the temple as the
paradise where the 'sons of man' shelter under God's wings and
feast by the fountain of life.

His testimony to God's love leads to the prayer for its continuing application (vv. 11f., p. 152): 'Continue thy fidelity to those
who know thee . . . let not the arrogant foot attack me.' The conclusion, v. 13, confidently points to the fall of the evildoers, and
we can well suppose that a symbolic demonstration of their doom
has taken place (cf. Weiser), a 'modelling' of God's covenant love
(p. 109).

Psalms 42–3
The unity of the two is generally accepted, especially because of
the distinctive refrain in 42.6, 12; 43.5. In 42 we have a lament of
great beauty and in 43 direct prayer.

The psalm tells of separation from the joyful encounter with
God at the temple and is apparently sung 'from the land of
Jordan, the Hermons, from Mount *Miṣʿār*' (v. 7), the region of the
springs of the Jordan, where the slopes of Mount Hermon re-
sound with waterfalls (cf. v. 8). If this is actually so, a royal

interpretation would think of a field-cult accompanying the king on campaign; or of a king on his way to give account of himself to an overlord, accompanied by cultic persons and objects so that he could hold intercessions for his safe return (similarly Mowinckel, *GT*).

But the location could well be figurative. The outstanding scene would readily become symbolic for the entrance to the under-world. The psalmist finds himself there inasmuch as 'all thy breakers and waves have flooded over me'. If we are to be literal, let it be noted that he does not depict himself as surveying the landscape, but as drowning in the waters! But this will surely mean, as Jonah 2.6, that he feels swept into the mouth of Sheol at the 'roots of the mountains'. It is a quality of experience, like the lament from 'the end of the earth' (61.3), from 'the gates of death' (9.14). We can then understand the other expressions of remote-ness from God and the joyful ceremonies of the temple as natural in penitential worship. Mourning rites are reflected in the refrain: the soul is bowed low, humiliated, moaning (also in 42.4, 5, 10; 43.2). The place could be some station off the temple hill, such as the Gihon spring and caves in the Kidron Valley. When God's favour is manifested, the worshippers can ascend the processional way to the temple (43.3).

Indications that the psalmist is the king are not lacking. He speaks boldly of God's relation to himself (p. 170): 'my God' (42.7; 43.4), 'God of my life' (42.9), 'I will say to *'ēl* my rock' (42.10), 'the salvations of my face and my God' (42.12; 43.5), 'thou art the God of my stronghold' (43.2). Likewise men say 'where is thy God?' (42.4, 11), elsewhere a taunt of foreign nations against the covenant people (79.10; 115.2). The enemy with whom he is personally in dispute is in fact described as a 'treacherous nation' (43.1). Notable is his prominence in the cult. He seems to have led in the dancing procession of the great feast (42.5), rather as King David did (II Sam. 6). So he would enter the holy place and look upon the face of God (42.3).[39] In 43.3f. he thinks of himself as led by the covenant angels to make solemn entry up to the altar and the divine presence (p. 153), there to make tes-timony with cultic music (p. 185). God's special appointment of covenant graces to attend him is also found in 42.9. It is exactly one in such high relation to God who in failure says reproachfully 'Why hast thou forgotten me?' (42.10), 'Why hast thou cast me off?' (43.2). Comparison of kings or princes to the hart or doe (42.2) is found also in Lamentations 1.6; Psalm 18.34 and perhaps II Samuel 1.19.

After Psalm 41 *leāwīd* is not found in the headings until Psalm 51. But Psalms 42–50, headed 'of the sons of Korah', do include one undisputed royal psalm (45), one royal/national psalm (44), and four psalms which could well come from the great festival of the royal period (46; 47; 48; 50). The New Testament may reflect a royal/messianic interpretation, echoing G's rendering of 42.6 in Mark 14.34, and of 42.7 in John 12.27.

Psalm 51

The concluding prayer for Jerusalem (vv. 20f.), according to Gunkel and others, is a later addition, revealed especially by its supposed contradiction of v. 18 regarding the acceptability of sacrifice. Even on this view, there would be a likelihood that the original psalm was already connected with official worship; why, otherwise, struggle to modify it? The text of vv. 1–19 in fact supports this latter observation. The distinctive expressions for guilt and cleansing are most nearly related to sayings about the nation in the prophets, where national ceremonies of atonement are probably reflected.[40] This fact encouraged Smend, Cheyne, Briggs etc. to be particularly confident that here the psalmist spoke for the nation. 'The speaker is clearly Israel personified or one who feels himself entirely united to his people in guilt and punishment' – so Cheyne. The theme of the 'spirit' in vv. 12–14 points beyond an ordinary Israelite, and in fact to the king. He stands before Yahweh's face, provided with his 'holy spirit', and supported by a 'princely spirit', *rūaḥ nedībā*, G πνευματι ἡγεμονικῳ.[41] The 'holy spirit', to judge from the only other occurrence, Isaiah 63.9–14, denotes the power or presence of God at the centre of Israel and working in his chosen ruler; in Isaiah 63.11 it is probably put in Moses.[42] The special gift of spirit to the king is well attested elsewhere (p. 156).

Several other points suit the royal style. A personal covenant is suggested by the appeal to God's fidelity and love (v. 3) and righteousness (v. 16), and by the expression 'God of my salvation' (v. 16). The king was exhorter and witness (vv. 15–17, pp. 181, 182). A comparison between the value of his obedience and of sacrifice (vv. 18f.) can be found elsewhere (p. 179). For the gift of wisdom direct from God (v. 8), we may compare Solomon, also the royal spirit in Isa. 11.2.

The conclusion that vv. 1–19 was a royal psalm is reached by Dalglish in an extensive study with special attention to Akkadian psalmody. He takes vv. 20f. to be an exilic addition.

Commentators who defend the unity of the psalm are inclined by the tenor of vv. 20f. to see the psalmist as an exilic or post-exilic leader praying for the rebuilding of Jerusalem. Thus Mowinckel (*GT*) thinks of Nehemiah, whose enemies threaten 'bloodshed' (v. 16) and towards whom he admits no offence (v. 6).

Certainly one must reckon with the possibility that vv. 20f. are original. If later than the monarchy, the psalm may still depend on a tradition of royal prayer in the great rites of atonement. But a pre-exilic date for the whole psalm is not impossible. The 'building' of Jerusalem's walls may mean their strengthening (p. 181), the prayer being, as in the parallel clause, for God generally to bless Zion (cf. 147.2, 13; Isa. 26.1; also the prayer for the repair of Babylon in the *akītu*-festival, p. 94). The sequence in vv. 18–21 would be that God does not accept animal sacrifice as itself sufficient for atonement; sincere penitence is required, the king's first and foremost. But now that his broken heart has been offered, he can pray for grace for the community and vow abundant sacrifices that will be offered in testimony for that grace (see also p. 180). Smend's explanation is on these lines; Dalglish, p. 191, objects that types of sacrifice cannot be so distinguished from the terms, but the explanation does not depend on the terminology but on the contexts and sentences as a whole.

In the title, *leḏāwīd* will be an ancient heading, later expanded with midrashic reference to David and Bathsheba. There is no reason to doubt that a rite of sprinkling water or blood (v. 9) was associated with the recital of the psalm. The absolute and general quality of the psalm's language, together with the parallels concerning national renewal, make it likely that it stems from the annual rite of atonement, where the king will have had the role which later fell to the post-exilic high priest (p. 177). Kirkpatrick notes that it is used in some synagogue liturgies on the Day of Atonement and in churches on Ash Wednesday; such usage at least shows sensitivity to the scope of the psalm.

Psalm 52

The psalmist addresses a man of might, arraigning him as over-weening in self-sufficiency, wicked, scheming, of harmful tongue, and he declares that God will eliminate him. God will extirpate him from the sphere of life, to the joy of the righteous people. In contrast the psalmist presents himself, trusting in God's covenant love. He will remain for ever like a lively olive in the temple, ever testifying to the act of deliverance in the assembly of Israel.

A threatening address to proud and powerful enemies is found elsewhere in the king's mouth (p. 181). Here the enemy is a single figure, designated *gibbōr*, 'mighty man'; there may be influence from the style of a challenge before combat; Bentzen (*DSK*, p. 87) compares I Samuel 17.44–47. There is emphasis on the enemy's damaging tongue; if a military foe has already launched the war of words (Num. 22f. etc.), the psalm makes good sense as counterblast (similarly Mowinckel *GT*). The foe is actualized and exposed by the descriptive address and then smitten with an execration. The tradition is probably close to that of cultic prophecy, but a royal psalm is indicated by vv. 10f., where the themes of eternal life in the house of God (p. 162) and of eternal witness (p. 183) and the comparison to a sacred tree (cf. p. 59) join with the heading (*lᵉdāwīd*) to indicate the king. The 'righteous ones' and 'covenanted ones' (vv. 8, 11) can well be taken of the community behind the king.

Psalm 54

It is very much the manner of a king when the psalmist thinks of God as his personal saviour ('God is helper to me, my Lord is chief among the supporters of my soul'), who will destroy his foes who have risen against him. He invokes salvation through God's name and power, which suggests the situation of the king in battle (v. 3, p. 155); it is this name that he will thank for delivering him from danger (vv. 8f.). By the covenant-grace of 'truth' also God will crush his enemies (v. 7, p. 153). These enemies seem to be terrible foreign armies (v. 5, but some Mss. *zēdīm* 'presumptuous'), who have no respect of God's dispensations and who 'seek' the king's soul. When God has crushed them, the king looks upon them in triumph (v. 9).

Somewhat lean in data, this short but sharp *lᵉdāwīd* psalm is

nevertheless entirely in conformity with the usual expressions
about the king and his enemies.

Psalm 55

It is the situation behind this *leḏāwīḏ* psalm rather than any royal
idiom which indicates that it is the prayer of a king. The case is
well presented by Birkeland, pp. 234–9. The psalmist's own person is well to the fore, but there are several indications that the
situation affects the community. Chaos afflicts the city; its good
angels are replaced by the spectres of Violence, Strife, Mischief,
Trouble, Ruin, Oppression, Fraud. That this could be the effect of
an attack by foreign enemies is suggested by the similarity with
Psalm 10, where the 'nations' have brought 'fraud, oppression,
trouble, mischief' (10.7). 'War' is mentioned in v. 22, cf. v. 19. An
act of treachery in v. 21 is against a plurality. It is characteristic of
the king's prayers that the communal distress is gathered up in the
personal, individual utterance which constitutes most of the psalm.

From the hostile forces emerges a figure whom the psalmist
especially accuses of treachery (vv. 13–15, cf. 21f.). He was a man
of comparable rank (*'rk*) to the psalmist, or whom he had treated
as such. They had conferred amiably together and gone together
to the 'house of God'. In spite of this brotherly covenant bond, the
man has now acted as an enemy and is subsumed under a curse
(vv. 16f.). He may have been head of a neighbouring state, or an
Israelite notable who perhaps had deserted the king during a
foreign invasion.

Verse 20 may have originally referred to desert peoples,
Ishmael, Ya'lam and Qedem (Gunkel, after Ehrlich). Perhaps
these were the invaders, or auxiliaries who had deserted the
Jewish king – as once befell Hezekiah in Jerusalem (*ANET*,
p. 288). But the detail must remain uncertain.

The psalm can thus be seen as the prayer of a king in a very
precarious situation. He repeats his supplication at the hours of
the temple offices (v. 18), while Jerusalem itself is in turmoil.
Flight to the wilderness, as in David's time, is contemplated (vv.
7f.). The psalm itself has a jagged, hectic character. Invocation,
prayer and lament culminate in a curse on the enemies (v. 16),
invoking a fate like that which befell those who challenged the
high prerogatives of Moses (Num. 16.30f.). Various motifs then
mingle, especially trust and further lament (vv. 17–22). In v. 23

the king hears, or himself quotes, the prophetic words of comfort and acceptance: God will nourish you (p. 148); he will never let the 'righteous one' stumble; *ṣaddīq* here is appropriate of the king (p. 151). The king's own rejoinder is confident prayer for the death of his wicked foes.

Psalm 56

The enemies are 'peoples' whom God is called upon to put down in anger (v. 8); they are numerous and martial (2f., 10). They bear upon the psalmist personally; peoples and armies are often represented thus to pursue the soul of the king (p. 137). Throughout the psalm use is made of the contrast 'God against mere creatures', as often in royal psalms (p. 192). The professions of trust make repeated reference to the praiseworthy word of God (vv. 5, 11), which would fit the thought of the royal covenant as above all a promise of grace (p. 154). The votive sacrifices of God are a special responsibility of the psalmist, which he gladly undertakes: 'On me, O God, thy votive sacrifices!' (v. 13). Above all, his final confidence is in terms which suggest the royal office: the defeat of the peoples (v. 10) will mean that his soul is delivered from death, to 'walk to and fro before the face of God in the light of life'. This suggests both the intimacy of God's special servant (such as Abraham, Gen. 17.1, Eli's family, I Sam 2.30, Davidic kings, I Kings 2.4; II Kings 20.3) and also the rich abundance of royal life (p. 160).

The heading *leḏāwid miḵtām* may indicate the setting of the psalm in royal expiatory rites (p. 47) and this is taken further by *ʿal yōnat ʾēlem reḥōqīm*. Mowinckel explained this in *Ps. st.* IV, pp. 22f. (*PIW* II, pp. 213f.) as 'over the dove of the distant gods' (*ʾēlīm*, G ἁγίων), the expiatory bird (cf. Lev. 14.4–7) being sent over the desert to remote spirits rather as the scapegoat was sent to the spirit Azazel. This suggestion was greatly strengthened by the subsequent appearance of 'the most distant of gods', spirits of the underworld in the Ugaritic texts: *rḥq ʾilm, rḥq ʾilnym*. It is likely that they appear again in Ps. 65.6, where 'the sea of the distant ones' is parallel to 'the ends of the earth', that is, the entrance of the underworld.

Psalm 73

Psalms 73–83 lack a *leḏāwid* heading, each one being headed *leʾāsāp*, 'pertaining to the guild of Asaph', which was supposed to have originated in the appointments of David (I Chron. 25). In this group almost all the psalms seem to belong to great convocations where the national assembly prays collectively or is in attendance; the king is heard in 75 (p. 55) and, I think, in 77 (p. 79). If Psalm 73 were a private meditation of a wisdom teacher, as some make out, it would be the cuckoo in the nest.

A link with Psalm 75 is in fact at once suggested, since both psalms deal at length with offenders who are described by the parallel terms *hōleˡlīm* and *reˢšāʿīm*, 'boasters' or 'upstarts' and 'wicked' (73.3; 75.5, p. 181); *hōleˡlīm* is found elsewhere only in 5.6 (p. 65), while a related expression is found in 10.3 (p. 32). The signs are that, as in Psalms 5, 10 and 75, so in Psalm 73 these wicked boasters are seen as arrogant rebels against the sovereignty of God and his king. That there is reference to great foreign powers in Psalm 73 seems likely from the description of their immense, albeit transient, might. In v. 9 they are pictured with mouth gaping wide enough to reach the heavens while the tongue rolls along the earth, a reminiscence of the chaos-monster opposing God (Ringgren, *VT* 1953). The expression 'everyone who goes whoring from thee' (v. 27) may refer to Israelite apostates who succumb to the prevailing temptation under foreign domination; but it could describe foreign oppressors themselves, since the psalms do regard such enemies as rebels against Yahweh's yoke (Ps. 2 etc.). The use of an ethical wisdom style to depict political domination is found in Habakkuk and Psalms 9–10 (cf. p. 49).

It is somewhat in the royal manner that the psalmist puts himself in pronounced individuality over against these offenders; note 'But as for me' in vv. 2, 22f., 28 and the themes of his personal indignation in vv. 2f., his suffering in v. 14 etc. The involvement of the nation is glimpsed in two places. First, there is v. 1, where 'God is good to Israel' (*MT*, Vss.) must have preference over the often proposed reading 'God is good to the upright'; the parallel 'pure of heart' presumably designates the people of God, rather as elsewhere 'the righteous ones', 'the faithful ones' etc., the term being chosen here to point the contrast with the enemies of God. A similar 'ethical' definition of opposing political entities occurs in Habakkuk 2.4. Second, the psalmist says that if he had spoken out in disillusion, he would have 'betrayed' (*bgd*) the 'generation'

or community of God's sons (v. 15). Such betrayal would presuppose a man with great responsibility for God's people, and
could well involve a covenanted relationship, as indeed bound the
king to the people (II Kings 11.17).

In vv. 23–28 the psalmist testifies to his intimate trust in Yahweh
and expresses confidence (a kind of indirect prayer) that the offenders will be destroyed by Yahweh, from whom they have gone
astray. The language is especially appropriate for the king: he is
perpetually beside God (v. 23a, pp. 143, 160f.), who has taken hold
of his right hand (v. 23b, p. 157; cf. royal names Ahaz, Ahaziah,
Jehoahaz, 'Yahweh has taken hold'). God conducts him by the
agency of his 'counsel' (v. 24a), which is here rather like the personified word and the covenant-graces which assist in guidance
(43.3, pp. 152–5). 'Counsel' itself is commonly associated with
kings and their political affairs.[43] Parallel is the remarkable assurance that God will take him up in glory; whether *'aḥar* is adverbial
('and *afterwards* in glory thou wilt take me') or has some preposi-
tional sense ('and *with* glory thou wilt take me'),[44] the mention of
'glory' certainly suits the reception of God's king. Verse 25 again
implies a very close relationship: God is 'for' him and 'with' him.
The relationship is 'for ever' (v. 26); God is 'the rock of my heart'
(cf. 'my rock' etc., p. 172) and 'my portion'. This last expression
has been discussed on p. 66 and found appropriate to the king's
bond with Yahweh, contrasting with the patrons of other kings.
The rejection of other gods (vv. 25, 27) also resembles Psalm 16,
as further do the themes of counsel and of eternal joy. The king
is pre-eminently the one who 'draws nigh' (*qrb*) to God (v.
28, cf. v. 17, Jer. 30.21,[45] p. 173), who also shelters in him
(v. 28b, p. 143) and who recounts the sum of his deeds (v. 28c,
pp. 182f.).

Engnell's confidence that the psalm is royal has been noted on
p. 18. Würthwein has also argued to this effect, while Ringgren, as
already noted, has seen a link with the mythology of the new-year
festival. Many authors, however, stress the psalm's relation to
wisdom literature. But this in itself does not exclude a royal interpretation; the various strands of the Old Testament tradition were
early penetrated by wisdom styles, and it was especially the kings
who were the patrons of the wisdom schools. Birkeland's interpretation of the psalm is similar to that given above,[46] but he
believes that it is post-exilic and that the leader in question is

probably the high priest. However, there are no sure grounds for
a post-exilic dating.

What is the purpose of the psalm? We may compare it in this
respect to psalms treated above as royal, such as 3; 4; 16; 23; 27;
61, where the king speaks warmly of Yahweh's care and of a close
bond, while along with this testimony there is (openly or implied)
an appeal for help; often some assurance, by rite or vision, has
been given. So too in the present case, the king testifies with a
story of grace bestowed on himself, and thereby instructs his
people, and at the same time implicitly moves God to continuing
protection and the destruction of the oppressors. The elaborate
story of how he almost lost faith in God's justice thus serves in
part as a subtle intercession; the onus is very much on God to
ensure that his new insights, publicly declared, are not proved vain.

His testimony is that God can still be trusted by Israel, in spite
of his seeming tolerance of foreign oppression. His personal story
(p. 88) is of how he almost lost faith and concluded that all his
efforts to please God were in vain. His ample description of the
presumption, cruelty and success of the wicked (vv. 3–12) may be
in part still a challenge to God's justice, and in part an arraign-
ment, preparing their doom (p. 197). He contrasts himself as a
pitiable sufferer in God's cause, toiling apparently in vain, chas-
tened daily (vv. 13f.); here there may be some connection with the
presentation of the king as sufferer in the cult (p. 179). Relief came
when he entered the sanctuary or 'holy rites' (v. 17); he then per-
ceived the certainty of the overthrow of the oppressors. This
could refer to his part in a festal demonstration of the doom of
God's enemies (p. 108), or to a vision in incubation or similar sign
from God (p. 175). We may translate the difficult v. 20 'As a dream
when my Lord awakes, when thou dost arise thou wilt despise
their image': when God 'awakes' and 'arises', he will regard them
as a fading dream; no greater substance will they have. This is
comparable to the king's direct calls for God to 'awake' elsewhere
(p. 175).

He then tells of his favoured closeness to Yahweh, upheld,
counselled etc. His being taken by Yahweh in glory may be 'afterwards' in the sense of 'after the destruction of the wicked' etc. But
he may go beyond this with reference to a transcendent life for
kings (p. 162). He treasures his grace of access to God (v. 28,
p. 173) and fulfils his duty of witness.

Psalm 77

This is a great intercession for the nation. Their protracted suffering is taken into the person of the intercessor as 'the day of my distress' (v. 3); he can therefore well be the king. He seeks to move God by calling attention to his own lamentation and affliction. Though the psalm is thus markedly in the 'I'-style, the personality has no obvious royal colouring. This may be partly due to the concentration on his desolation, partly to the psalm's concern being the long sorrow of the nation. A faint clue may be found in the final sentence, 'thou didst lead like a flock thy people by the hand of Moses and Aaron', which has force as a rather abrupt and unexpected ending. Since psalmists do sometimes end with an allusion to themselves as though 'signing off' (p. 151), the psalmist may imply a prayer that now under his shepherd-rule God will again save his people.

The king would thus appear in this psalm as carrying in his own person the nation's suffering, as the reciter of the tradition of God's ancient work (p. 192), and as the great intercessor. It is not far removed from the role of the prophet-leader, and in Habakkuk 3 a visionary intercession for king and people uses some of this psalm's material about the ancient salvation.

Dahood considers the psalm to be one of the earlier ones, much of the language being archaic. Mowinckel suggests that the heading *'al yᵉdūtūn* refers to the ritual setting, a ceremony of 'confession' of Yahweh's name with intercession and penitence (cf. p. 49).

Psalm 86

The heading seems to indicate a royal supplication. It is not unfitting for a king to depict himself as 'humble and poor' (v. 1, p. 180). In v. 2 he stresses his relation to Yahweh: *ḥāsīd* (p. 151), 'thy servant' (p. 149), 'my God' (p. 170); in v. 4 'thy servant . . . my Lord'; in v. 16 'Give thy power to thy servant and bring salvation to the son of thy handmaid'. This association of divine power and servanthood would certainly fit the king well (p. 145) as also does the repeated mention of 'fidelity' and 'truth' (vv. 5, 11, 13, 15, p. 152) and God's 'name' (vv. 9, 11, 13, p. 156). By his great fidelity God has delivered the psalmist's soul from the remotest region of Sheol – an allusion perhaps to royal passion rites. The enemies are 'my haters' (v. 17), 'presumptuous men' who 'have risen against me', 'an assembly of terrible ones' who 'have sought

my soul and have not set thee before them' (v. 14); they will be
discomfited if only God will signal his support for the psalmist
(v. 17). The picture agrees fairly well with the traits commonly
found in the king's enemies (p. 137). In keeping with the king's
lofty role of witness, he praises Yahweh's uniqueness among the
gods and envisages that all nations will converge to worship
Yahweh (p. 182f.).

Psalm 102

This is a good example of the supplication of a leader who bears
in his own person the suffering of his community. Appearing as a
pathetic figure in the penitential rites, he laments in the style of an
individual (vv. 2–12, 24f.) and then broadens his prayer explicitly
to cover Zion and God's servants (vv. 13–23, 26–9). Apart from
this representative character of the psalmist, there is little to iden-
tify a king. But we may note to this effect how in a contrast he
couples himself with the heavenly ruler – he so frail, God enthroned for ever (vv. 12f., 24); also that he is one who can 'say
"My God" ' (v. 25, p. 170); that the cutting off of his days (v. 24)
resembles royal Psalm 89.46; and that the enemies of v. 9 suit the
king. In such a penitential rite, little would be left of the king's
dignity; he is 'poor' (title), 'stripped' (v. 18a), and the glimpse of
glory to come centres on Zion itself.

Resemblance to the language of Second Isaiah does not in itself
entail a post-exilic date, since the prophet uses older language
from Zion's worship (p. 107). As Weiser points out, allusions to
Zion's stones and dust (v. 15) and prisoners (v. 21) are not necessarily references to conditions after 586 BC. We may compare the
Babylonian prayer for the repair of the bars, bolts and bricks of
city and temple in the new-year festival (p. 94). If, however, an
exilic or later date is preferred, it is likely that an older pattern has
been followed. A similar style is used in Lamentations 3. That the
psalm discloses to us something of the tradition of the great rites
of penitence in the autumn festival is likely from references to
God's kingship (v. 13) and creation (v. 26) and the new era of
salvation accompanying his epiphany at the appointed season
(vv. 14, 16f., *HTC*, pp. 84f.).

The title is difficult to evaluate because of its uniqueness. Some
think it indicates that the psalm came to be used by any sufferer
(Birkeland, p. 328); others wonder if the *'ānī* is the king or other

leader in his penitential role (p. 180). Bentzen (*DSK*, p. 53) makes a case for the latter view, noting the application of '*nh* = '*ānī* to the king in the inscription of Zakir,[47] but he finally prefers the former explanation. Mowinckel (*GT*) leaves both open.

Psalm 109

The psalmist's bond with Yahweh is indicated by his appeal for 'fidelity' (vv. 21, 26, p. 152), his expressions 'God of my praise' (v. 1), 'Yahweh my Lord' and 'my God' (vv. 21, 26, p. 170), and 'for the sake of thy name (v. 21, p. 37). 'God of my praise' may indeed mean 'source of my praise' (cf. 'God of my salvation' etc.) and indicate a man endued with glory (22.26a?); otherwise it could fit the royal role of witness in the great assembly (cf. v. 30, p. 184). That he depicts himself as poor before God (vv. 22, 31, cf. 16) need not mean that he is a pauper (p. 180)!

He prays against enemies who requite evil for good, break covenant and go to war against him without cause (v. 3). He is especially concerned with the enemy's harmful words, which may include execrations accompanying a campaign and damaging accusations. For this reason he counters with an exceptionally strong cursing prayer, appealing to God's justice. It is likely that the king's efforts in this regard were thought to carry special weight (p. 197). In this curse his enemy appears mostly as a single figure, no doubt a leader (cf. Ps. 55); *p*^e*quddā*, v. 8, could refer to his office of authority, though the meaning 'property' is possible.

The old theory that the curse of vv. 6–19 is a report to God of the enemy's curse has been adopted by Schmidt, Weiser and Kraus, but there is no justification whatever for avoiding the natural direct meaning, however it may jar one's pious senses. Birkeland, pp. 203–9, interpreted the psalm as a king's prayer against military enemies on the lines suggested above; his view failed to convince Bentzen (*DSK*, p. 100) but was adopted by Mowinckel (*GT*). The heading includes *l*^e*dāwīd*.

Psalm 116

The beginning of this thanksgiving resembles royal Psalm 18: the psalmist expresses his love of Yahweh (p. 169), who has accepted his prayer (p. 194) and saved him from the bonds of death and Sheol. In his thankful testimony the psalmist appears as a prominent figure before the representative assembly at Jerusalem, himself sacrificing and raising the 'cup of salvations', perhaps a drink-offering (p. 174), with proclamation of Yahweh's name. Gunkel and Kraus compare the stele of Yeḥawmilk, king of Byblos; in robes and headdress he stands before his goddess, his left hand holding up to her a bowl, his right making a gesture of respect (*ANET*, p. 502; *ANEP*, no. 477).

The psalmist designates himself Yahweh's servant, and with emphasis (v. 16, p. 150); he is one who 'walks to and fro before the face of Yahweh' (p. 75), having been brought from death to life. A hint of the participation of his community in his experience may be found in the 'our God' of v. 5 and the plural 'praise ye Yah'; 'the simple ones' (v. 6) could illustrate the custom of generalizing from the king's case (p. 190). That Yahweh has loosed his bonds (v. 16) may well be metaphorical for deliverance from 'the cords of death' (v. 3); a literal interpretation (as Birkeland, pp. 293f.) would in any case not exclude a royal interpretation, since Judean kings were sometimes so afflicted by imperial overlords. If Psalm 117 is really the conclusion of Psalm 116 (Schmidt etc.), its address to the nations and its testimony to Yahweh's fidelity and truth would suit a royal psalm (p. 152).

The psalm has often been adjudged late in view of Aramaisms and supposed literary borrowings and freedom of style (Mowinckel, *GT*). However, there is no solid reason to date it later than the monarchy; such features, including Aramaisms, occur in royal Psalm 144. Engnell (*Studies*, p. 211) describes the psalm as a royal passion liturgy and understands v. 15 as a direct reference to the king's vicarious death: 'precious in the eyes of Yahweh is the death for his covenanted ones'. But it would be rash to build on this explanation, for which there is no phraseological parallel; 'death of his covenanted ones' seems more likely in view of the similar construction in v. 14b. The point would be that Yahweh does not lightly discard to the fate of death those in covenant with him (cf. 72.14 of the king's care for the poor).

Psalm 120

The balance of the psalm favours its interpretation as a lament (Gunkel, Mowinckel, *GT*) rather than as a thanksgiving (Kraus, Weiser). Since the peoples mentioned in v. 5 belong to widely separated regions (Armenia and the Syro-Arabian desert), the allusion is best taken metaphorically; Gunkel and Birkeland take

it literally only at the cost of speculative emendation. The psalmist
is thus beset by enemies bent on war (v. 7, cf. 4), whom he compares to distant tribes renowned for their belligerence. That he
sees himself as bearing the warfare individually is in accord with
royal style (p. 137). The emphasis on their 'false tongues' may
relate to a breach of alliance or injurious accusations. A connection
with official worship is indicated by the fact that the psalm begins
the series headed 'song of the stairs' (or 'song of ascent'). This title
possibly connects with ceremonies on the temple *steps* in the
autumn festival or with processional *ascent* at the same festival.
The former possibility appealed to Engnell (*SBU* II, col. 635);
Delitzsch discusses the sources behind this tradition, but inclines
against it. The latter possibility gains support from Psalm 132 and
title, as argued by Mowinckel (*Ps. st.* II, pp. 4f.).

Psalm 121
Indirectly through his cultic minister, Yahweh the 'Creator of
heaven and earth' and 'keeper of Israel' here pledges some person
complete and everlasting protection. So far as this text goes, the
promise is unconditional, once trust has been expressed. Surely the
person in question is most likely to be the king, to whom such
elaborate pledges are given elsewhere (p. 157). Yahweh is at his
right hand (v. 5, p. 157). Corresponding to the style of royal
avowals of trust ('Yahweh is my ——', p. 170), the minister assures
him 'Yahweh is thy keeper, Yahweh is thy shade'. The expression
'go out and come in' is often (though not exclusively) used of
kings, especially of warfare (Berridge, p. 47). The help will be
'from now and until eternity' (cf. p. 160).
   The opening verses may be related to the festal theophany,
heralded over the eastern mountains at sunrise (cf. Isa. 52.7f.;
Nah. 2.1 [EVV 1.15]; Hab. 3.3f.; Mal. 3.1, 20 [EVV 3.1; 4.2];
Ps. 22 title). The king looks yearningly for Yahweh, rather as in
101.2, 'Oh when wilt thou come to me'. A hint of the 'new-year'
setting may be found in vv. 3f., which stresses the incessant
vigilance of the ever-living Yahweh, as though in contrast to the
summer death-sleep of Baal (cf. Kraus). The title 'song of the steps'
is also a pointer to the festal setting (p. 83).

Psalm 139
The psalmist seems to be drawing near to God to seek an encounter,

from which he will gain strength against his enemies; he is concerned to invite God's search of his inner being, confident he will be found loyal, and also to pray God to slay the wicked assailants. Accordingly the psalm reaches its goal in vv. 19–24, while vv. 2–18 are preparatory, praising God as able to know him and prove him thoroughly. The psalm, which is headed *leÚdāwīd*, is thus similar in purpose to some claimed as royal above (Ps. 17, p. 33; Ps. 63, p. 50).

Indications that the psalmist is in fact a king may be found in the enemies being God's as well as his (p. 137); in his claiming special merit in the fierceness of his opposition to them (vv. 19–22); in his request to be conducted by God on the way of eternity (v. 24, p. 160); and in the remarkable elaboration of his relation to God (vv. 2–18) – God knows him like the closest of companions, embraces him, has him constantly in his presence ('face', 'spirit', cf. p. 71), lays his hand on him, leads him with his hand, grasps him with his right hand (v. 10b, p. 157), formed him wonderfully in the womb. The theme of his creation in the womb of the earth (v. 15) may derive from the identification of kings with the 'first man' (Bentzen, *DSK*, pp. 104f.). Certainly the concentration on God's work with him before birth is reminiscent of traditions of royal predestination (Labat, pp. 44f.).

A royal interpretation has been favourably considered by Bentzen (*DSK*, pp. 104f.) and advocated by Danell; they suggest a setting in the annual rites. Mowinckel (*GT*), following Birkeland, analyses the psalm on lines like those above, but thinks the psalmist will be a post-exilic leader (also in *PIW* 1, p. 68); as Kraus points out, however, the psalm may be quite early, the reflective style of the hymnic section being indebted to ancient Egyptian compositions; affinity with the hymn to the Aton is also noted by Holman, p. 309.

Psalm 141

The psalm is headed *leÚdāwīd* and, as Delitzsch shows, is related to 140, 142 and 143. As in these others, so here the psalmist can well be a king, for he appears to be in a situation of war, presented mostly as his personal struggle. In the received text of v. 7 he laments slaughter suffered by his people: 'As when one works and breaks up the earth, our bones have been scattered at Sheol's mouth.' Another reading (11 Q Ps) gives 'my bones', and another

(G^{mss.}, S) 'their bones'; the last would predict the enemies' doom as in v. 6.

He looks for the overthrow of the enemy rulers, their followers then being ready to treat with him (v. 6). Here 'when their rulers are cast down on the edges of rock' suggests a campaign in territory like that of Edom, and *sela'*, 'rock', is perhaps a pun on the name of the Edomite capital Sela'. In this case, the point of v. 2 would be that the king prays on campaign away from Jerusalem, and asks that his prayer and raised arms may be as acceptable to God as the regular sacrifices in Jerusalem. Delitzsch interprets v. 2 similarly, thinking of David fighting far from Jerusalem during Absalom's revolt.

In vv. 3f., rather than directly protest his innocence, the psalmist modestly asks God to keep him from sin, which, he continues, is amply found in his enemies.

Psalm 142

As remarked on the preceding psalm, there is similarity between Psalms 140–3, and here again the title includes *l^edāwīd*. The lament speaks of enemies laying traps and of the psalmist's lack of helpers other than God; both traits can be found in a king's prayer (pp. 140, 180). His bond with God appears in v. 6, 'I say, thou art my shelter (p. 172), my portion in the land of the living' (p. 66). In close resemblance to royal Psalm 18.18 he says of his enemies, 'Deliver me from my pursuers, for they are too strong for me.' The phrase 'thou wilt act on my behalf' (v. 8b, cf. 18.21; 116.7) resembles the kind of promise-formula reflected in 57.3 and 138.8. The celebrating of the people of God ('the righteous') about him (v. 8b) well fits a leader, whether we render with RSV ('will surround me') or NEB ('shall crown me with garlands'). That his soul is to be brought out of 'prison' (v. 8) is probably metaphorical, to judge from the psalm as a whole (cf. p. 82).

3. *Psalms not to be used*

In addition to the ten royal psalms of Gunkel and the groups of thirty-one and twenty-three added in the preceding discussion, there remain nearly forty psalms which in some way present an 'individual', quite a few of them having been taken as royal by one scholar or another. While most of these show little positive deviation from the psalmody already treated, their indication of an individual is too vague or indirect to build on in the present work. In a few cases, moreover, a psalm has peculiar features, which make its provenance difficult to assess.

Psalm 1, which has been thought to portray the king as responsible for God's law,[48] is in itself quite general. Hardly less so is Psalm 15, which Koole has imagined in a coronation rite. The same applies to a number of psalms which fall under Bič's theory of Psalms 1–41 as a continuous royal liturgy (above, p. 19), such as 6, 13, 26, 38. There is little to build on in Psalms 64 and 88 except analogy, though Birkeland, p. 264, speaks for the former, while Engnell describes 88 as a very characteristic royal passion psalm.[49] Psalm 8 is rather general or indirect, although the cautious Bentzen makes great use of it in his *King and Messiah*. The creation features in another 'I'-psalm, 104, which echoes hymns of the Pharaohs, but is again somewhat general.

Possible royal elements in 19 and 119 ('thy servant' etc.) are barely sufficient to clarify the psalmist's person, in view of their peculiar development of praise for God's word or law; 119 is taken by both Birkeland and Mowinckel (*GT*) of a post-exilic head; Widengren (*SK*, p. 31) thinks of a young prince, whose psalm was re-worked later.

In other cases there is little or nothing to distinguish the psalmist from a spokesman of prophetic type: 12; 14; 53; 58; 78. Difficult to place also are some with didactic features: 25; 32; 37; and the distinctive 49, one of Engnell's 'royal passion psalms' (p. 18). Little can be said of the speaker in the great psalms 78; 103; 106; 145 (*leďāwīd*); 146; or in the smaller pieces 122; 123; 129; 130; 131, except that a festal setting is mostly probable.

Such psalms, then, are best not used in the task of reconstructing the royal ideal in the psalms, unless the perspectives of scholarship change considerably. It is interesting, however, to observe that even in these cases there is little firm sign of a 'private' psalmody. The style and setting remain preponderantly those of Jerusalem's official cult.

III

THE ROYAL RITES

The study of the setting of Gunkel's 'royal psalms' over the years has given rise to important questions. Royal ceremony within the autumn festival is often envisaged, but its character is much disputed. I begin this chapter with the hope that a valuable contribution to the discussion may be made with the help of the extra psalms I have claimed as royal. However, it will first be necessary to consider the autumn festival in general. Since comparison has often been made with foreign rites, especially those of Babylon, we shall first gather some relevant information from recent study in those fields. We shall then estimate the abiding contribution of Mowinckel to the clarification of the festival and note his disagreement with Johnson concerning the rites of the king. With this disagreement in mind, we shall examine Gunkel's 'royal psalms' in turn. Then we can bring the results of chapter II to bear and hope to resolve the important argument. So the preliminaries for the study of the royal ideal in chapter IV will have been completed.

1. *Rites of new year and enthronement outside Israel*

(a) Mesopotamia
Most commonly compared with the Israelite festival are the *akītu* celebrations, attested in various forms and places in Mesopotamia in the first three millennia.[1] The word *akītu* remains unexplained. It sometimes refers to a particular festival or part of a festival, and

sometimes to the special sanctuary outside the city to which procession was made as an essential item in the celebrations. We know
of such sanctuaries with chapels and courts and situated by a canal.
A complete picture of the celebrations for any one city or period
eludes us. But it is fair to say that the greater part of our information shows the *akītu* rites as belonging to the observances of new
year. In some cities they took place at the beginning of Nisan
(about April). In others they were held both in spring and in
autumn, where Tishri (about October) could also be regarded as
new year.

The theme of renewed fertility in new-year festivals is best
evidenced in the Neo-Sumerian period and a little later at Lagash
and Isin, where the marriage of the god and his goddess-consort
was enacted. A beautiful account of a new-year festival (not
explicitly *akītu*) at Lagash when a new temple came into service no
doubt reflects some features of the normal annual rites.[2] The
inscription of Gudea, ruler of Lagash, relates: 'The year was gone
by, the months completed; a new year entered the heaven, the
month of this house entered; three days of this month passed; (the
god) Ningirsu comes from Eridu . . .' When all was prepared,
Gudea led Ningirsu, king and hero, into his temple. The goddess
Baba awaited him in her chapel like 'a good wife who takes care of
his house'; on her bed she was 'the Tigris in flood', and 'a fair
garden of fruits'. From the god's entrance the festival continued
seven days and the sacred marriage was concluded. In the city all
disharmony was forbidden. The poor were exalted. All the gods
joined in a concluding festal banquet. A prominent feature of
akītu ceremonies in general was the grand procession of gods to
and from the shrine outside the city, and it is likely that part of its
meaning was to convey the blessing of fertility to the fields. These
journeys through sacred streets and gates and by canal would
increase public participation, and the festivals were marked with
general rejoicing and feasting. The participation of the king was a
principal feature. Even in the great days of empire, the king would
make the utmost effort to be present; his absence often necessitated
the curtailment of the rites (Labat, pp. 173f.).

A much fuller portrayal of a new-year festival, though still far
from complete, can be given for Babylon during the first millennium. The chief sources (*ANET*, pp. 331–4) are the remnants of
what was evidently a massive record of rites; the copies are from

Seleucid times, but no doubt descend from texts at least as old as the Neo-Babylonian empire (Assyrian sources show that the observances were essentially the same from about 750 BC, Lambert, *JSS* 1968, p. 106). The rituals were originally detailed here for the successive days of the festival extending from 1 to at least 11 Nisan, but only the account from the 2nd to the 5th has survived with any clarity.

Until the entry of the king on 5 Nisan, the chief priest takes the leading part in the temple. Two hours before dawn on 2 Nisan, this priest washes himself and enters the great temple within the city to recite praise and prayer before the image of Marduk, who is also called Bel, 'lord'. He praises the god as supreme king of all, irresistible in wrath and valour, pacifying and subduing the gods, providing for the life of mankind, giving light, oracles and law, granting mercy, taking the hand of the fallen. He asks for grace towards Babylon, the temple and the people, 'your city', 'your house', 'your subordinates'. This address to Marduk was of peculiar solemnity, uttered in solitude. Only when it was completed were the other priests and singers admitted to the temple to perform duties before the god and his consort Beltiya ('my lady', also called Sarpanitu). Prayers against enemies followed, but much is here lost.

The beginning of 3 Nisan, poorly preserved, resembled that of the 2nd. Then we learn how two small wooden figurines were to be made according to detailed prescriptions. In their left hands one held a snake, the other a scorpion, while their right hands were raised towards the god whom they would meet on 6 Nisan, namely Nabu, son of Marduk. Anticipating the events of the 6th, the text tells us that when Nabu arrives in the temple (his image having been brought from its temple in Borsippa), the figures are to be beheaded and burnt in his presence.

Resuming at the beginning of 4 Nisan, the text prescribes that the chief priest must rise and wash still earlier, three and a third hours before dawn. Alone in the temple, he again recites praise and prayer before Marduk. He praises him as king above all gods, controller of waters, cultivator of fields, decreer of destinies, bestower of authority on the king. He begs for 'release' for Marduk's city, mercy for his temple, light for his people. He then prays before the consort-goddess. He praises her supremacy among goddesses, her brightness among the stars; she makes poor the rich and enriches the poor, strikes down irreverent enemies, releases the prisoner, takes the hand of the fallen. He begs her to appoint a good destiny for the king and life for the people of Babylon, pleading for them before Marduk. Before admitting the other priests as on previous days, he utters further prayers in the open court, apparently blessing the temple. In the evening of the 4th, the chief priest recited the great story of Marduk's creator-kingship, Enuma Elish, a poem of over a thousand lines, happily preserved elsewhere (*ANET*, pp. 6of.). This he addressed to Marduk, while covers were placed over the tiara of the god Anu and the seat of the god Enlil, perhaps symbolizing the eclipse of their more ancient glory by the ascendant Marduk.

The significance of this recitation at this point in the proceedings must be assessed with reserve, as Lambert has recently stressed (*JSS* 13). It took place before the entry of the king and several days before the ceremonies in the *akītu*-house, where, as will be mentioned below, Marduk's victory was ritually actualized. Moreover, it has recently come to light that a similar recitation of the same poem took place on 4 Kislimu, November–December (Lambert, *JSS* 13). The composition of the poem is probably to be dated in the second millennium. Its original purpose and sources remain an open question. The epilogue envisages its use outside the cult. On the other hand, major elements of its story, such as the god's supreme kingship, his enemies, his victory, the involvement of the other gods, his creative work and provision for life, and the twofold determination of destinies, are known to be embedded in the other proceedings of the festival, irrespective of the poem. There was thus a close relationship between the poet's raw material and the cult. Indeed the value of the poem for the study of the festival can be said to lie in its showing the coherence of these major elements of the festal ideas. In the poem's present application in the cult, its recitation is directed not to an audience of worshippers but to Marduk, as though contributing to the preparation of the victory that was to be enacted a few days later.

The poem begins with the origin of the oldest gods from the Abyss and Sea. Dissension among them leads to the triumph of Ea, god of subterranean regions, who establishes his dwelling over the Abyss with his wife Damkina. To this pair is born Marduk, surpassing all the gods in might. Dissension is renewed when the Sea, Tiamat, threatens the gods with an army of monsters under the command of her spouse Kingu, to whom she has given the tablet of destinies. Only Marduk can deal with this threat. The gods hasten into the hall of assembly and appoint the destiny of Marduk to be their king and champion. They erect for him a royal throne and convey to him the fullness of power. This is to be especially effective in his word, and when he forthwith gives a demonstration, destroying and re-creating a constellation by his mere utterance, all do homage and cry joyfully 'Marduk is king!' Soon the opposing forces join in battle. Marduk assails Tiamat in a manner suggestive of storm and lightning striking the sea. He slays her and seizes all her helpers. He recovers the tablet of destinies from Kingu and fastens it on his own breast.

The carcase of Tiamat now serves Marduk for acts of creation. Splitting it like a dried fish into two, he forms the sky above and the earth beneath. In the sky he fixes the order of the heavenly bodies and forms the system of the seasons, the years, months, day and night. Presiding over a fresh assembly of the gods, Marduk examines his captives. Kingu is sentenced, executed, and from his blood mankind is created by Ea. Marduk then gives the gods their allotted places in the new creation. In gratitude for their deliverance the gods build Marduk a temple in Babylon. Here they gather to feast and rejoice, to perform their rites and fix the destinies, and they confirm Marduk in his kingship over all the gods. The fifty names of Marduk are proclaimed and expounded, to the further exalting of his royal supremacy, mighty acts, and bountiful provision. It is notable that the story does not contain any death and resurrection of Marduk, nor a union with his consort.

On the following morning, 5 Nisan, the hardy chief priest resumed his duties four hours before dawn. As on the previous mornings, he washes, enters the temple alone and recites prayers before Marduk, then before his consort. He hails Marduk as king of the countries, the only lord, and addresses him under the names of various planets and stars, the sun and the moon, praying him to be calm. The prayer before the goddess likewise identifies her with various heavenly bodies. The chief priest then admits the other priests to proceed with their usual duties. Two hours after sunrise an elaborate purification of the holy places is carried out. From this the chief priest is excluded, lest he be contaminated. The rite includes sprinkling with water, beating a drum, censing, torchbearing, smearing of doors with cedar resin, and the recital of

incantations. In a ritual to prepare a chapel for the imminent arrival
of the god Nabu, a ram is beheaded and made in some way to
draw upon itself the impurities. The body and head are then cast
into the river, and the officials concerned (the incantatory priest
and the slaughterer) have to leave the city and remain in the open
country until 12 Nisan when, with the completion of the festival,
Nabu has returned to Borsippa. Three and a third hours after sunrise, the chief priest and craftsmen make further preparation for
Nabu's arrival, erecting a canopy in his chapel and praying further
for the banishment of evil powers. The chief priest then personally
serves food and drink to Marduk, the items being carefully prescribed. He beseeches him, as exalted over the gods and creator of
the laws, to show favour to the one who will take his hands, that
is the king, who is shortly to enter and who will later take the hand
of the god to invite him to begin the procession. There follow
some instructions for the serving of Nabu when he disembarks.

The king now comes to the temple and approaches the presence
of Marduk. At once the chief priest takes from him his royal
insignia and deposits them before the god. He strikes the king's
cheek, drags him by the ears before the god and makes him bow to
the ground. The king has to declare to the god that he has not
ruled wickedly or neglected the divine requirements:

I did not sin, lord of the countries,
I was not neglectful of the requirements of your godship.
I did not destroy Babylon, I did not command its overthrow.
I did not . . . the temple Esagil, I did not forget its rites.
I did not rain blows on the cheek of a subordinate . . .
I did not humiliate them.
I watched out for Babylon; I did not smash its walls.

(*ANET*, p. 334)

After a gap of some five lines, we hear the priest expressing the
god's favourable response: he will listen to the king's prayer and
exalt his kingship; he will bless him for ever and destroy his
enemy. The king is reinvested. It is again prescribed that the priest
strike the king; if tears flow, the god is pleased; if not, he is angry
and the king's enemy will overthrow him. In the evening the king
and the priest conduct a rite in the courtyard involving a white
bull and an offering in a great blaze of reeds; they offer a prayer to
'the divine Bull, brilliant light which lightens the darkness'.

The detailed account is not preserved further, but a number of important items in the remaining days emerge in outline from a variety of sources. Discrepancies in the day given for the visit to the *akitu*-house may reflect changes in the programme from time to time.

The images of the great gods were conveyed to Babylon from their respective cities and eventually they went in procession with Marduk along the stations of the sacred way, with its streets, gates and waterways, to the complex of the *akitu* sanctuary outside the city. Before they set forth, however, the first fixing of destinies took place in a special chamber of destinies in the main temple. This could be supposed to signify, on the analogy of the story in Enuma Elish, the appointment and equipment of Marduk by the gods as their champion in the battle to be fought in the *akitu*-house (cf. Gadd, *MR*, p. 55). The gods then proceeded in carefully prescribed order, and recitals were addressed to them at the various stations of the sacred route (Zimmern I, pp. 136f.; II, pp. 42f.). They accompanied Marduk as an army goes forth with its king (Zimmern II, pp. 49f.). That Marduk rode out as to war is also indicated by a text dedicating a war-chariot to his use in the procession (Zimmern I, pp. 153f.). The same text shows how the king hoped that the outcome of the ritual would be for him a destiny of joyful life, conquest of enemies and an eternal destiny.

That the procession culminated in Marduk's combat with Tiamat at the *akitu* shrine is sufficiently established by other sources, some relating to Assyrian celebrations imitative of Babylon's. An inscription of Sennacherib describes the restoration of the *akitu*-house at Ashur and how its gate carried a representation of his god Ashur (instead of Marduk) fighting Tiamat from his war-chariot. The combatants are accompanied by their armies and King Sennacherib himself is portrayed in some capacity. Lambert (*Iraq* 1963) has combined with this evidence several other texts to establish the conclusion that this battle was indeed symbolically accomplished in the annual rite in the *akitu*-house. An Assyrian ritual fragment lists the deities preceding the god to the *akitu*-house and they correspond exactly with the battle-order of the gods on the gates in Sennacherib's representation; evidently the procession was a setting-out to battle with Tiamat. Other texts combine to depict the triumphant god as sitting or placing his feet on Tiamat in the *akitu*-house. 'The Sea (Tiamat)', writes Lambert, 'was no doubt a small cultic structure in the *akītu*-house (probably a dais) and when the statue of Marduk was taken there, it was set on the dais to symbolize victory over Tiamat.' He further points out that the presence of the gods in the shrine and their lavish bestowal of gifts on Marduk is entirely consistent with the idea that Marduk delivered them from danger by taking up their part in fighting with Tiamat; the *akītu*-house was also called in Sumerian *E-siskur*, Akkadian *bīt ikribi*, 'house of benediction', which can be related to the congratulations given by the gods to Marduk on his victory; the rejoicing of the whole community also fits into this picture.

It was on 10 Nisan, so Nabonidus relates in an inscription, that he presented offerings when Marduk, king of the gods, and the other gods had taken up residence in the *akītu*-house (Falkenstein, 'Akiti-Fest', p. 161). An important event attested for the 11th is a second gathering of the gods at the temple in Babylon to fix the destinies.[3] Whether or not the earlier meeting for fixing the destinies had regard to the ensuing battle (p. 93), the later gathering presupposed the victory and looked out upon the prospect of ordered life in the established kingdom of Marduk. The Babylonian king, to judge from the dedication of the chariot mentioned above, would hope for the securement of his life and throne and the prosperity of his people. The ritual drama had 'repeated'[4] or actualized the salvation which lay beyond the first creation.

The omen of the king's tears described above reminds us that the beneficial effects of the rites were not taken to be automatic. The pleasure of the god could not be taken for granted or coerced, as experience indeed would prove. It is not surprising, therefore, that an example of a prayer recited on 11 Nisan before Marduk on his return to his temple expresses a mood not of gay abandon, but of earnestness. Its frequent refrains are 'Be appeased!' and 'How long?' It ends with supplication for his cities and temples concluding:

> The bolt of Babylon, the lock of (the temple) Esagila,
> The bricks of (the temple) Ezida restore thou to their places.
> 'O Lord be appeased' may the gods of heaven and earth say to thee.   (*ANET*, p. 390)

The features of the festivals that have now been mentioned are probably all that is sufficiently established for purposes of comparison with biblical materials. In his influential studies, Zimmern drew upon a number of problematic texts to bear out his view that the festival also reflected the assimilation of Marduk to a dying and rising fertility god. His reconstruction was widely followed, for example by Pallis, Gadd (*MR*, pp. 58f.), Labat and Frankfort. Von Soden (*ZA* 1955) has re-edited the main texts in question and finds that no death and resurrection of Marduk is mentioned and that a connection with the festival has not been demonstrated. He suggests rather that a myth of the god's ill-treatment was a theological version of Sennacherib's annihilation of Marduk's city, Babylon, in 689 BC. Lambert (*JSS* 1968) further declares that he has been unable to find evidence that Marduk was involved in a sacred marriage in the course of the new-year festival, though he acknowledges that other sacred marriages are attested under the Third Dynasty of Ur. The presentation of such supposed festal events for comparative studies was evidently premature.[5] It is interesting to note, however, that Mowinckel, who was stimulated by Zimmern's work as a whole, as he mentions in the preface to *Ps. st.* II, and who later gave an account following Frankfort (*HTC*, pp. 41f.), does not depend on these problematic elements for his own biblical reconstructions.

The rites of the king's enthronement are attested by a poorly preserved Assyrian text (Müller; Labat, pp. 81f.). The essential ceremonies take place in the temple, supplemented by some in the palace. The heart of the rite is the acceptance, authorization and empowering of the king by the gods. The king is thus made the instrument of the gods' rule, as is vividly indicated when the king is first carried into the temple preceded by the priest of the god Ashur, who strikes an instrument and calls repeatedly 'Ashur is king, Ashur is king!' The king prostrates himself before Ashur and the royal insignia are deposited before the god, along with offerings and a golden cup of oil, presumably for the anointing. The priest of Ashur then crowns and invests the king, pronouncing the blessing-wishes for his reign and priestly service to Ashur. Other officials add their prayers and kiss the king's feet. After returning to the palace, the king takes his throne. The officers surrender to him their symbols of office and mingle out of station; at the king's command they retake their insignia and resume their order of precedence. Presents are exchanged and musicians play.

Some features of this rite are easier understood if the enthronement it describes is not an *ad hoc* accession but a new-year enthronement. In particular one notices the smallness of the offerings (explicable if this were but part of a festival) and the assumption that all the officials will keep their offices. But Müller (pp. 53f.) thinks such arguments insufficient.

That full enthronement might be linked to the new-year festival is a deduction based on the practice of dating reigns from the month Nisan following the death of the previous king, to whom the broken year was attributed (p. 113; Smith, *MRK*, p. 29); the deduction is supported by reference to the Babylonian new-year festival, where the king gave up and received back his regalia (p. 92). This Babylonian rite has similarities with the Assyrian enthronement, repeating essential items of enthronement: the king's prostration before the god, the depositing of royal insignia before the god, the expression of the god's favour, the investiture, the words of blessing. The general similarity of Assyrian and Babylonian enthronement ceremonies is also indicated by allusions in royal inscriptions (Labat, pp. 87f.).

Representations of enthroned figures receiving a drink from the gods, as in the case of the Sumerian ruler Gudea, suggest that the bestowal of a drink representing supernatural life may sometimes have been part of enthronement ceremony, but are not sufficient to establish the point (Labat, p. 89).

(b) Egypt

The materials from Egypt relevant to kingship and the great festivals have long been profuse, including vivid pictorial records. But it is still difficult to win a coherent understanding of the cultic myth and ritual, since Egyptian sources offer little in the way of connected interpretation. While the understanding of the king's divinity is still a matter of dispute (Soggin, pp. 133f.), the emphasis on the humanity of the Pharaoh in the studies of Posener and Goedicke has helped to maintain the comparability of the Egyptian institution with the Israelite. The significance of the annual burial rites of Osiris remains disputed. In the influential works of Moret and Frazer the basic purpose was seen as the fertilization of the earth. In contrast stands the recent work of Chassinat. Favouring the moralistic interpretation of Plutarch, he understands the rites to show the triumph of piety over evil by commemorating the piety of Isis, who secured the reconstitution and burial of Osiris' body as a mummy, after he had been killed and dismembered by

Seth. But though Osiris presents many problems, there is much evidence that he came to be linked with the renewal of the divine order given in kingship (A. R. David, pp. 217–59). The complexity of Egyptian gods is further illustrated by a recent study of Seth by te Velde. On the positive side, we are indebted to modern study of the temples built in the Ptolemaic period for a wealth of data. In spite of their late date, these well preserved sanctuaries throw much light on the ancient ceremonies and structures. Their texts include long descriptions of the temples and the nature and purpose of each part, together with records of the annual programme of festivals; their reliefs add ample illustration (Fairman, 'Worship and Festivals', p. 165).

The Egyptians divided their year into three seasons: inundation, winter, summer. (The correspondence of the festal calendar to the natural seasons was maintained by the use of an ancient lunar calendar with intercalation, not the solar calendar used for finance and law; see Parker.) Each of these seasons was inaugurated with festivals of foundational and renovatory significance.

The beginning of inundation, when the Nile rose in June, was obviously rich in promise of extended renewal. A new-year festival from the end of the old year to perhaps the fifth day of the new year. Fairman gives reasons for thinking that the ceremonies included the annual rededication and renewal of the temple. From the evidence of the Ptolemaic temple of Horus at Edfu, he describes the main ceremony on new-year's day as a procession of the statues on to the roof to be united with the rays of the midday sun. In the afternoon the statues were probably displayed from a balcony to a privileged congregation. In these and all great rites, the chief officiant in principle was the king; the unity of kingship in the divine and human spheres also entailed that such ceremonies of the gods had direct bearing on the king's life and welfare.

The beginning of the season of winter, about October, was the favoured time for a king's full enthronement, his coronation. His accession would have taken place ideally in the dawn following his predecessor's death, when his titulary was drawn up and proclaimed (Frankfort, pp. 102f.). From the Ramesseum Dramatic Papyrus it has been deduced that between accession and coronation the king travelled through his realm enacting a play of some forty-six scenes to exhibit his succession (Frankfort, pp. 125f.).

The interpretation of the document is difficult, but no doubt it reflects elaborate ceremonies connected in some way with the succession (Fairman, *MRK*, pp. 81f.; Bonnet, p. 400). The coronation, effected by the gods (Bonnet, pp. 396f.), began with the king's baptismal purification, conveying divine life and power (*MRK*, pp. 78f.). The king was later invested with the insignia of crown, crook, flail, and a casket containing his testament of office or title-deeds; the gods affirmed his legitimacy, proclaimed his titles and inscribed his years (*MRK*, p. 79). He was given dominion over the two parts of Egypt and 'over all plains and all mountain-lands' (Bonnet, p. 397). The king was recognized as son of the god, usually as actually begotten by the sun-god Re; but a distinction still remained between his divinity and that of the 'great gods' (Bleeker, p. 127).[6]

The renewal of the king's office at this season is attested in the first place by the *sed* festival (*MRK*, pp. 83f.). Its incidence remains problematic; it particularly marked a king's thirtieth anniversary, but there were times when it was celebrated every three or four years (Bleeker, p. 114). After much construction and preparation of sanctuaries and five days of illuminations, the festival proper began with processions of the king and the gods, whose statues had been brought from all over the country. All the leading persons had likewise assembled, reaffirming their loyalty. The king danced over a field, perhaps sanctifying his country and renewing his dominion over it (cf. Frankfort, p. 85). He was enthroned and proclaimed to each of the four points of the compass, to which also an arrow was shot. Bleeker (*HR* I, p. 90) considers that it was especially the king's high-priesthood which was renewed in this festival.

As regards an annual renewal of kingship at this season, valuable evidence can now be drawn from Ptolemaic Edfu (Fairman, 'Worship and Festivals'). The ceremonies involved the king, the falcon-headed statue of Horus, and a real falcon selected by oracle for a year's 'reign'; in all three the same kingship is manifest. The renewal of the kingship is effected by the god's choice and presentation of the sacred falcon as his 'heir'. Litanies were sung in prayer for a happy year and for the safety of the falcon. The bird was anointed, invested with a ceremonial collar, given the symbol of eternity and other divine and royal emblems. It was put with the image of Horus, which was similarly invested. At a banquet the king presented pieces of meat to the falcon, signifying the destruction of his enemies. The bird then took up residence in its own temple adjacent to that of Horus. The populace celebrated with joyful feasting.

This annual renewal of coronation lasted five days; the first day, the beginning of the season of winter, is named in the calendar 'the day of the new year feast of Horus the Behdetite'. Fairman ('Worship and Festivals', p. 192) is surely right in bringing this into relation with the rites of Osiris in the previous month, completed on the last day. Osiris first represents the dying power of kingship. Through his pious burial, however, his eternal life is ensured. The king hauls a sacred pillar, the *ded* column, upright; vengeance and victory are represented by mock battles and processions (*MR*, fig. 4). The continuance of the royal and divine order is ensured. All is ready for the son of Osiris, Horus, to be crowned on the first day of winter, his 'new-year feast', and thereby for the coronation of the Pharaoh to be renewed.

The beginning of summer (about February) was also marked by a new-year and harvest festival, the festival of the god Min. There are impressive pictorial records of the festal scenes (*MR*, fig. 5). Themes of harvest and kingship mingle. The king was first carried on a splendid sedan-throne into Min's temple, where he made offerings. The god's image was then carried out, preceded by the symbols of the royal ancestors, the white bull which was a form of Min, and the king and queen. A shrine was set up in the fields and here the king ceremonially reaped corn; rites on behalf of the kingship included the loosing of geese to the four points of the compass. Such announcement of a 'new' reign seems in this context to have reference to the fertile power seen in Min and in the king and his ancestors (*MRK*, p. 86).

Another festival with the character of a new-year and harvest celebration, including a sacred marriage, is known at Edfu, where its position in the calendar seems inappropriate (Fairman, 'Worship and Festivals', pp. 196f.). The main observance lasted from new to full moon in the third month of summer. The image of Hathor was brought by boat from Dendera to be met by that of Horus; together they entered the temple of Horus to spend their marriage night. There followed processions to the necropolis for the cult of the ancestors and rites of harvest. Arrows were shot to the compass points, to which geese were also sent bearing the message of renewed kingship: 'The King of Upper and Lower Egypt, Horus the Behdetite, great god, lord of the sky, has possessed himself of the White Crown and has assumed the Red Crown.' Defeat of enemies was represented by attacking a hippopotamus of red wax inscribed with their names, a papyrus list of enemies, and other models. In other festivals yet more forms of ritual victories are known, such as the trampling of grain, the netting of birds, animals, and figurines of prisoners, and recitals over inscribed figurines (*MRK*, pp. 88f.).

Through all this abundance of rites the main theme is reasonably clear. At the great transitions – the change of ruler, the turn of the seasons – the rites of kingship represent the overcoming of the threat of chaos and the renewal of the divine cosmic order. That order is the essence of kingship, a unity manifest in the gods and in the office of the Pharaoh.

Finally, it must be remembered that if in many respects Egyptian religion and kingship were remote from the Israelite, there is no doubt that through Egyptian domination of Syria–Palestine in the second millennium BC ideological influence was exerted on Canaanite cities and so bequeathed to Israel. The influence could be quickened by such contacts as are recorded in the case of Solomon, I Kings 3.

(c) Hittites

Similar influence could be expected from Hittite penetration of the area, a circumstance which Ezekiel understood as late as the sixth century, when he said of the royal Jerusalem, 'Your father was an Amorite and your mother a Hittite' (16.3).

The Hittite king took a leading part in the *purulli* festival in the spring (Gurney, *MRK*, pp. 106–8). There are some resemblances to the Babylonian festivals. A myth of the god's victory over the *illuyankas* dragon was connected with this celebration, which also included the assembling of all the gods and the fixing of destinies. The destinies were especially those of the king and queen and then of the world as a whole, the gods being called upon: 'Pronounce the life of the king and queen! Pronounce the life of heaven and earth!'

An autumn festival (*nuntariyašhaš*) extended over sixteen days; the king, with his queen and his heir, made processions from city to city with sacrifices and assemblies (*MRK*, p. 109). The ceremonies are in some respects the counterpart of those which the king performed in the spring, as appears from materials recently presented and discussed by H. G. Güterbock. A tablet outlines the programme of a spring festival (AN.TAḪ.ŠUM), which lasted thirty-eight days, the king and queen accomplishing many journeys and rites. The rites included the opening of storage jars which had been filled in the autumn festival, processions of a shield which may have represented a protecting deity, a visit to the temple of the dead, offerings before the images of dead rulers, and celebrations at a sanctuary situated in a grove outside the capital.

A ceremony of mock battle is known to have been held at Gursamassa, apparently in the autumn (Gurney, *The Hittites*, p. 155). Before an image and a sacred stone there was feasting and singing and a combat between two groups of young men; the group representing the home side carried copper weapons, easily vanquishing the enemy whose weapons were of reed, and devoting a captive to the god. The colourful nature of Hittite festivals is indicated in another text which tells of a procession reminiscent of the Babylonian egress to the *akītu* shrine (op. cit., pp. 156f.). An ornate chariot is brought to the temple and decked with red, white and blue ribbons, the god's image is seated in it and so progresses behind a column of sacred women, dancers and torch-bearers to a woodland shrine.

Little is known of the Hittite king's enthronement. He was apparently installed in rites which included anointing, robing, crowning, and the giving of a royal name; there was emphasis on his appointment as the god's chief priest (*MRK*, p. 118; Kümmel, pp. 43f.). The perpetuity of royal life is seen both in a kind of identification of the current king with the dynasty's founder (T/Labarnas; *MRK*, pp. 114f.) and in the phrase 'he became a god' to refer to a king's death (*ANET*, p. 393a; Dussaud, p. 352).

(d) Canaanites

For Canaanite festivals we have much suggestive material in the OT and in Ugaritic literature and we can draw points from other archaeological materials. Yet we still lack direct coherent information relevant to our present enquiry.[7] It is true that an interesting picture has been built up from the Ugaritic texts by some scholars. Thus A. S. Kapelrud (*Ras Shamra Discoveries*, pp. 48f.) feels able to summarize how Baal took his throne at the autumn new-year festival:

> He sat upon his throne at the new-year festival . . . He had returned
> from his sojourn in the underworld and was greeted with the cultic
> shout, 'Our king is Aliyan Baal; our judge and none is above him!'
> . . . Baal's worshippers saw in him the powerful king who drove
> across the sky on the clouds and let his mighty voice be heard in the
> crash of thunder. In violent conflicts he triumphed over his opponents.
> He sent the rain and promoted fertility; but the heat and drought of
> summer compelled him to withdraw and descend into the depths of
> the earth. When autumn came and the rains began, it was Baal who
> returned to ensure fertility and ascend the throne . . . The entire
> annual cycle was then presented in the cultic drama, the climax being
> Baal's enthronement and the dedication of his temple, which took
> place anew each year.

As for the part of the king, a few deductions have been made from
those Ugaritic texts which seem to concern royal ancestors and
dynastic continuance. Kapelrud can thus say (op. cit., p. 74):

> The king played an important part in the cultic action. In the Krt-
> text there is an account of an offering which the king brought . . . He
> is said to have washed himself and made himself red. Presumably this
> was a ceremony of purification in which the king washed away his
> sin and ritual impurity with the blood of the sacrificial animal and
> thus consecrated himself for the sacred acts which he was about to
> perform . . . He took with him a lamb and a bird for sacrifice, poured
> wine into a silver cup and mounted to the top of the tower . . .

On the whole, however, the texts are too problematic to be of
direct assistance in our enquiry.[8] The same lack of direct information besets the question of Canaanite enthronement, in spite of the
glimpses afforded by Ezekiel 28.12–14 and discussed by Widengren
(*MRK*, pp. 165f.).

2. *The Israelite autumn festival as clarified by Mowinckel*

(a) *The chief annual festival*

Of Israel's three annual pilgrimage festivals (Ex. 23.14f.; 34.18f.;
Deut. 16), that in the autumn was clearly the most important in the
time of the kings, as already recognized by Wellhausen, Volz and
others, and subsequently confirmed by Snaith and Kraus.[9] Its pre-
eminence is clear enough from its designation as 'the festival of

Yahweh' (Lev. 23.39; Judg. 21.19; Hos. 9.5) or simply 'the festival'
(I Kings 8.2, 65), from its use for the inauguration of the temple
(I Kings 8), and from Jeroboam's rival institution (12.32). The
other festivals remain in obscurity. There is just a trace of the
thrice-yearly pattern in I Kings 9.25, while Josiah's reform is said
to revive the passover from the time of the judges (II Kings
23.21f., cf. Josh. 5.10f.); the Chronicler seems to have read Josiah's
action back into Hezekiah's reform (II Chron. 30; cf. Kraus,
Worship, p. 52).

The Pentateuchal references to the festivals are difficult to use
as evidence for Jerusalem under the kings, since they may in part
be too early and hence from other sanctuaries, or in part too late
and hence reflect the Assyro–Babylonian calendar introduced
around the exile. The latter applies to Exodus 12.1f., where the
month of passover, the Nisan of the Babylonian calendar, is
emphatically designated as the first of the year. That there was a
tendency to think of the spring as the beginning of the calendar
even in the early periods is suggested by the order of the festivals
in all the Pentateuchal sources (spring, summer, autumn). As in
Babylonia and Egypt (pp. 87, 96) and in later Judaism,[10] it seems
that aspects of 'new year' could be attached to the beginnings of
several seasons. Nevertheless, the evidence as a whole shows that
the autumn was a major annual turning-point under the kings.
The Pentateuchal sources chime in by placing the autumn festival
at the 'coming round' (*t^eqūpā*) of the year (Ex. 34.22) and the
'going forth' (*ṣē'ṭ*) of the year (Ex. 23.16). Whether the latter
expression means 'entrance'[11] or 'exit',[12] the decisive transition of
the seasons is indicated. Exodus 23.16 and 34.22 put the feast in
the season when produce is brought in from the open; this marks
the end, but also looks forward, since it was occasioned by the
approach of the new-year rains. The Gezer calendar, commonly
assigned to the tenth century BC, lists 'ingathering' (*'sp*) first in the
round of agricultural seasons. And in fact the climatic conditions
of Palestine make it certain that this was the appropriate point in
the cultic calendar to pray with full solemnity for the sometimes
fickle winter rains, the means for a new year of life. This function
of the festival is still clear in the post-exilic period (Zech. 14.16f.)
and at the end of the era, when elaborate ceremonies of water-
pouring and rites with green branches are attested (Mishna,
Suk. 4). It is notable that Volz (1912) had already depicted the

festival without use of the controversial enthronement psalms and
had reached conclusions similar to those which Mowinckel was to
formulate independently. In fact, before recourse is had to the
psalms at all, it is clear enough that the dominant festival under
the Jerusalem monarchy was the autumn pilgrimage, and that this
would be the context for the society to renew its foundations,
purifying and re-sanctifying men and institutions, re-experiencing
the divine salvation which had created its world and life and hope.

Deut. 16.13 calls this festival 'the feast of booths (*sukkōt*)' and depicts
it as an observance of seven days. In Lev. 23.23f. and Num. 29 there is
a more precise dating. The relevant month, in accordance with the
Babylonian calendar, is here counted as the seventh (its name Tishri is
not found in the OT); the pilgrimage feast of booths takes place from
days 15–22; it is preceded by two one-day observances: on the first of
the month a 'day of acclamation (with trumpets)', and on the tenth a
'day of atonement' (cf. Lev. 16). This first day of the seventh month is
called 'head/beginning of the year' (*rōš haššānā*) in the Mishna tractate of
that name. But in the OT this expression occurs only in Ezek. 40.1,
where its application is disputed; here some take it to mean the whole
seventh month,[13] others only its tenth day.[14] The tenth day is in fact
given in Lev. 25.9 for the fanfare announcing a jubilee year, and in the
Mishna (*Taanit* 4.8) its ceremonies include a dance of maidens (cf.
Judg. 21.21).
Mowinckel saw these later Jewish developments as stemming from
the change to the Babylonian calendar around the exile.[15] He saw the
pre-exilic festival of harvest and new year as essentially the week beginning with the full moon. In the old calendar the months may well have
begun with the full moon.[16] But in the new calendar the months began
with the new moon, so the festal week, tied to the full moon, now began
on the day counted as the fifteenth. Naturally the preceding new-moon
day, reckoned now as the first of the month, gradually drew to itself
some elements of new-year observance. As for the Day of Atonement,
falling on the tenth in the new calendar, Mowinckel was inclined to see
here a day of penitence and purification which in the pre-exilic calendar
had marked the end of the old year. In *Ps. st.* II, p. 22, he suggested that
the days intervening between it and the great festal week were perhaps
intercalary days, resembling the five epagomenal days added in the
Egyptian civil calendar after twelve thirty-day months.
The details of such developments in the calendar must remain rather
uncertain, though in outline Volz, Mowinckel, Snaith and Kraus agree.
The main festival was the week that we see beginning at the full moon;
the post-exilic first and tenth days may have had forerunners as holy

days of some kind in the old calendar.[17] The festal ideology would naturally spread into preparatory and concluding days, just as it extended over twelve days for the Babylonians (p. 89) and thirty-eight for the Hittites (p. 101).

(b) The celebration of Yahweh's kingship

Mowinckel argued that throughout the time of David's dynasty this autumn festival included a special celebration of Yahweh as King.[18] Gunkel's classification of the psalms had brought into relief the hymns in which Yahweh is proclaimed and manifested as King in something like an act of enthronement (*Einl.*, pp. 94f.). Mowinckel saw that such texts had belonged to a regular ceremony of worship and that this must have been part of the supreme festival, that of autumn. The ritual actualized the original exertions of Yahweh's superiority, over chaos in creation and over enemies in history. It signified his epiphany, when the loyal encountered him afresh as Saviour and Provider. Even the nucleus of the relevant texts, which Mowinckel took to be Psalms 47; 93; 95–100, amply displayed the themes of Yahweh's kingship: the new song of the new era, the triumphant judgment of gods and men, salvation for the loyal (*Ps. st.* II, pp. 3f.). It is true of these 'enthronement' psalms, as of all Gunkel's classes, that there is much variation within the general homogeneity of the class, as Lipiński emphasizes; but the common core remains substantial and indicates a particular cultic context. Since the ceremonies would not be restricted to one isolated scene but comprise processions, acts of homage, sacrifices, purifications and the like, it was correct to seek for other psalms which, though of different form, were likely to have belonged to the festival. Mowinckel's choice is based mostly on solid reasons of content, comparability and Jewish tradition; especially relevant for us is his inclusion of Psalms 24; 29; 46; 48; 76; 81; 82; 84; 118; 149; and in his later work 68. The wider selection of festal texts serves to add clarity to the peculiar complex of ideas already present in the narrower group.

This complex of ideas is also much illumined by foreign, especially Mesopotamian festivals. Nothing from the foreign worship should be read into the Israelite, but the *akītu* ritual does help us to see how a god's kingship and epiphany, his triumph over waters and other foes, his creating, judging, saving and providing could form a pattern and supply content to the principal annual festival of a kingdom. The location of such a pattern in Jerusalem's autumn festival tallies well with Jewish tradition, which associates these ideas with the autumnal new year and booths (*Ps. st.* II, p. 82) and uses here some of the relevant psalms (Volz, pp. 42, 60). The rooting of this Jewish tradition in OT times is proved by the post-exilic Zechariah 14.16f., where the themes of Yahweh's kingship, control of the waters and universal dominion are firmly attached to the keeping of the autumn festival in Jerusalem. And that the pattern existed in pre-exilic worship is shown by the way it is used by pre-exilic and exilic prophets.

Thus it is used by Nahum to predict the doom of Nineveh which occurred in 612 BC. Yahweh here manifests himself in fury to combat his enemies, Yahweh whose roar destroys the sea and affrights all the world; he routs the death-powers led by Belial and overwhelms the residence of the hostile goddess;[19] the feet of the messengers are swift over the mountains to carry the good tidings of Belial's destruction; they announce the era of peace and urge Judah to celebrate her festivals. All this is tantamount to the proclamation that Yahweh is proved King, victor over all rivals, as comparison with Isaiah 52.7 shows.

In about the same period, Habakkuk likewise applied the festal story to history. Though the end of the summer sees a parched and bare land, the festival brings confidence that Yahweh will show his supremacy over the chaos-powers and bring salvation to his anointed and to his people; this will include the overthrow of the current political enemies.[20]

Another pre-exilic prophet, Zephaniah, also reflects the festal ideas, even though his message begins with God's purifying wrath bearing upon Jerusalem. Yahweh comes on his 'day' for his sacrificial feast, here given a sinister aspect (1.7). Throughout the world and in the midst of Jerusalem the wrathful Yahweh destroys corruption. His sovereignty is expressed in words against the nations,[21] execrations which, like the arrows in Egyptian kingship festivals, are aimed at the four points of the compass.[22] His dread godhead, as in the psalms of his kingship, is manifest in supremacy above the foreign gods (2.11) and all nations worship him. To purified Zion he then comes as King, victorious and saving champion, loving spouse, restorer of the happy state (3.14–19).

In Jeremiah also the festal events are reflected (8.19): though the harvest and summer are ended and Yahweh is supposed to be present in Zion as her King and bringer of salvation, the faith of his worshippers continues to be sorely tried by hardships.

The eighth-century prophets likewise made use of the festal scheme. Amos begins with Yahweh's royal roar from Zion (Lipiński, p. 140) and directs the imperial execrations to the four points of the compass;[23] he hymns Yahweh's control of the creation (4.13; 5.8; 9.5–6); the people wait for Yahweh's 'day' in expectation of the light of salvation and think to please him with their festal celebrations; their hope of rains is transformed by Amos into a demand for torrents of righteousness (5.18–24, Volz, p. 45). As for Isaiah, he sees Yahweh manifest as King in his Zion temple, hymned as dominating all the world in radiant majesty, pronouncing the destiny of his people (ch. 6). There is indeed hardly a chapter in Isaiah 1–39 where the festal ideas are not apparent.

It is therefore not surprising that in the exile Isaiah 40–55 should still depend on the festal tradition. Mowinckel showed in *Ps. st.* II, pp. 193f., how these chapters blend psalmic and prophetic forms and hence could hardly be the source of the 'unmixed' psalms 93, 96–99; and he showed how the relevant concepts in Isaiah 40–55 are given a secondary application.[24] The very proclamation of Yahweh's kingship is still embedded in a cultic procession into a guarded Zion (52.7f.), not the historical ruins.

The prophetic literature thus gives abundant support to the essentials of Mowinckel's account of the autumn festival under the Davidic monarchy. The correctness of his choice of this festival for the celebration reflected in his psalms is certainly borne out by the climatic factors mentioned above. For not only Zechariah 14.16f. but also the psalms in question, such as 29; 68; 84; 93; show Yahweh's kingship at Jerusalem as bound up with his mastery of the rain-sources. Such psalms have every appearance of antiquity and there is no justification for denying the existence of the autumnal celebration of Yahweh's kingship in the early and great days of Israelite Jerusalem. Indeed, the early dating is required by the evidence of some continuity with pre-Israelite Jerusalem traditions,[25] and it accords with the essential nature of the monarchy as the organ of Yahweh's kingship.

Attempts to find a different setting for the psalms of Yahweh's kingship have made little headway. Mowinckel's *Zum isr. Neujahr* sufficiently refuted theories that they are hymns of sunrise or sabbath. Gunkel's complicated explanation (*Einl.*, pp. 100f.) was already seen to be invalid by his co-author Begrich, p. 421! Kraus soon saw that his own adaptation of Gunkel's view was untenable (below, pp. 110f.).

(c) The dramatic character of the celebration

The proclamation of Yahweh's kingship in Psalms 93, 96–99 etc. presupposes his triumph over rivals and is received with excited joy. It is all part of a gospel of victory and a new era. Admittedly there is some difficulty in the plain translation of *Yahweh mālak* as 'Yahweh has become King' and in speaking of God's 'annual enthronement'; such expressions do not reveal the distinction of a cultic event from a historical event, nor of a deity's reign from a man's. But the dramatic nature of the cultic scene must not be denied.[26] It was this which enabled it to be applied to great turning-points of history by Nahum, Zephaniah, Deutero-Isaiah and the rest (pp. 106f.) and to the eschatological drama of the apocalyptists.[27]

We have already seen that the festivals of Mesopotamia and Egypt had such a dramatic character and actualized archetypal events by easily executed movements and manipulations. There is plenty of evidence that the Israelites employed similar rites. Especially prominent are the processions which betoken the divine warfare, triumph, exaltation and epiphany (Pss. 24; 47; 68; 132 etc.), while a rich variety of symbolic acts, including the destruction of the doomed, is evidenced in the prophets. It is true that the monotheistic and aniconic nature of Israelite worship would put certain restrictions on the ritual and its mythology, except in the periods of extreme syncretism. But the psalms show that, within such limits, the worship could continue to convey an exhilarating experience of divine actions made present.[28]

The triumph underlying God's exaltation as cosmic King assumes various forms: he mastered the waters (Pss. 29; 93; 89; 74); he destroyed Pharaoh's hosts in the exodus (Ex. 15; Ps. 114); he conquered the inhabitants of Canaan and made Jerusalem his sanctuary (Ex. 15; Pss. 47; 132; 76; cf. 78). One way in which Yahweh's supremacy was dramatized in the festival was by a ritual demonstration of his routing all the kings of the earth as they are imagined to converge against Jerusalem. Psalm 48 is good evidence for this rite, with support also from 46 and 76. Since a victory in just this form was not part of the national historical traditions, it is likely that, as in the prophetic acts and some Egyptian customs,[29] the intention was rather towards the future: such would be the fate of all enemies who might assault Yahweh's city. Psalm 48.9f. stresses that the worshippers have seen and heard Yahweh's work of salvation in the midst of his city, having depicted or 'modelled' his covenant-keeping in the midst of his temple. The use of 'modelled' (*dimmīnū*) here would certainly be appropriate for a symbolic representation, as Johnson has recognized (*SKAI*, p. 88). We may compare Plutarch's use of *eikones* 'likenesses' and *mimēma* 'copy' to describe the Egyptian rites of Osiris (*De Is. et Os.* 27).

(d) The involvement of the Davidic kingship

What was the king's part in all this? Although Mowinckel presented a comprehensive view of the festival, marshalling his texts at the outset and examining all the main ingredients of myth and ritual, he did little to integrate the royal psalms into the picture. He included Psalms 75; 118 and 132 in his general material for the festival (*Ps. st.* II, p. 4). Further, he considered it likely that the king's enthronement was re-celebrated annually in connection with the new-year festival (*PIW* I, pp. 60, 66) and thus that Psalms 2; 72; 101 and 110 would have a place there. He also made the generalization that 'the king stands at the centre of the festivals, and from the power and blessing he there obtains from Yahweh, vital force and blessing radiate to the people' (*PIW* I, pp. 61f.). But it remained for H. Schmidt (*Die Thronfahrt Jahves*) and more especially A. R. Johnson to take the matter further.

In his first study ('The Role of the King in the Jerusalem Cultus'), Johnson accepted that the festival provided a context for the celebration of Yahweh's original work (triumph over chaos, enthronement, creation), and then concentrated his attention on a part of the festival, a dramatic sequence which stood out in this context and which displayed Yahweh's recreative work, replenishing society for the new year. In this drama Yahweh defeated the forces of darkness and death, which were represented as the kings of the earth attacking Jerusalem. But since the divine warfare was here projected on the earthly plane, it would be likely to involve Yahweh's ruler in Jerusalem, the Davidic king. So Johnson expounded Psalms 89, 18, 118, 2 and 110, in that order, as belonging to this drama; the king is seen as leader of Jerusalem's forces against the hostile kings; he succumbs at first (a trial of faith) and is then rescued by Yahweh and re-installed in glory.

In *Sacral Kingship* (1955, 1967) he uses more texts; the king's ordeal now includes Psalm 101 and his re-enthronement Psalm 21. But the chief difference is that he now understands this dramatic sequence as concerned with eschatology rather than the annual revival of society. Rather like a prophetic symbolism, it prefigured the consummation of God's kingdom, which will come to pass if and when the challenge of Israel's vocation is met. The glories shown in the drama were potential and challenging; the well-tried and exalted king, represented in the drama by the present king, was likewise an unrealized ideal: this is what the kingship would be if the true response were given to Yahweh.

Johnson's use of Psalms 89; 18 and 118 of such ritual humiliation and exaltation is discussed by Mowinckel in *PIW* II, pp. 253f. and rejected. Much of the latter's argument, however, could be countered by using his own insights into ritual. For Psalms 89 and 18 he asserts the historical interpretation without facing the problems this involves. He agrees that Psalm 118 belongs to the new-year festival, but he strangely asserts that the king's combat in the psalm must be referred to all the historical disasters which had befallen Israel throughout her history. He also rejects Engnell's proposal to place Psalm 22 and other psalms in similar rites. He concludes:

> As long as the 'suffering' of the king in a majority of psalms must be referred to actual historical distress, or to real prosaic illness, strong positive arguments are needed in order to prove that the suffering in other psalms, in which it is described in a perfectly analogous way, has to be referred to ritual sham suffering.

Kraus first presented a view of the festival which under the kings gave prominence to the election of the dynasty and Jerusalem by Yahweh; the celebration of Yahweh's kingship he then moved to the post-exilic age with dependence on Deutero-Isaiah (*Königsherrschaft*, 1951). Mowinckel pointed to the arbitrary way in which Kraus selected his texts for the early period and to the fallacy of making the rites of Yahweh's kingship derive from Deutero-Isaiah (*PIW* II, pp. 230f., 237–9). In fact Kraus soon

changed his theory, accepting the antiquity of the celebration of
Yahweh as King but denying that it involved an annual throne-
ascension of Yahweh (*Psalmen*, 1960, pp. xliiif.). His commentary
on the royal psalms is close to Mowinckel's position, in that he
ascribes some to the king's enthronement rites in the festival but
does not follow up the matter very far, and certainly does not
envisage ritual suffering in 18; 89; 101; 118.

Thus a position is reached where Mowinckel and many others
recognize a festival of great ideological importance and further see
that most of the royal psalms have some connection with it, yet
cannot accept the most significant work that has been done to
elucidate this connection, the work of Johnson. Johnson's theory
has such far-reaching implications that it is most desirable that its
validity should be tested from every point of view. I shall therefore examine the matter in the light of my wider definition of royal
psalms; but first we must look carefully at the core of the relevant
material, Gunkel's royal psalms.

3. *The interpretation of Gunkel's 'royal psalms'*

Psalm 2

There seems no cause to assume, with Schmidt and Johnson
(*SKAI*, p. 129), any change of speaker in the psalm. With Gunkel
and Mowinckel (*GT*), therefore, we should consider the Davidic
king as the speaker throughout, referring to himself in the third as
well as the first person (cf. p. 48). Imagining a world audience, he
portrays the beginnings of a general revolt; he sees the kings of
the earth planning to break the yoke of Yahweh's reign, which he
represents. From the outset his speech is clearly intended to issue
a warning. He continues by depicting the easy supremacy of God,
whose measures centre in the establishment of his king on Zion,
his sacred mountain. In vv. 7–9 he recites from the decree which
God has given him, to the effect that God has 'today' declared him
his son, entitled to rule over all nations and equipped with the
necessary power. In vv. 10f. he concludes his warning by directly
summoning the kings of the earth to the wiser course of
submission.

It is clear enough that the king speaks within the context of his
enthronement or related rites. The schematized picture of revolt,
the reference to his installation in v. 6, the contents of the decree,

– all point to such a context. This has become all the clearer since Gunkel's time by the clarification of the function of the decree as a royal document of legitimation (p. 43). The king's speech in Psalm 2 thus occurs in succession to major items in the enthrone-ment ceremonies. Anointing (cf. v. 2), installation (v. 6), legitima-tion (v. 7) and empowering (v. 9, sceptre etc.) seem already to have been represented. After such dealings with God, the king here turns to speak to the world. Von Rad (*OT Theology* I, p. 319) and Mowinckel (*PIW* I, p. 62) even think the scene of the main cere-monies in the temple has now been left behind, Psalm 2 being delivered after procession to a throne in the palace. Schmidt thinks such looking back on the acts of enthronement shows that the psalm belongs rather to an annual remembrance or renewal of his enthronement, comparable to the Egyptian and Mesopotamian practices, and situated in the autumnal new-year festival.

This latter possibility takes a special form in the work of Johnson (above, p. 109). Within the autumnal festival, Johnson reconstructs a drama which year by year showed the ideal Davidic king standing against the evil forces, brought to the verge of disaster, and then restored in God's intervention and triumph. He places Psalm 2 in the final stages of this drama, along with 110 and 21; the ritual battle has been won and is here followed by a re-enthronement. He translates, 'Why did the nations become insur-gent . . .' and thinks the reference is to 'their abortive attempt throughout the years to thwart Yahweh's plans' (*SKAI*, pp. 128f.). But this does not do justice to the psalm's urgency and unity as a response to a current threat. It is hardly correct to say that the psalm shows us the kings 'being compelled to acknowledge the universal sovereignty . . .'.[30] Rather, they are being urgently warned, and it is therefore more natural to understand vv. 1–3 as portraying the current and urgent situation. More convincingly Bentzen (*KM*, pp. 16f.) places the psalm before the ritual combat, believing also that elements of enthronement had preceded as preparation for the ordeal.

There are indications outside the psalms that the king's en-thronement was celebrated at the autumn festival. This seems to have been the best time for usurpers to get themselves proclaimed, as Snaith (*JNYF*, pp. 75–80) argues from the cases of Absalom,[31] Adonijah and Solomon. Mowinckel points out that the Israelite system of dating events according to regnal years implies a uniform starting point for reigns (*Zum isr. Neujahr*, p. 19). The period from the death of the old king to the festival would then have a preliminary status for the new reign, as is indicated by the expression *rēšīt mamleket* (Jer. 26.1 etc.) corresponding to the Akkadian *rēš šarrūti*.[32] An annual commemoration or renewal at this season would then be likely, somewhat in the manner of the Babylonian and Egyptian customs.[33] The linking of the king's enthronement with the festival was indeed a necessary corollary of the doctrine of the unity of the kingship wielded by the god and his chosen king, a kingship asserted at the new year.

Psalm 2 is wholly in accord with this. The event of the Davidic king's installation is here enclosed in a presentation of God's kingship. The entire unified sovereignty, moreover, is projected in a highly imaginative, dramatic fashion. Gunkel (*Einl.*, p. 145) remarks that the psalmist 'imagines a whole drama', while de Vaux, p. 109, sees a similarity with the sham fight at coronation feasts in Egypt. We have seen that the autumnal festival contained a dramatically conceived assertion of God's Creator-kingship (pp. 105–9); this psalm strongly suggests that basic rites of the Davidic kingship were involved in it, as Johnson recognized. Restrained comparison with foreign rituals of kingship is supported by the fact that the psalm, thoroughly Israelite as a whole, yet preserves a considerable foreign inheritance. This could well descend from the rites of pre-Davidic kings in Jerusalem, influenced in turn by the great empires of Egypt, the Hittites and Mesopotamia. Such an inheritance includes the vivid conception of world-wide sovereignty, the title-deeds of divine sonship (p. 98), the figure of the pots (cf. p. 101) and the kiss of submission (p. 95).

The psalm, then, illumines the rites establishing the king at Jerusalem. It shows that these had a dramatic character. It also indicates that they were linked to the presentation of Yahweh's kingship. The setting was most likely the autumn festival. These connections raise the possibility that the royal rites in question were not just a once-for-all installation but also an annual renewal.

Psalm 18 (*cf. II Sam. 22*)

It is now generally agreed that this is the thanksgiving of a king who speaks throughout. For the most part it is a testimony about God in the third person, dealing especially with the salvation and eminence he has bestowed on his king. The view of Gunkel and

others that it is from near the end of the monarchy seems to depend
mainly on dubious views of the development of Israel's religious
ideas. Against this is the conclusion of Cross and Freedman ('A
Royal Song') that considerations of orthography and idiom point
to an early date, the tenth century being not at all improbable.
Their view suits the archaic grandeur and confidence of the
psalm.

In vv. 2f. the king makes a preliminary statement, accumulating
the epithets which present Yahweh as the personal deliverer of his
king. Verse 4 seems to give the essence of the testimony that is to
follow: he had called on Yahweh and been saved. Perhaps we
should render, 'Wailing I called on Y.' (the first word being pronounced *meḥēlil*, hiph. participle of *yll*).

From v. 5 he tells the story of his deliverance. He had sunk into
the mouth of Death, overwhelmed by the waters at the entrance
of Sheol. But Yahweh had heard his prayer and descended from
heaven, the irresistible warrior God, in full demonstration of
power over all creation, smiting the earth with his storm-bolts and
volcanic blows, cleaving through to the underworld. So he had
drawn his king up from the great waters, the mouth of Sheol, and
saved him from his enemies, the death-powers.

From v. 21 the significance of all this is brought out. It showed
that God's pleasure in him, the basis of his appointment, still holds
good. Yahweh has approved him as right in conduct, loyal,
obedient. Verses 26–8 remind the listening people that there is a
lesson here for them all. At v. 29 the psalm returns to its prevailing
concentration on the king's own position before God. Yahhew
gives him light and strength. Yahweh, Israel's God without compare, makes him an agile warrior, trains him in the arts of war,
shields and supports him. In vv. 33-46 some find a resumption of
the preceding story: having been saved from near death, the king
went on to rout opposing armies (Gunkel, RSV). But the verses
could be taken more generally, expressing the capacity for
triumph which Yahweh has now bestowed on his king, to be
translated with present and future tenses (NEB, Johnson). We
hear that God has appointed him 'head of the nations', to be
served by the remotest peoples. The king's testimony rings out
among the peoples of the world, celebrating Yahweh as the faithful fulfiller of his covenant with David and his descendants for
ever.

To what deliverance is the king referring? Some think of an unknown historical battle (so Mowinckel, *GT*), others of the characterization of a whole career (e.g. David's, so Delitzsch), others of a ritual. Against the first view is the lack of any clear indication in the text or in tradition to this effect; even if vv. 33f. are understood as the concrete version of the event that has first been rendered poetically in vv. 5f., it is hard to think of any occasion in Israelite history remotely suitable.[34] The second view is even further from the narrative in vv. 5f., though it could claim support from the title if Davidic authorship is envisaged. To be plausible, either of these views would need to assume that the narrative of vv. 5–20 was *ultimately* traceable to another use, for it reads as pure and intact myth, which could not have been created directly for these supposed purposes. Is it necessary or proper to assume such a secondary application, unless a primary force, as a myth interpreting ritual, is implausible? If other psalms show the existence of appropriate rites, such a primary force must have the preference.In fact we shall see that one of the psalms which most clearly establishes such rites, Psalm 144, is strikingly related to Psalm 18. The historicizing interpretation in Psalm 18's title is readily understandable in view of the end of the monarchy and its rites in 586 BC.

These observations are in harmony with Weiser, who takes the psalm (as Schmidt had taken part of it) as a text from the renewal of the king's salvation in regular festivals. He thinks of the rite as actualizing the king's historical rise to power, and here he seems in danger of leaving the direct interpretation of the text. Bentzen (*Jesaja*, p. xv) came to reject a reference to history; he sees the narrative as the myth of the primeval election and salvation of the king, represented in the rites of his enthronement. The clearest treatment is that of Johnson (*SKAI*, pp. 117–23), who includes the psalm in his annual drama of kingship; the king had been presented as almost defeated in his battle with the forces of darkness, before the intervention of Yahweh was signified at dawn and the king brought forth in triumph; perhaps there had been a baptismal scene in the caves of Gihon, now to be followed by procession up the sacred hill; the whole was a kind of acted parable of faith, humility and righteousness, a challenging demonstration of Yahweh's will for Israel and the world.

The title refers to the king as 'servant of Yahweh' (so also Ps.

36), denoting his high office, but not necessarily his role as sufferer (p. 150).

At the end of the psalm the stress on the king's appointment to rule the earth would certainly suit a context of enthronement or related rites. The cry 'Yahweh lives' (v. 47) points to the autumn festival's assertion of Yahweh's own kingship; similarly v. 47b ('and the God of my salvation is ascended'). Widengren (*SK*, p. 69) has compared the use of the phrase 'Baal lives' in the Ugaritic texts, and one can allow force to the comparison without equating the celebration of Yahweh's kingship in all respects with that of Baal.

To sum up: the psalm is best taken to describe a liturgical salvation, if other psalms also indicate the existence of such rites. The psalm expresses the confirmation of the king as Yahweh's vicegerent and so was probably connected with the enthronement or renewal rites. There is evidence also of its integration in the annual liturgy asserting the Creator-kingship of Yahweh.

Psalm 20

In vv. 2–6 the psalmist addresses the king, expressing his people's blessing-wish for him. He anticipates a 'day of distress' (cf. 18.7, 19) and desires that Yahweh will answer the king's cry and send help from the holy place; may the king's offerings, plans and prayers be acceptable to Yahweh, so that the king and his people will experience salvation! In vv. 7–9 the psalmist, referring to the king in the third person, expresses confidence that the desired salvation will be given. Yahweh has granted salvation to his anointed and will respond to his cry from heaven with mighty acts. Those who trust in their own power will go under, but king and people will triumph by invocation of the name of Yahweh. Verse 10 seems to be a summing up, renewing the prayer ('Yahweh, save the king') and restating the confidence ('He will answer us on the day when we call'). The wording of v. 7 ('Now I know . . .') suggests that in some ritual, which the psalm accompanies, a sign of God's readiness to save has been given after v. 6. The psalmist will be a cultic minister with prophetic and priestly authority. (Gunkel thinks of a choir in vv. 2–6 and 10, with vv. 7–9 being contributed by an individual under oracular inspiration.)

Gunkel confidently describes the situation of the psalm as on a day of prayer before battle; sacrifices have been offered and the king's own prayers presented. Mowinckel (*GT*) agrees. Other commentators, however, have judged the psalm's character to be more appropriate for festal ceremonies. Duhm thought of a king's enthronement and H. Schmidt of an annual festival of Yahweh's kingship and royal anniversary. Weiser agrees essentially with Schmidt, finding the psalm too general and colourless, too calm and measured to originate in the hectic circumstances of real warfare. He thinks a more probable setting is a new-year feast, which combined the celebration of Yahweh's kingship with the enthronement of a new king. Our studies in chapter II suggest that a view like Schmidt's or Weiser's is the more probable. The mood and style of Psalm 20 are indeed in great contrast to the pieces I have connected with prayers before battle (p. 131). The latter are freer in form, passionate, urgent, and often reflect particular circumstances. It is significant that Gunkel himself describes Psalm 21 as parallel to this one, and Psalm 21 he understands as belonging to an annual celebration.

The psalm thus seems to add to the evidence that there were rites of inauguration or renewal of kingship with a highly dramatic character, in particular as portraying warfare. As Bentzen (*KM*, p. 25) observes, the psalm would suit the preparations for the ritual combat.

Psalm 21

In vv. 2–7 address is made to Yahweh, acknowledging the grace he has bestowed on the king. What God has done is spelt out at length, as though the words are designed to support and clarify an immediately preceding ceremony. Thus the king is portrayed resplendent in the divine salvation; his prayers have been granted; God has brought him all blessings, placed on his head a golden crown and granted his prayer for everlasting life. This section is rounded off by v. 8, where God is named in the third person.

Verses 9–13 are best understood as an address to the king (Gunkel; Kraus; Mowinckel, *GT*), not to God (Weiser; Johnson, *SKAI*). In the style of prophetic blessing, the speaker declares how the king will vanquish all his foes. Verse 14 rounds off the whole, invoking Yahweh, whose power alone gives victory.

The psalm is obviously connected with enthronement or related rites, as is generally agreed. Gunkel thinks of a celebration of the king's birthday or the anniversary of his enthronement. Mowinckel thought first of prayers before battle (*GT*; *PIW* I, p. 70) but in the end declared for 'festivities at the annual celebration of the day of anointing and enthronement' (*PIW* I, p. 224). Weiser sees the psalm as part of the coronation ritual, while Johnson places it at the end of his annual drama. On Johnson's view (*SKAI*, p. 133), the ritual 'earnest' of salvation is completed and the promises of victory look out into the real future. However, the psalm's retrospect makes no explicit mention of the king's terrible ordeal, so Bentzen (*KM*, p. 25) may be right in supposing that this is still to come; the question is like that raised by Psalm 2 (p. 112), though in this case Johnson's view seems the more probable of the two. The experience of Yahweh's majesty, salvation, advent with blessings, gift of eternal life etc. (vv. 2–7) would seem to belong to the culmination of the rites.

The psalm certainly indicates that the rites of royal inauguration or renewal were richly sacramental. For his part, the king must pray for life and show his trust, while God imparts to him glory, salvation, blessings and life; he is made secure against plotters and capable of routing his enemies in the field. The concluding reference to Yahweh's majestic exaltation suggests that the rites are associated with the celebration of his kingship, especially when comparison is made with Psalms 2 and 110.

Psalm 45

Some connect this with northern kings, such as Ahab or Jeroboam II. But there is no adequate reason to separate it from the other royal psalms. The allusions to ivory and to Tyre are as appropriate to the Solomonic kingdom as to Samaria. A recent study by Mulder rightly links the psalm with the Davidic house. Mulder's suggestion of Josiah, however, has no firm support; his evidence for such a late date is drawn especially from the Akkadian royal tradition, where the fortuitously extant examples cannot establish dates for the origin of the phraseology.

That the psalm was situated in a royal marriage is clear enough. The singer begins by calling attention to the force of his inspiration. The bulk of his address is to the king, praising him as exalted above all other men through the grace bestowed on him by God; he is beautiful, eloquent, a majestic and triumphant warrior, occupying an eternal throne as representative of God's kingship (v. 7, p. 143). Having found him righteous, God has anointed him to distinction above his fellows (v. 8). As Gunkel notes, the allusion here is first to the anointing of enthronement, while in v. 9 it relates to the wedding festivities. Comparison with Canticles 3.6; 4.14; Proverbs 7.17 indicates that the perfumes are seen as a preparation for the marriage bed; no doubt the music also helps to this end (v. 9b). In v. 10 the address to the king at last mentions the queen. While the king has other wives, who include daughters of kings, the new consort takes the chief place at his right hand, resplendent in gold.

The speech is now addressed to her (v. 11), with a striking change of tone. She is admonished to forget her own people and family and yield herself wholly to the king's desire. Verses 13–15 are unfortunately difficult. Mention of a bridal procession continues into v. 16. In v. 17 the address is again to the king, promising him sons comparable to his ancestors, sons who will assist his rule over all the earth. The praise of the king sustains its hymnic style to the end; the singer would celebrate his name for ever, prompting the peoples to praise him to all eternity.

Widengren (*SK*, p. 78) thinks the psalm shows that the king's wedding had a fixed place in cultic ritual and from other OT books he gathers the evidence that in some periods Israelite theology and ritual were much influenced by Canaanite fertility religion; in such periods, he argues, Yahweh had a consort (Anat, Astarte, the Queen of Heaven etc.) and their union would be represented by the sacred marriage of the king and queen at the feast of booths, legitimizing sacred prostitution and promoting fertility. That there were such periods is clear enough from the prophets and the histories. But Psalm 45 is not of this character and does not reflect the theology of fertility cults. What is possible, however, is that the influence of the ancient sacred marriage rites has caused the Davidic king's wedding to be associated with the rites of enthronement or its renewal. This would explain why there seems to be reference to his anointing both as king and as lover, as noted above. The theological point of the association was that among the blessings conferred on the faithful king was the begetting of sons to extend the divinely chosen dynasty. Further than this the text does not take us, even though the prayer for healthy growth and fruitfulness was present in some form in the festival and even in other royal psalms (72; 132 and 144).[35]

Mowinckel's suggestion (*PIW* II, p. 214) that the 'lilies' of the

title belonged to an omen-rite concerning the fruition of the royal
union is plausible.

Psalm 72

The speaker first prays God to impart his righteousness to the
king (v. 1). In the remainder there seems to be oscillation of mood
between *prayer* that the king may then rule successfully and
declaration that he will then do so. Even so, the extensive and brilliant portrayal of royal prosperity in vv. 2–17 seems in effect to
have much in common with the conferment of blessings on the
king in Psalms 21 and 45. Mowinckel rightly notes that the peti-
tion becomes a description of future blessings. As a result

> The psalm becomes a formula of blessing which reminds one
> strongly of the promises of the prophets as it oscillates between
> blessing and prediction. The officiating priest, who recites the psalm,
> to begin with speaks on behalf of the congregation and in the form
> of a petition. But he is also the representative of Yahweh and pro-
> nounces strong and effective words with a ring of certainty (*PIW* I,
> p. 69).

The king, enabled by God, is to rule with compassion, bringing
prosperity to society and nature and enjoying lasting, world-wide
dominion.

Such a broad prospect of ideal rule would best belong to the
rites of enthronement. With this ceremony probably set in the
autumnal festival (p. 112), the psalm's themes of an ideal kingdom
and fertility would be all the more appropriate. The designation of
the king as 'son of the king' (v. 1) seems to fit the inauguration of
a new king, who was but recently a prince. But an extension of
usage to annual rites of renewal cannot be ruled out, especially as
'son of the king' might idiomatically denote a 'member of the
dynasty'.

Peace reigns also among the commentators. Mowinckel (*GT*)
thinks of the king's inauguration, anointing and enthronement;
Johnson (*SKAI*, p. 9) says the psalm bears every appearance of
having been composed for use on the king's accession to the
throne. Gunkel suggests either this occasion, or more particularly its festal anniversary (and cf. *Einl.*, p. 145). Kraus thinks either
of these possibilities lies near to hand, while Schmidt favours the
latter.

Psalm 89

Gunkel's understanding of this psalm has been outlined on p. 57.
He supposes that a post-exilic head of David's family laments the
fallen dynasty, using an ancient hymn and oracle as introduction.
The artificiality of this view is especially apparent when the singer
emerges as himself the humiliated anointed (vv. 48–52). Moreover, as Weiser notes, there is no reference to the deportation of
king and people, a difficulty which Gunkel hardly evades by posit-
ing a fifth-century date.

More common today is the view that a reigning Davidic king
laments some humiliating defeat. But here we meet the difficulty
of identifying the occasion, which tradition has forgotten. While
Mowinckel (*GT*) can only speak vaguely of 'the late monarchy',
Kraus asks if it might be one of the successors of Josiah, subjected by Egypt. Schmidt treats vv. 20–52 as prayer at the anniversary of enthronement in some period of suffering. It is no wonder
that more precision is not attempted, since the situations in question have no real relation to the text. The arbitrary breaking up of
the psalm has recurred in some recent studies.[36]

As it stands, the psalm is presented by Yahweh's anointed himself,
who first appears in his characteristic role as Yahweh's chief witness
(cf. pp. 185f.) and with measured fullness testifies to Yahweh's
sovereign power and fidelity and to his irrevocable election of
David's dynasty. All this is designed to achieve the maximum
contrast with his subsequent lament (vv. 39–52), which will show
this praiser of God's fidelity as forsaken, and the guaranteed kingship as broken and rejected. In his lament, Yahweh's anointed and
servant complains that God has spurned his covenant and defiled
his royal headpiece in the dust; he has breached all his defences
and made him an object of scorn, given triumph to his foes, rendered him feeble in battle, deprived him of his glory and hurled
his exalted throne down to the ground; he has terminated early
his days of vigorous life and enveloped him in shame. So the king
pleads for an end of Yahweh's hiddenness as Saviour, an end to
the blazing of his wrath. He points to the brevity of man's life and
pleads for the fulfilment of the Davidic covenant-promises. Let
Yahweh take heed and act for his anointed, the shepherd of all
peoples, now pursued by mocking foes.

Even allowing for pathetic exaggeration, it is difficult to imagine
a king in such a desperate situation presenting his prayer in such

an extended and stately form as we find in this psalm. He depicts himself dethroned, hunted and virtually done to death, yet he can still begin with a splendid song of royal witness and a lengthy unfolding of the Davidic covenant. Even the lament has a measured, rounded quality, contrasting with the alarmed and hasty tone of other royal prayers in crises (p. 117). There is therefore reason to favour the interpretation of Johnson (*SKAI*, pp. 106f.), where the psalm expresses royal humiliation in the festal drama. In such a treatment the coherence of the psalm is particularly striking, since it represents so beautifully the autumn festival's themes of Yahweh's creator-kingship and the Davidic covenant.

Some weight is added to such a ritual interpretation by the comparisons made by Widengren (*SEÅ* 1945) and Ahlström (pp. 146f.), connecting the language of dethronement with Tammuz traditions, though of course such an argument cannot be conclusive in itself. A further argument is that the consideration of human frailty is thrown into the king's plea in 89.48f. just as it is in 144.4, the latter being very probably from rites of the king's humiliation (p. 128); also, both psalms make subtle and calm use of the motif of royal witness. Finally, it is noteworthy how Psalm 89 complains by citing the full scope of the dynastic promises, including that of world dominion. Elsewhere the laments about what should have been do not go so far. It might well be a context of idealizing ritual which has induced this absolute treatment in Psalm 89 (cf. p. 160).

In short, the character of the psalm would be best explained if it belonged to rites broadly of the kind proposed by Johnson. We should, however, look to other psalms to secure the foundation of the theory of such rites.

Psalm 101

The lack of any designation of the king here has not impeded a general recognition that the psalm is a king's utterance. In the main part (vv. 2b–8) he pleads his adherence to royal duty, though it is not certain whether he is making a vow for the future (Schmidt; Mowinckel, *GT*) or a claim about his rule hitherto (Johnson, *SKAI*, p. 115). The vow would suit the inauguration of his reign, while the claim can be well imagined in rites renewing his office. The tenses are not decisive, but would favour a vow; a claim could be compared with the Babylonian king's annual protestation (p. 92). Certainly the psalm's methodical exposition of royal duty points to a basic royal ceremonial, enthronement or its renewal, as is widely agreed.

The psalm is mostly in the 3:2 rhythm favoured for dirges, a feature which tallies with the pathetic question linking the introduction to the main part: 'O when wilt thou come unto me?' (KJ). The obvious conclusion is that the king is making his plea of righteousness in a situation of ritual ordeal and humiliation, as indeed is also the Babylonian king. This has been clearly recognized by Johnson (*SKAI*, pp. 114f.) and supported further by Kaiser (*ZAW* 1962). That Gunkel, Schmidt, Weiser and Kraus find it necessary to obliterate the plaintive question in v. 2b by conjectural emendation indicates a deficiency in their general approach to these psalms.

The exact meaning of the first three clauses is debatable. We could understand the king here to announce his theme – the loyalty and justice required of kings; as Johnson has it:

> Of devotion and justice will I sing;
> Unto thee, O Yahweh, I will raise a psalm.
> I will make my theme 'A Faultless Way'.

Here *hiśkil* is taken as 'to sing a *maśkil*-psalm', which has been explained as an efficacious song (Mowinckel, *PIW* II, p. 209); we could as well render: 'I will sing movingly of the perfect way.'

Alternatively, we could understand the first two clauses with Kaiser as an undertaking to praise Yahweh and his fidelity (cf. 89.2); the king would in effect be saying, 'I am ready, in accordance with my calling as thy witness, to praise thy faithful salvation when it comes to me.' Verse 2a might then anticipate the main section: 'I will rule wisely in a perfect way'; *hiśkil* is often connected with the action of a charismatic leader (p. 45 and p. 204, n. 24).

Mowinckel (*PIW* I, pp. 67f.) takes the beginning as actual homage to Yahweh's goodness, with a shift at v. 2:

> I will sing of goodwill and righteousness
> and play unto thee, O Yahweh.
> May I get insight in the perfect way –
> when wilt thou come to me?

Having overcome doubts similar to Gunkel's about the text (*GT*), he now remarks: 'In this introduction the tone of the hymn and of the psalm of prayer harmonize perfectly.'

In spite of this rather ambiguous introduction, it remains that the psalm offers important evidence for the scene of humiliation in the enthronement sequence or related rites.

Psalm 110

Gunkel's treatment refuted the objections to linking this with the Davidic kings. He sets out the evidence for the priesthood of David's dynasty and recognizes the continuity of tradition from the Jebusite kings. De Savignac sees a relation to the Egyptian king, who in the pattern of the sun-god 'rises' at dawn to begin his reign, emerging from the waters on to the holy hill.

The psalm consists of oracles and related declarations of blessing conveyed to the king by a leading priest or prophet. Items from the king's initiation are well reflected. Thus in v. 1 there is allusion to the enthronement proper. In v. 2 the sceptre is mentioned; it seems to be held out in a gesture denoting world-dominion (cf. de Savignac, p. 115). In v. 3 the king seems to be portrayed as glistening with the 'dew' of a ritual rebirth (see p. 147) and we might think here of his anointing or his emergence from a baptism at Gihon, Jerusalem's spring which featured in the inaugural rites (I Kings 1.33). The bestowal of priesthood, v. 4, might have included ceremonies of robing. In vv. 5f. Yahweh's smashing of the enemies may correspond to some ritual demonstration. If v. 7 relates to the king now in the third person, it could refer to his drawing strength from a ritual drink of the 'water of life' (cf. p. 96; Kraus).

It may seem that the text belonged to the concluding phase of the enthronement ceremonies, when the main themes of the kingship had already been established and the prophetic words set the seal upon the glorious status that Yahweh had granted his king. On this view the defeat of the enemies has already been accomplished in symbol (vv. 5–7); in so far as they remain to be dealt with (cf. vv. 1f.), this is a prospect in the real world. Johnson (*SKAI*, pp. 130f.) sees the psalm somewhat in this way, placing it at the end of his annual drama. On the other hand, Bentzen (*DSK*, p. 24) believes that the ceremonies reflected in the psalm all serve as a preparation for the ritual combat; the peculiarity of v. 7 arises from its being the culmination of the psalm, focusing attention on the communion-drink which gives the king strength for his imminent ordeal. In discussing the similar difficulty of placing Psalm 2 (p. 112), we noted that acts of anointing, enthronement, legitimation and empowering could well have preceded an ordeal of combat, so Bentzen's view of Psalm 110 is not impossible. However, this psalm is not so clearly dominated by the feeling of imminent confrontation as is Psalm 2, so Johnson's placing may have the advantage.

Whether the psalm was used in annual royal rites in the festival, as Schmidt and Johnson believe, cannot be proved from the text itself. However, as in the case of Psalm 2, we note a striking unity in the presentation of God's sovereignty and that of his king. God too is enthroned (v. 1), holds the sceptre (v. 2), is the king's father (v. 3) and strikes the hostile kings. This again indicates that it would be appropriate for the royal rites to be tied to the autumnal festival.

Psalm 132

Most commentators, with good reason, connect this with a festal procession which re-enacted David's epoch-making work of making Jerusalem the residence of the ark and the Presence of Yahweh (cf. II Sam. 5.6–12; 6). Verses 1–10, in general, address prayer to Yahweh for the reigning heir of David (note v. 10) and for priests and people (v. 9), on the strength of David's ascetic piety with regard to the ark and Jerusalem. Verses 11–18 respond with re-affirmation of Yahweh's promises to David, Jerusalem, priests and people.

The details of the first part, however, are not so clear. It is of little moment whether we change 'his affliction' (v. 1) to 'his humility' ('*anwātō*') as Johnson prefers (*SKAI*, p. 20), since the implication is spelt out in what follows: David vowed not to sleep until he had secured a place for Yahweh's sanctuary. But in vv. 5–7 we meet several problems. In v. 5 it seems that David was seeking a sanctuary for Yahweh, such as he in fact found at Jerusalem, whereas in v. 6 what is 'heard of' and 'found' is indeterminate, but is most probably the ark, which is named in v. 8.[37] The fields of Jaar, in view of the context, can with great probability be linked with Kiriath Jearim (I Sam. 7.2). Delitzsch has made a case for regarding Ephratha here as yet another name for this area, but we can more safely understand it, as in Ruth 4.11 and in

Micah 5.1, of Bethlehem, David's home. Thus in this verse we would hear a voice or choir, representing David's men, declare that they heard news of the ark while they were in Bethlehem, then took possession of it in Kiriath Jearim. The implication is that not only did David need to secure a site; he also had to seek out the ark, and this, as now announced in the re-enactment, has been accomplished. The text has not spelt out the full story, because in the context of the sacred drama the matter was sufficiently clear. This reconstruction might be supported by the studies of Bentzen (*JBL* 1948) and Porter (*JTS* 1954), which claim affinity of the story of the ark in I Samuel 4–7, II Samuel 6 with foreign cult-myths of finding and reinstating a god's image.

In v. 7 the call for obeisance before the ark, Yahweh's footstool, seems best interpreted as a call to proceed first to the sanctuary of Zion (*miškᵉnōtāw*), where the ark will be brought to rest and obeisance made.[38] This call is then accompanied by v. 8, the prayer for Yahweh to arise as the ark is lifted for the procession.[39] Verses 9f. are governed by a certain apprehension at the dangerous task of conveying the ark: may the priestly bearers, the accompanying people and the anointed himself be acceptable to Yahweh and no omen of wrath be given (cf. II Sam. 6.7). Indeed this apprehension may provide the momentum for the whole psalm. Re-enacting the original story by procession of the ark from outlying stations, the worshippers are careful to seek the favourable co-operation of Yahweh on the strength of his original acceptance of David. In vv. 11–18 Yahweh happily reaffirms his enduring covenant with David, his continuing pleasure to reside in Zion and his will to bless people, priests and king.

Such a re-enactment belongs to the fundamentals of Jerusalem's worship in the time of the kings. It is as though the whole basis of the sanctuary were being renewed, and with it all the hopes of the people for life and blessing. The essence of the sanctuary is the Presence of Yahweh, and Yahweh's will in this respect is closely bound up with his relation to David, resulting in his eternal (but not unconditional) covenant-promise. Accordingly, the psalm can with confidence be placed in the chief annual festival, though it is not so easy to explain its relation to other moments of the feast. Like the processional Psalms 24 and 68, it may imply that Yahweh enters fresh from defeating his foes, since the stories of the ark in I and II Samuel include the triumph over the Philistines and their god. Martial triumph is promised to the dynasty in vv. 17f., while the theme of agricultural abundance appears in v. 15.

The psalm joins Psalms 2 and 110 in indicating a close connection between the autumnal festival and the themes of the king's vocation, and further in showing the dramatic character of the celebrations. Here is a good example of how the ceremonies actualized ancient salvation and sought its effects for the future.

Psalm 144

The king opens with witness to God's fatherly bond with him (vv. 1f.), and thereby he prepares the ground for his appeal. In vv. 3f. he adds the consideration that mankind, whom he represents, is so feeble. Now he is ready to launch his prayer: 'Yahweh bow thy heavens and come down . . .' (vv. 5–8). He asks for God's intervention in a scene like that on which Psalm 18 looks back in testimony. Yahweh is to descend in might of storm and earthquake to pluck him from the grip of the forces of death and evil. In vv. 9f. he supports his prayer by promising to sing the 'new song' (cf. p. 43) of royal witness, telling of Yahweh's salvation of his king. Then he stresses his prayer by repeating its essential clauses (v. 11). Verses 12f. indicate the consequences which should follow the king's deliverance, healthy growth in population, crops, flocks and herds, no cry of distress in the streets. The dependence of such benefits on a kingship approved and established by God is a common feature of ancient Near Eastern thought and is expressed also in Psalm 72 (cf. also Ps. 4, p. 30). The psalm's coherence of thought is all the clearer if vv. 1–10 relate not to a particular military crisis but to the symbolic enemies of the festal rites, the comprehensive dangers that threaten the life of king and society. Verse 12 may be translated without difficulty as 'so that our sons shall be like . . .', a well-established usage of *'ašer* (cf. BDB, p. 83 8b); it is hardly necessary to pronounce *'aššēr*, 'Bless our sons . . .', with Kraus. The details of the hoped-for blessings are spelt out vividly, perhaps in the tradition of 'creative words', and the 'we-style' could indicate that a prophetic choir here takes up the chant. The section is rounded off with the beatitude of v. 15, affirming the good destiny of Yahweh's people; a similar formula concludes royal Psalm 2. Aramaic influence in the psalm's vocabulary is not now thought to require a post-exilic explanation.[40]

The psalm is of great significance for the present enquiry and it is remarkable that it has been so little used by the leading students of royal psalmody. Gunkel gave no consideration to it as a whole, severing vv. 12–15 from the preceding verses which he related to a military crisis. Mowinckel's approach was similar. Johnson does not mention the psalm in *SKAI*.

Schmidt and Weiser, however, consider the whole psalm as from the liturgy of the royal rites, without pressing far into the implications. Kraus likewise declares himself open to this view; on v. 7 he perceives that it may be a question, not of specific dangers, but of the motif of chaos-enemies, as in Psalm 2, from the tradition of the royal festival. But he still thinks the setting *may* be a particular military crisis and takes the matter no further.

The importance of the text should emerge clearly once it is considered as a whole. Since the result of God's epiphany to save his king is pictured chiefly as health and abundance in the natural order, the epiphany in question is similar to that described by Mowinckel in his reconstruction of the autumnal new-year festival. The forces of death there routed by God must afflict not only 'Zion', as Mowinckel generally supposes, but also the king, as Johnson maintains, and as indeed is only to be expected. But, as we have seen (p. 110), Johnson sees the king's humiliation and restoration as an eschatological challenge, the Israelites having here moved beyond the nature-religions' rituals of annual revival. But this lucid psalm, which he leaves aside, shows that the older meanings were not wholly lost. The representation of God's intervention for his king and people could still be seen as a sacrament of health for all aspects of life in the new year, even though this was but part of the meaning.

The similarity to Psalm 18 is particularly valuable.[41] If Psalm 144 shows the king praying before his ritual deliverance, it is all the more likely that Psalm 18 is the thanksgiving which follows that deliverance. Psalm 144 also shows how comprehensively we need to see the king's enemies in similar psalms. In Psalm 18 the death-powers of vv. 5f., although later presented in military character, may thus include threats in the 'biological' order (cf. p. 116 on 'Yahweh lives'). No doubt the theme of the king's contribution to this biological order is greatly subdued in Israel, but it is not eliminated, as Psalm 72 shows.

In brief, then, the psalm points to a drama of humiliation and restoration in the royal rites, connected with the autumnal festival, and indeed part of its annual repetition.

4. The setting of the king's psalms

(a) The setting of Gunkel's 'royal psalms'

We can now bring together what has just been said regarding the original function of Gunkel's 'royal psalms'.

A setting in the inaugural or renewed enthronement of the Davidic kings is virtually certain for Psalms 2; 21; 72; 101; 110. Already in this group there are strong indications that the accompanying ritual had a dramatic and imaginative character, including scenes of the king in confrontation with his enemies and fallen into pathetic need; further, that this ritual was part of the celebration of God's kingship in the autumn festival. To these psalms can be added with probability Psalm 20, illustrating further the scenes of martial challenge. Psalm 132 does not link so directly with the enthronement, but can still be placed with great probability in the autumn festival, where it shows both the integration of the Davidic office within the main themes of this festival and also the use of drama for this purpose.

From this basis, which involves little that is controversial, we can advance some way in accordance with the preceding interpretations. Psalm 144, taken directly as a unity, is further evidence of a drama in the autumn festival; the king's ordeal and restoration mean a renewal of his office and so of God's blessings of health for society given in connection with that office. Consequently, the related Psalm 18 should be explained in the same setting, which in fact it fits well. The rite of the king's ordeal before his enemies now appears vividly as depicting his near-expiry in the jaws of Sheol and his rescue by Yahweh, who brings him up from the waters and scatters all his foes; and the rite is emphatically expounded as demonstrating Yahweh's faithfulness to the faithful. At this point in the argument it is fair to add Psalm 89. Granted the ritual context so far established, this great psalm is best explained as a lament of the king in his scene of humiliation before his enemies.

Psalm 45 has been found to stand rather apart as a royal marriage-blessing, but even so there appeared some reason to think of the wedding as attached to the king's rites in the autumn festival, the emphasis falling upon the king's grace and glory and the extension of his dynasty.

Thus the conventionally accepted 'royal psalms' can all be connected with the great rites of the Davidic kingship. Leaving aside Psalm 45, they combine to show how a king was installed as mediator of Yahweh's kingship and established by sacramental scenes of promise, suffering and exaltation. The integration of the king's office into the festal theology is shown very clearly in these texts, and this combines with other evidence (p. 112) to make it probable that the royal rites belonged to the autumn festival. A king's immediate accession on his predecessor's death would thus be confirmed in his first autumn festival with the ceremonies reflected in these psalms, and thereafter it would be renewed annually in some similar fashion.

(b) The setting of the other royal psalms

It will now be helpful to co-ordinate the studies of chapter II, having regard to the function and setting of the additional psalms there claimed as royal.

A distinction may be attempted between those psalms which seem to have been created purely for regular rituals, and those which, whether rendered in festivals or not, were designed to seek help or give thanks for some historical event. The former are the minority: 51 (and perhaps 102), which may belong to the annual day of atonement; 91 and 121, which convey God's assurances to his king; 75, where the king warns of judgment; 22, which shows him in rites of suffering succeeded by restoration, and 23, his subsequent testimony; 118, where he looks back on the rites of chastisement and deliverance as he proceeds into the temple. These could well be from the major ritual sequences of the autumn festival. To them might be added 36, where the king prays for the destruction of the wicked, and 92, where he testifies to the triumph of God in which he participates.

Psalms occasioned by some particular event are most clearly 41 (the king sick and insecure) and 71 (the king old and insecure); then many that reflect warfare: 7; 11; 17; 27; 31; 35; 40; 42–3; 44; 54; 55; 56; 59; 60; 62; 63; 66; 69; 70; 108; 109; 140; 141; in several others the military aspect is not brought out but can reasonably be assumed: 5; 16; 28; 142; 143; in several the enemy seems to exert a lasting domination: 9–10; 73; 77; 80; 94; in Psalm 4 the crisis seems to include a dearth.

There are a few others which should probably be included in the preceding paragraph, but which, on account of their more schematic character, could otherwise be added to the ritual group, though this seems less likely. In some, warfare is prominent: 3; 57; 120; in some, just 'enemies': 52; 86; 139; and still vaguer, 61; 116; 138.

The distinction of the historical from the ritual psalms is, of course, somewhat tentative, and it is all the harder to establish since the psalms evoked by a crisis still present the matter largely in ritual stereotypes and quite easily passed into regular usage. Nevertheless, in most cases a certain jaggedness or abruptness and sudden glimpses of affairs point to a real crisis, which most commonly involves the king in war. In such wars or oppressions he often faces external peoples, as seems probable in Psalms 7; 9–10; 11; 16; 17; 31; 35; 42–3; 44; 54; 56; 59; 60; 69; 73; 77; 94; 108; 141. In some cases insurrection may be involved: 4; 5; 41; 62; 71; 141.

It is interesting to note that incubation may have been the occasion for a number of psalms, where the king seeks help through encounter with God: most clearly 17 and 63, but also perhaps 3; 4; 16; 57; 139. The seeking of oracular guidance or an augury may be detected in 5; 27; 143.

(c) Conclusions for the royal rites

Comparing the conclusions of the last two sections, we note that while almost all Gunkel's 'royal psalms' concern events on the ritual plane (especially enthronement), the majority of our additional royal psalms originated as responses to particular crises (especially war). This broad difference in origin goes a long way to explain why many scholars set the latter group apart from their class of 'royal psalms', the characteristics of which were defined in terms of the former group.

We have seen, however, that a few of our additional royal psalms can best be identified as essentially ritual texts, which then make a direct contribution to the clarification of rites discerned in Gunkel's 'royal psalms'. Of great importance in this respect is Psalm 118, which depicts a procession so appropriate to the ritual situation deduced from Psalm 18, as Johnson recognized. The ordeal is over, the king having survived sore chastisement and overcome 'all nations' by invocation of the name of Yahweh; now he proceeds (from Gihon?) amid acclamation into the temple; he has passed from rejection to supremacy, and all the people rejoice in the light and life which God's great work has thus created among them in this festival, surely that of autumn.

Another major contribution comes from Psalm 22 (with 23). Here we have the ultimate in humiliation, the cry from the dust and dissolution of death, followed by a great scene of restoration, where the emphasis is on the enhancement of God's kingship and the access of life in the farthest regions. This text thus belongs to the very centre of a sacrament of death and life, covering the moment of transition. Whether it belonged to precisely the same sequence as those already discussed in this chapter is difficult to say; it does not share the obvious affinities, say, of 144; 18 and 118. No doubt the rites varied in different periods and items of diverse origin accumulated. Still, Psalm 22 certainly supports our conclusion from Gunkel's 'royal psalms' that the celebration of God's choice of his king was elaborated with a sequence of affliction and restoration, heavy with significance for all the world.

The complexity of festivals must further be borne in mind with regard to Psalm 51. There is no obvious connection of this great confession of sin with the psalms of ritual combat and enthronement, but it would be appropriate as the king's representative confession in some early form of the Day of Atonement among the holy days of the autumnal new year. In Psalm 102, representative lamentation goes with several features indicating this season. Several other psalms could have fitted quite easily into the dramatic enthronement rituals: 91 and 121 with their rich promises of protection, 75 with its warning to the enemies, and perhaps 36 with their doom and 92 with its celebration of the victory of the divine kingdom. In several respects such psalms supplement the major contributions of Psalms 22 and 118 to the ritual interpretation of Gunkel's 'royal psalms'. We may instance the death and life themes of Psalm 23 (p. 38), the king as executive of the divine judgment in Psalm 75, the linking of God's victory with the king's anointing, triumph and vitality in Psalm 92.

But important contributions of this kind are also made by the mass of the king's psalms responding to historical crises, since these texts often reflect items from the regular festal rituals. The most notable case is Psalm 40 (p. 42). Here a series of rites is reflected, remarkably similar to those deduced from Gunkel's 'royal psalms'; the king's humiliation in the waters of Sheol, his deliverance, his exaltation on Zion's rock, his 'new song' of festal witness and proclamations of God's victory, his receipt of the scroll of divine sonship, his hearing of an oracle, his procession of self-offering.

Of comparable importance is Psalms 9–10, which again seems deliberately to point to the autumn liturgy. Here we especially note that this liturgical foil for the psalm's lament comprises both the victory of God the King over the nations and the exaltation of the Davidic king from 'the gates of death'. Psalm 71 is also rich in such allusions: the king's exaltation from Sheol and endowment with greatness, his festal testimony and proclamations, his position before the congregation as exemplar of God's grace. Psalm 61 also implies his exaltation from Sheol to Zion's rock. His deliverance from the bands of Sheol is also well reflected in Psalm 116, while the horror of Sheol's waters appears in Psalm 69. Frequently there is reflection of the cultic deliverance through Yahweh's world-shaking epiphany, as in 7; 9–10; 57; 94. In Psalm 3 the reflected scheme includes encompassing by beast-like foes, the cry to Yahweh, the answer from the holy hill and the exaltation. Less obvious are allusions to the procession signifying the king's salvation (5.9; 23.3; 43.3–4; 143.10).

We can now draw together our conclusions with regard to the basic problem of the royal rites described on pp. 109–11. From two directions our argument has found Johnson's position in the main more satisfactory than that of Mowinckel. Firstly a survey of Gunkel's 'royal psalms' pointed to this conclusion (p. 130), and secondly we have found that the extra psalms of the king add valuable corroboration. With reasonable clarity we see that the dramatic celebration of Yahweh's kingship in the autumn festival entailed also a dramatic presentation of the Davidic office. In symbol the king was beset by enemies from all quarters and brought to the realm of death; his humble fidelity was thus proved and Yahweh answered his prayer, exalting him above all dangers and foes. While the order of the ceremonies and texts remains uncertain, the chief elements of the royal suffering and exaltation are strongly attested, as is also the close relation to the assertion of Yahweh's own kingship.

Our studies, however, would not support an entirely eschatological interpretation of this ritual. The king prays in Psalms 40; 9–10; 3 etc. as though he himself had personally experienced the rites as a sacrament, a replenishment of grace, not just as a prophetic parable. The rites have relevance for the future and certainly tend to the ideal (p. 160); they are full of promise and challenge. But the aspects of the royal legitimation and empowering and of social renewal are well maintained. As Psalm 144 in particular shows, the royal humiliation is more than a lesson; it is a means of grace for the contemporary society. Through the royal righteousness there demonstrated, Yahweh is ready to send health into all parts of society. Not that the mere performance of the rites was thought to guarantee the blessings, any more than it was in Babylon (p. 94). But those who undertook God's ceremonies with faithful hearts would receive the gifts of his faithfulness.

The intersection of the ideal and the circumstantial in the royal rites may be compared with a certain duality in foreign kingship. According to Goedicke (above, p. 26), the office of king in Egypt expresses the divine will and has a transcendent quality; but the particular ruler, bearing office for his allotted time, retains the limitations of his humanity. Labat (pp. 361f.) finds duality also in the Assyro-Babylonian monarchy; sometimes the king is illumined by a quasi-divine glory, sometimes he is deeply humiliated; the kingship is in effect, he says, the expression of a divine power which the gods have temporarily entrusted to a predestined mortal.

IV

THE IDEAL OF THE KING'S OFFICE IN THE PSALMS

1. *Davidic rule lies within God's kingdom*

As we now examine the royal ideal on the basis of the preceding chapters, we begin with a feature of all-pervading importance. The Davidic king is considered to serve within the sphere of God's own kingship. God remains the active king of all, not least of the community centred at Jerusalem; Davidic rule is his instrument.

This view of a single kingdom, which is God's, dominates the psalms relating to the king's ordination, 2 and 110. The imagined rebellion is against a dominion exercised jointly by 'Yahweh and his anointed' (2.2). The king is to take the throne beside Yahweh, who will crush opposition to this joint sovereignty (110.1, 5; 2.12).

When king and people implore God's aid, stress is laid on the kingly responsibility of God himself. Prayer rises to him who is ruler of the universe (89.7–15; cf. 11.4f.) and in particular king of Israel:

> Yahweh himself is our shield,
> the Holy One of Israel is indeed our king[1] (89.19).

To God as eternal king (10.16), ruling all nations (9.9), enthroned in Zion (9.12), the Davidic king presents the case of the fatherless and oppressed (9.13; 10.18), the special care of kings.[2] Again, in Psalm 94, where Yahweh is described as Creator of man (vv. 9f.) and ruler of the earth (v. 2), his kingly responsibility is appealed to most sharply in this description of conditions:

> Widow and sojourner they slay,
> and the fatherless they slaughter   (94.6).

With reference more particularly to his own plight, the king likewise appeals to the kingly power of God: may God rise up in majestic epiphany, assert his kingship over all the world, and thereby save the Davidic king (7.7f.; 18.7–20; 57.6; 59.6; 144.5f.).

The king also stresses the active reality of God's kingship when he prays to God as 'my king' (5.3; 44.5), or when he depicts himself in the care of God the royal Shepherd (23.1–4 and p. 171). The king's thanksgiving for his own deliverance is likewise bound up with the prospect of God's kingdom (22.29).

It is notable that the king usually speaks of the people not as his own, but as God's subjects. He prays Yahweh to act as their shepherd-king, pasturing and carrying the lambs:

> Save thy people and bless thine inheritance,
> and pasture them and carry them for ever   (28.9).

With such expressions the king puts all his trust in God's ownership of the people:

> On thy people be thy blessing   (3.9).

> Thy people, O Yahweh, they crush,
> and thine inheritance they afflict   (94.5).

The cases where he designates the people by reference to himself are rare and mostly dubious: 'those who delight in my righteousness' (35.27); 'my people' (59.12; 144.2?); 'every one that swears by him' (63.12). With many expressions, however, he designates them by relation to God: those 'seeking him' (22.27; 9.11), 'fearing him' (22.26), 'sheltering in him' (2.12; 5.12), 'fearing thy name' (61.6), 'loving thy name' (5.12), 'knowing thy name' (9.11), 'knowing thee' (36.11), 'in covenant with thee' (*ḥᵃsîdēkā* 52.11).

Such expressions on the king's lips show how lively was the sense of God's rule precisely in the time of the monarchy. The king was foremost in confessing:

> God is ruler from within Jacob
> to the ends of the earth   (59.14).

> Blessed are the people
> who have Yahweh as their God   (144.15).

2. *The enemies of God as personal enemies of the king*

By contrast with his usual designation of the loyal people as God's, the king frequently speaks of the enemies as 'mine'. Even so, it is evident that in general he faces such foes on behalf of God's kingdom.

Sometimes the enemies of the kingdom are designated absolutely: nations, peoples, kings, rulers, death, Belial, Sheol, the man of violence, speakers of falsehood, violent or false witnesses, the enemy, the son of perversity, the great waters (or 'their lordships the waters'),[3] the foreign ones, the wicked, the boasters, the workers of iniquity, the man of blood and deceit, the disrupter, the assembly of harmers, bulls, lions, serpents, Violence, Strife, Mischief, Trouble, Ruin, Oppression, Fraud (p. 74), the rebellious, the proud, the evil man. But it is very common for the enemies to be denoted with reference to the king: 'the enemies of the king' (45.6), 'my enemies', 'those hating me', 'those rising against me', 'his enemies', 'my adversaries', 'my pursuers', 'those surrounding me', 'those lying in wait for me', 'those that contend with me', 'those that seek my soul', 'those that plot my calamity', 'those that make great show against me', 'those that fight against me', 'he that pants after me (?)', 'those that exalt themselves against me', 'those that besiege my soul', 'those that oppose my soul', 'those that seek my calamity', 'those that rage against me', 'those that are sworn against me', 'adversaries of my soul'.[4]

The impression we gain is of the king as the unique representative of God and of God's people, and hence the target for all the evil forces which assault earthly society. In danger and suffering, the king is very conscious that the enemies, albeit against God, are especially bearing upon 'me', and the promises of God likewise anticipate this situation. (Most of the above expressions are participles; 'my enemies', for example, is rather 'those acting in enmity against me'.) The king's enemies and God's promises against them are presented most schematically in the psalms from the great rituals; the schematism persists in more broken forms in the prayers which rise from the many contingencies of the king's practical life.

Thus in the ordination psalms, 2 and 110, the simple theory of the king's role is dramatized. In Psalm 2 the king confronts the hostile peoples and rulers confident that the weight of God's power is entirely behind him. In 110.2 the absolute word given to him is 'Rule in the midst of your enemies!', and God himself slays the enemy kings and their hosts (vv. 5f.). Similar absolute assurances are conveyed in 18; 21.9f.; 45.4–6; 72.8–11, 15; 89.23–26; 132.18.

In the king's prayers from particular situations of need, he sometimes bases his appeal on this simple scheme, asking for the destruction of those who are 'my enemies' and who must therefore without more ado be deemed liable to God's wrath. Thus 143.12, with reference to the status God's covenant has bestowed on him:

> And in thy fidelity (*ḥesed*) destroy my enemies
> and cause to perish all the adversaries of my soul,
> for I am thy servant.

He may make a simple antithesis between those assailing him and those who adhere to Yahweh, as in 40.15f. More often, however, the pressure of the situation leads him to underline the wickedness of his enemies and the unprovoked character of their aggression (7.4f.; 35.12; 69.5). Sometimes he explicitly points out that they are God's enemies too:

> In the multitude of their sins thrust them out,
> for they have rebelled against thee (5.11).

> For aliens have risen against me,
> and terrible ones seek my soul,
> that do not set God before them (54.5).

> Wonderfully work deeds of fidelity,
> O saviour of the trustful
> from those that make insurrection against thee (17.7).

> The insults of those who insult thee
> have fallen upon me (69.10).

Even in the psalms glorifying the king, he is not often pictured as himself active in conquering his enemies, and when he is so depicted the point is that God empowers him. The most vivid example is 18.29–51, where the king appears as a marvellously skilled and potent warrior, fighting on foot with wonderful agility, a deadly archer, routing and pursuing his foes single-handed; clearly the passage testifies to God who has 'lit his lamp', dressed

him in might, guided his feet, trained his hands, shielded and upheld him (and similarly 144.1f.). It is also in a testimony to God
that the king in 118.10 describes how he cut down the nations
who swarmed about him like bees, – he achieved it by invocation
of the name of Yahweh. The essential part for the warring king is
to trust in Yahweh:

> It is better to trust in Yahweh
> than to trust in man.
> It is better to trust in Yahweh
> than to trust in princes   (118.8f.).

This thought is echoed in 20.8 by the people whose confidence is
that Yahweh will grant success to the king's stratagems. In 44.5–9
we glimpse the king using sword and bow, and, with his people,
pushing and trampling the enemies like a mighty bull; but the
point again is testimony to Yahweh, through whose name such
feats are achieved; the king must not trust in his own bow and
sword, but in Yahweh the true king above:

> Thou art my king, O my God,
> commanding[5] the salvations of Jacob.

Psalm 21, before depicting the conquering power of the king,
stresses its basis as trust:

> Truly the king is trusting in Yahweh,
> and in the fidelity of the Most High
> he will not be cast down   (21.8).

It is the divine blessing invoked by the subsequent words of the
sacred spokesman which endows the king with unerring aim and
a fiery, consuming presence (21.9–13). In Psalm 45 also, the portrayal of the king as riding in his chariot, girt with sword, shoot-
ing arrows straight into the hearts of his enemies, is a prophetic
blessing, unfolding the graces given by God's anointing (45.8).

There is a tendency to show the king as passive while God wins
him his victories:

> Sit at my right hand,
> while I make your enemies
> a footstool for your feet   (110.1).

> You shall but look on with your eyes
> and see the recompense of the wicked   (91.8).

In Psalm 2, it is with Yahweh's wrath that the king threatens the rebels (2.12). God himself, who makes the horn of his king to sprout and his light to shine, will envelop the enemies in defeat (132.17f.).

In keeping with this perspective, it is characteristic of the king's prayers of distress to call for Yahweh's action, while the king's own efforts fall from sight. His weapons are prayer and execration;[6] he invokes the name of Yahweh and his promises,[7] and sharpens his pleas by depicting his weakness (p. 180) and the evil of the enemies (p. 169). The situation of battle is sometimes clearly indicated (Pss. 3; 27; 35; 54; 55; 56; 57; 59 etc.) but hardly ever does the king envisage himself in action. The action is to come from Yahweh, the omnipotent warrior.

It is as the unique representative of God's kingship that the king is pictured solitary and assailed by so great a range of enemies. This lonely figure (35.17; 69.9) is assailed by all nations (118.10; 2). Enemies surround him in myriads (3; 69.5); multitudes plot against him (2; 31.14). Danger looms by day and night (3; 4; 91; 121). Enemies hunt him, as they do the anointed in Lamentations 4.20, with nets and traps.[8] They strike at him with lies and evil words.[9] The archetypal nature of the enemies appears especially when they assume a sinister character, using black arts,[10] assuming bestial shapes,[11] demonic,[12] the very forces of Belial, death and Sheol.[13] The basic enemies of the life of society, such as appear in national defeat or anarchy, in famine or plague, are depicted as concentrating their hate against the soul of God's king.

The aim of the king's foes is to strike at him in a moment when he may have incurred God's displeasure. They are ever watching, lurking and plotting, until they can say:

> God has forsaken him.
> Pursue and capture him,
> for there is none to deliver   (71.11).

> There is no salvation for him from God   (3.3).

And with mocking reference to the formula in the king's ordination (p. 146):

> He depended on Yahweh.
> Let him rescue him.
> Let him deliver him,
> for he delights in him   (22.9).

The Israelite king's view of his enemies can be compared with that of other sacred kings. The Assyrian king, for example, considered his enemies as enemies of his gods, guilty of impious rebellion; his wars were always undertaken with such a religious justification and were waged under oracular guidance and with observance of taboos; the king might send a report on the campaign to his god, as though to the commander-in-chief; victory redounded to the glory of his gods (Labat, pp. 253f.).

3. *The laws of the kingdom are God's*

Further acknowledgment in the royal psalms that the kingship is really God's is made in respect of the laws by which the society is to be governed. These psalms are clear that the laws must be from God, conveying his will and his justice. By God's laws and directions the king must govern himself, his household and his society. At the outset or renewal of a reign, prayer is accordingly made that the king may be a true mediator of divine law and justice for this people, which, it is stressed, is God's people:

> Give, O God, thy judgments to the king,
> and thy righteousness to the royal one.
> May he judge thy people with righteousness,
> and thy humble ones with justice   (72.1f.).

In Psalm 75 the line is drawn from God's oracle of judgment ('at the set time . . . I will judge with equity . . .') to the king's execution of God's justice ('All the horns of the wicked will I cut off . . .').

The king must keep Yahweh's stipulations (*'ēdōtay?*) which he is ever teaching him (132.12). He keeps 'the ways of Yahweh' (18.22). He should be able to say:

> All his commandments are before me
> and his statutes I never put aside   (18.23).

Such laws of Yahweh appear more concretely in Psalm 101; the king follows a 'perfect way' (*mišpāṭ* and *ḥesed?*, p. 123) as he orders his palace and government and sits in judgment; it is Yahweh's city which he purges, and it is obviously Yahweh's laws which he aspires to keep and enforce. His daily sitting in judgment in the early morning aligns his work with the sending out of divine light

and order through the sun (cf. II Sam. 23.4).[14] He must answer to
Yahweh for his zeal in putting down the wicked (101; 17.4;
p. 176).

In 89.31f. Yahweh enjoins his law on the dynasty with the
expressions *tōrātī, mišpāṭī* (or *mišpāṭay*), *ḥuqqōtay* and *miṣwōtay*.
Tōrā, which seems to depend on the king in Lamentations 2.9,[15]
occurs again in 40.9 when the king affirms his readiness to act
according to God's pleasure and law:

> To do thy pleasure, my God, I delight,
> and thy law is in my inner parts.

In the same spirit the king asks in times of perplexity that God will
show him his way and his pleasure:

> Cause me to know the way I should go . . .
> Teach me to do thy pleasure   (143.8, 10).

In similar passages the verb *hōrēnī* could imply guidance by revelation of a *tōrā*:

> Teach me (by *tōrā*) thy way
> and lead me in the path of equity   (27.11).

> Teach me (by *tōrā*) thy way, Yahweh.
> I would walk by thy truth . . .
> Make for me a sign for good   (86.11, 17).

It is the ways of Yahweh which the king undertakes to inculcate
in his subjects:

> I will teach thy ways to the rebellious   (51.15).

For king and people the pattern of law and life is the way or path
(*derek, 'ōraḥ*) decreed by Yahweh, the true authority; protesting
their innocence they can say:

> Our heart has not slid backwards
> nor our steps slipped from thy path   (44.19).

4. *The king is drawn into God's aura*

Other ways in which the Davidic kingship is presented as the
instrument of Yahweh's kingship include ideas about the king's
throne, glory and sanctity. We may translate 45.7 (in line with the
thought of I Chron. 29.23; 28.5):

> Your throne, the throne of God,[16]
> is for ever and ever.

In some way the king appears as occupant of Yahweh's throne on Zion, his deputed representative. The picture is clearer in 110.1, where the king is to sit at God's right hand, presumably sharing the throne with God in a manner known in Egypt (Gunkel; de Savignac). The king is thus within the orbit of the divine Presence and it is especially appropriate for him to be depicted as covered by God's shadow or wings:

> He who is enthroned in the covert of the Most High,
> In the shadow of the Almighty he nestles.
> With his plumage he covers you over,
> and beneath his wings you may shelter[17]   (91.1, 4).

Similarly the Assyrian king, Ashurnasirpal, says that at his enthronement the god spread his shadow over him and gave him his insignia (Labat, p. 91). Ashurbanipal says that Ishtar spread her enduring shadow over him (Labat, p. 62). A Hittite king declares 'The bird takes refuge in its nest and lives; I have taken refuge with the storm-god . . . my lord' (*ANET*, p. 398). Egyptian kings are also represented under the deity's wings or shadow (*ANEP*, nos. 377 and 389).

Psalm 61 pictures the king as enthroned eternally in the presence of God, flanked by the guardians Fidelity and Truth (v. 8, p. 153). The king says:

> I will reside in thy tent for ever;
> I will shelter in the covert of thy wings   (61.5).

His closeness to God is also expressed as being in the embrace of God's right hand:

> Truly thou art my succour
> and in the shadow of thy wings I rejoice.
> My soul cleaves to thee
> and thy right hand has grasped me   (63.8–10).

> Because of my integrity thou hast grasped me
> and stationed me in thy presence for ever   (41.13).

As the king journeys about his tasks, God maintains this close companionship, leading and guiding him, ever at his side.[18] We may compare the striking prayer of the Hittite king:

Walk on my right hand,
team up with me as a bull to draw (the wagon),
walk by my side in true storm-god fashion   (*ANET*, p. 398).

The Hittite king Tuthalija IV is accordingly depicted in the reliefs
of the sanctuary of Yazilikaya as walking closely with his god; the
king's head nestles in the shoulder of the god, whose arm passes
round the king's neck and upholds his hand by clasping his wrist
(Akurgal, pp. 106, 113).

In Israel such closeness suggests the simile of the reflection in
the eye, the tiny replica of one who stands near, and the king
prays:

> Keep me as the little one in the eye.[19]
> Hide me in the shadow of thy wings   (17.8).

In Psalm 2 the unity of the divine and the Davidic kingship may
be indicated more in the fashion of 'correspondence', – a conception where the earthly institution tends to be a replica of the
heavenly.[20] Yahweh is enthroned in the heavens (v. 4), while he
has installed his king on his holy mountain of Zion (v. 6). This is
expressed more fully in Psalm 89: as God was *'elyōn*, Most High,
above the heavenly beings, so he had made the king *'elyōn* above
earthly rulers (v. 28), his hand reposing with authority on the
water-powers as did the Creator's in heaven (v. 26). And as the
Creator had crushed the monsters of chaos, so Psalm 91 depicts
the king placing the victor's foot on lion, snake and dragon (v. 13).
The same psalm seems to apply to the king the notion of the divine
throne borne on the hands of celestial attendants (vv. 11f.). The
king's dawn judgments (101.8) correspond to the radiation of
divine order with the sunrise (p. 141).

Drawn into God's aura, the king is enveloped and penetrated
by God's holiness and glory. The king's glory is hence a holy
splendour derived from God, a manifestation of the same sovereignty. This is signified especially in the anointing of the king,[21]
where God himself is thought to inundate his chosen one with
holiness:

> With the oil of my holiness
> I have anointed him   (89.21).

> Therefore God your God has anointed you
> with oil of gladness above your fellows   (45.8).

The proper place for God's anointed must therefore be on the sacred mountain; God says:

> But I have installed my king
> on Zion, the mountain of my holiness   (2.6).

The divine aura conveys majesty, glory, power and salvation:

> Yahweh, in thy power ('*ōz*) the king is glad
> and in thy salvation how greatly he exults!   (21.2).

> Great is his glory in thy salvation;
> honour and majesty thou hast laid on him   (21.6).

While it conveys beauty (45.3), it may also appear as a blazing heat to consume enemies (21.10, text difficult).

Hidden and preserved in the covert of God's pavilion, the king is able to gaze upon the beauty of Yahweh (27.4f.); thereby he replenishes himself with glorious strength, rather as Moses came out from God's presence with a radiant face. In time of danger he turns to God athirst for such replenishment:

> So in the sanctuary I would gaze on thee
> to see (*or* drink in)[22] thy power and thy glory   (63.3).

The king's glory or lustre (*thr* 89.45) is not his own; it is a reflection or extension of God's own majesty, a sign of God's own kingship. The king seems to indicate this when he confesses in prayer:

> Thou art my glory and the exalter of my head   (3.4).

> From[23] God is my salvation and my glory.
> He is the Rock of my power.
> My shelter is in God   (62.8).

All the more poignant, therefore, are his laments that this glory is trodden down:

> And my glory (the enemy) makes dwell in the dust   (7.6).

> O men, how long shall my glory be reviled?   (4.3).

> Face towards me and show me grace.
> Give thy power to thy servant
> and salvation to the son of thy maid   (86.16).

The glory expressed by the king's insignia is also seen as from

God. God makes the king's headpiece shine (132.18) and is the power behind the glory-laden sceptre:

> The sceptre of your power
> Yahweh shall extend from Zion   (110.2; p. 124).

An acknowledgment of the king's divinely originated splendour may be seen in the prostrations made to him by his subjects (72.11), even his own queen (45.12).

The basis for the glorious condition given to the king is God's pleasure in him. He is God's chosen one (89.4). The divine favour has marked this man out for such elevation. The expression of this favour in I Kings 10.9, Isaiah 42.1 and Mark 1.11 points to the rites of ordination as the main setting for God's declaration to this effect.[24] The humiliation of the king in the enthronement ceremonies (chapter III) issued in a demonstration that God maintained his favour, having tested the king's humble faith:

> He delivered me
> because he delighted in me   (18.20).

Against the enemies' report that he has lost God's favour (3.3; 22.9 in irony), he claims that he retains it (4.4; 35.27; cf. II Sam. 15.26).

5. *The king as God's son*

The preceding sections have clearly shown how the psalms think of a single dominion, the kingship of God, within which the Davidic king is chosen to play a part. It is a very exalted part, leading him into the intimacy of God's presence. How is this part defined?

One definition is in terms of sonship. The king is proclaimed by God to be his son, and moreover one that has a unique relation to his father. He is the first-born (89.28), the one most entitled to represent the father's kingship. In Psalm 2 God's decree resembles an adoption formula (Cooke, p. 210); the sense in any case is strong: at his installation the king enters into the fullness of the role of God's son.

> He has said to me: You are my son,
> today I have begotten you   (2.7).

The psalm as a whole clearly involves the uniqueness of this sonship; he is the sole representative of God's kingdom over all nations.

In Psalm 110 it seems that the ordination rites are linked imaginatively with a godlike birth; the king, freshly anointed with holy unguent, is greeted as new-born and glistening with the vital graces of God:

> With you is royal grace
> on the day of your birth,
> a holy apparition from the womb of Dawn!
> On you is the dew of your fresh life.[25]

In Psalm 89 the sonship is a status to which 'David' is raised and which is bound up with the dynastic covenant:

> For his part he shall call to me,
> 'My father art thou,
> my God and the Rock of my salvation'.
> For my part I will make him the first-born son,
> The most high over the kings of the earth   (89.27f.).

Thereby God covenants to make the dynastic throne eternal as the days of heaven, though he will inflict fatherly blows on kings who forsake his laws (vv. 29–38). Psalm 118 may show that such chastisement of God's son was symbolized in the annual rites:

> Yah has chastised me severely,
> but to death he has not delivered me   (118.18).

Also from such passion rites (according to p. 132) comes the vivid treatment of the theme of sonship in 22.10f., where the king appeals to God as his birth-helper and adoptive father,[26] who drew him from his mother's womb, receiving him, then placing him at his mother's breasts:

> Yea, thou wast the one to draw me from the belly
> and confide me to the breasts of my mother.
> Upon thee was I cast out from the womb.
> From the belly of my mother thou art my God.

Very similar is 71.5:

> Truly thou art my hope, O my lord,
> my confidence from my childhood, O Yahweh.
> On thee was I supported on leaving the belly.
> Thou wast the one to sever me
> from the inner parts of my mother.

The king's formation before birth was God's special care (139.15f., cf. p. 84).

In 27.10 the king seems to imagine himself as a child abandoned by father and mother but gathered up and so adopted by Yahweh.[27] The thought may resemble Isaiah 49.15: Yahweh's love of his chosen one exceeds even that of human parents; should they – it is almost inconceivable – abandon their child, Yahweh gathers it in his arms (cf. Ezek. 16.4f.). We may compare the prayer of a Hittite king: 'I was but a mortal . . . my father begat me, but thou, storm-god . . . tookest me from my mother and rearedst me . . . thou madest me priest . . . king' (*ANET*, p. 398).

In Psalm 27.11 the king continues with a prayer to be taught God's way. Similarly Psalm 71, already quoted for its theme of sonship, contains the statement:

> O God, thou hast taught me from my childhood (71.17)

Several other references to God's teaching his king can be seen as aspects of fatherhood. God teaches him the arts of war, especially archery, where the training of 'hand', 'arms', and 'fingers' (18.35; 144.1) suggests the overlaid hands of the father.[28] Each successive heir of David is taught by God his requirements, *'ēdōt* (132.12). The king asks for such teaching:

> Teach me to do thy pleasure   (143.10).

> In the hidden place (?) cause me
> to know wisdom   (51.8; cf. Isa. 11.2).

Some form of parental sustenance may be referred to in 55.23, the king being told:

> Cast[29] . . . upon Yahweh!
> He himself will nourish you.

Perhaps also Yahweh has the parental role when he nurses a sick king, thoroughly remaking his bed:

> Yahweh tends him upon the couch of sickness.
> All his bed thou turnest over in his illness   (41.4).

Yahweh's parental role is also implicit in the passages already cited (p. 142), where the king nestles against Yahweh as a bird under its parent's feathers.

A fairly literal notion of the divine sonship is found commonly in Egyptian kingship and sometimes in Mesopotamian. But in the latter there exists also a vaguer metaphorical expression; it may be said rather that the gods have fashioned the ruler physically and spiritually in the womb and favoured his birth to fit him for his commission; his birth is a manifestation of the divine, accompanied by omens, for he comes from the hands of the gods; the gods may be said to have accepted the child by a kind of adoption; he grows up in the lap of the goddess and is nourished by her (Labat, pp. 53f.). In Ugarit it can be said of the king of the heroic age: 'Is Keret the son of El, the offspring of the Kindly One and the Holy?' and his eldest son is described as one 'who sucks the milk of Aṭirat, sucks the breast of the Virgin Anat' (Gray in *Ugaritica* 6).

6. *The king as God's servant*

Another designation of the king's role is as Yahweh's servant (*'ebed*). The word is particularly expressive of a relationship between persons.[30] When used of a pre-eminent servant of Yahweh, it denotes one whom God has chosen for a position of intimacy and trust, with authority as his chief minister and the executive of his will.[31] Thus 78.70–2 relates how Yahweh put his people Jacob, his heritage Israel, into the care of his chosen 'servant' David to feed and lead them as a shepherd tends a flock. Likewise David is described as 'the servant of Yahweh' in the title of Psalm 18, and by Yahweh as 'my servant' in 132.10 and in 89.4, 21. This pre-eminent office is linked to the divine choice which has enthroned the king; this 'servant' is the chosen one (89.4; cf. 78.70 and p. 146 and n. 24, p. 209). In Psalm 89 a successor of David is presumably intended in v. 40, which refers to the covenant and crown which were marks of such a servant:

> Thou hast defiled the covenant of thy servant.
> Thou hast profaned his crown on the ground.

Yet again, according to one reading in v. 51, the reigning king stresses that he is Yahweh's servant, carrying in his bosom like sheep the many peoples:

> Remember, Lord, the reproach of thy servant,
> my carrying in my bosom all the many peoples.[32]

The high dignity of this servanthood makes the title combine well

with the sonship theme prominent in the same psalm (pp. 146f.): the
king, by the election and covenant of Yahweh, is raised to be his
representative to the nations; whether designated first-born son or
servant, as most high and shepherd he embodies the sovereignty
of Yahweh.

The same tone sounds in 35.27; those who desire the king's
welfare will bless God when he helps him, saying:

> Glory be to Yahweh,
> who takes pleasure in the well-being of his servant!

In several psalms the king describes himself as 'thy servant' to
stress the relationship, his belonging to Yahweh through the covenant. In Psalm 116 he does so in thanksgiving:

> Truly Yahweh, I am thy servant,
> I am thy servant, the son of thy maidservant.
> Thou hast loosed my bonds   (116.16).

Here all the stress falls on his utter belonging to Yahweh; he was
born in such a relationship, and Yahweh has even more claim
upon him now as his redeemer. The reciprocal claim sounds in the
king's petitions, where the high privilege of his servanthood may
still be apparent. Thus as Yahweh's servant he can claim God's
promises to destroy his enemies:

> And in thy fidelity destroy my enemies
> and cause to perish all the adversaries of my soul,
> for I am thy servant   (143.12).

This servant has a right of access:

> Hide not thy face from thy servant   (69.18).

On the other hand, the connection of the term 'servant' with a
role of humiliation and suffering is not so evident, though the use
in Psalms 18 and 89 just noted, coupled with Isaiah 52.13f., could
indicate the double sense: the servant both humble and highly
privileged.

7. *The king as God's covenant-partner*

It is significant that Psalm 89, which gives prominence to the
king's servanthood and sonship, also makes much of the covenant
God has created with the dynasty. The climax of the psalm is the

contrast between the king's present distress and the promises of
this covenant. The word 'covenant' (*berīt*) occurs in vv. 4, 35 and
40, while other vocabulary of covenant relations is also prominent,
such as *ḥesed* (fidelity, constancy) in vv. 3, 15, 25, 29, 34. In v. 35 a
parallel to 'covenant' is 'that which has gone out of my lips'; here,
as elsewhere, the dynastic covenant centres especially on the oracular word sent to David and renewed to his descendants. It is
likely that this oracle was represented in a document presented in
the rites of installation (p. 43).

By this covenant God has bound the king in special relationship
to himself. If the king says now 'my God', 'my father', 'my king',
'my rock', etc. (p. 170), so God refers to him as 'my king',[33] 'my
anointed',[34] 'my chosen'.[35] More specifically, the king is God's
pre-eminent covenant-fellow (*ḥāsīd*):

> Thou wilt not make thy covenanted one
> see the grave   (16.10; cf. 116.15).

> Know that Yahweh has exalted me
> to be his covenant-fellow;[36]
> Yahweh will hear when I call upon him   (4.4).

The expression 'thy covenant-fellow' may also be used of David
in 89.20 as recipient of revelation, if the singular reading,
laḥªsīdᵉkā, is preferred.

Somewhat similar to such use of *ḥāsīd* is the designation of the
king as *ṣaddīq*, 'the righteous one', pre-eminent in God's favour
and blessings.[37] Since there is a tendency for a psalm to end with
an allusion to the one who is offering it (Gunkel, p. 66), it is
likely that in 75.11 *ṣaddīq* is a designation of the king, a single
figure standing over against the plural 'wicked', confident of
martial triumph:

> And all the horns of the wicked will I hew off;
> thou wilt exalt the horns of the righteous one.

A similar example may be found in 5.13. Plural expressions have
just been used of the enemies and of God's people; now the king
denotes himself as the *ṣaddīq*, crowned in the protection and favour
of God:

> Thou thyself wilt bless the righteous one, Yahweh;
> thou crownest him with the protecting band of favour.[38]

The blessings enjoyed by the king as *ṣaddīq* are depicted also in 92.13. He has just described himself as vitalized by his anointing and with triumphant 'horn'; he continues:

> The righteous one will flourish like a palm tree,
> like a cedar of Lebanon he will tower up.

That the 'righteous one' is here the king is supported by the sequence from the preceding verses and also by the fact that the tree is a favourite image of a king (p. 59). Then the continuation in v. 14 generalizes the thought:

> Those that are planted in the house of Yahweh
> flourish in the courts of our God . . . (92.14f.).

As *ṣaddīq*, the king is also responsible for good order (II Sam. 23.3f.), and so the term may well denote the king in Psalm 11.3:

> When the foundations are torn down,
> The righteous one – what shall he do?

As Yahweh distinguished Israel by choosing them as his 'portion' (Deut. 32.9), so the covenanted relation was completed by their willingness to have him as their 'portion' (Jer. 10.16). The king naturally takes the lead in the confession that Yahweh 'is my portion' (Pss. 16.5; 73.26; cf. Lam. 3.24), expressing his loving and exclusive bond in contrast with the cults of other kings (p. 66). It is his responsibility to keep his people from other cults (Pss. 4.3; 31.7; 73.27).

8. *The king assisted by the personified covenant-graces*

As foremost covenant-partner of God, the king makes frequent reference in his psalms to *ḥesed*, *'emet* and *'emūnā*, the faithful keeping of covenant, especially on the part of God towards his king. Thus in Psalm 89, as the king begins his exposition of God's covenant with the Davidic dynasty, he announces his theme as the *ḥesed* and *'emūnā* of God (89.2f.). The subsequent citation of God's oracle to David stresses the same terms:

> I will ever maintain for him my fidelity (*ḥesed*),
> and my covenant will stand firm (*ne'ᵉmenet*) for him (89.29).

> Yet my fidelity I will not withdraw from his side,
> and I will not go back on my faithfulness (*'emūnā*) (89.34; cf. v. 25).

The king can elsewhere praise God as:

> He who excels in salvation for his king
> and practises fidelity towards his anointed,
> towards David and his seed for ever   (18.51).

It is appropriate that in 118.1–4, 29 the theme of God's *ḥesed* introduces and follows the king's testimony of deliverance. In 63.4 the king can utter no greater praise than to declare God's *ḥesed* to be 'better than life'. He takes the lead in praising and praying for God's *ḥesed* in relation to the nourishment and care of all creatures and the downfall of evil forces (p. 69).

A tendency to personify the covenant-graces appears fairly clearly in a number of passages; they take the form of angelic beings commissioned by God to accompany and guard his king.[39] Thus:

> (The king) shall be enthroned before God for ever.
> Appoint Fidelity and Truth that they may guard him   (61.8).

> Thy Fidelity and Truth shall guard me continually   (40.12).

> By day Yahweh shall command his Fidelity,
> and by night (he will send) his vision[40] to be with me   (42.9).

> He will send from heaven to save me . . .
> God will send his Fidelity and his Truth   (57.4; cf. 18.17).

> As for my God
> his Fidelity will come to meet me   (59.11).

> Thou sendest blessings of goodness to meet him,
> thou placest a crown of gold on his head   (21.4).

> His Truth shall be (thy) shield and buckler   (91.4).

> Send thy Light and thy Truth!
> It is they that will lead me.
> They will bring me to thy holy mountain,
> and to thy sacred dwelling   (43.3).

> Goodness and Fidelity will closely attend in my train[41]
> all the days of my life   (23.6).

> By thy Truth destroy them!   (54.7)

There is a correspondence between the king thus guarded and escorted and the heavenly King of whom it is said:

> Righteousness and Judgment are the base of thy throne.
> Fidelity and Truth go before thy face   (89.15; cf. 85.14).

9. *The king aided by God's word*

Similar to such personification of the covenant-graces as helpers of the king is the treatment of God's word.[42] In the covenant with David and his dynasty, the essential is the oracle, oath or decree which issued from God's lips.[43] The king's praise of God's word in several psalms seems to have reference to such divine utterance on which the election and salvation of the dynasty rest:

> Here is the God whose way is perfect!
> The utterance of Yahweh is well-proved.
> He is a shield to all who shelter in him   (18.31).

> In God whose word I praise,
> in God I trust, I fear not
> what flesh can do to me   (56.5).

> In God – I praise the word –
> In Yahweh – I praise the word –
> in God I trust, I fear not
> what man can do to me   (56.11f.).

Among all the angelic graces the word is made supreme:

> Over thy fidelity and over thy truth,
> truly over all thy revelation
> thou hast magnified thine utterance   (138.2).

With the aid of God's word, the king restrains the trouble-makers:

> Regarding the deeds of men,
> by the word of thy lips
> I keep watch on the paths of the violent   (17.4).

In distress he relies on Yahweh's having spoken for his salvation:

> Lift up thyself against the raging of my adversaries,
> and rouse[44] for me the judgment thou hast commanded   (7.7).

> Be thou to me a rock of shelter for constant resort.
> Thou hast commanded to save me.
> Truly my rock and my refuge art thou   (71.3).

But there are times when the word, like God's fidelity, may seem absent:

> Has his fidelity vanished for ever?
> Has the utterance come to an end for all time?   (77.9).

hesed and utterance are thus easily linked, and sometimes become one, as when the king prays that with the break of dawn God will cause him to hear *hesed* (143.8).

10. *The king aided by God's name*

Help also comes to the king in the form of God's name. Rejecting the names of all other gods (16.4), the king shows his close adherence to Yahweh by confessing his name alone, and on this basis is promised exaltation:

> Because he cleaves to me I will deliver him;
> I will set him on high because he knows my name   (91.14).

But it can be said that it is the name itself which effects this exaltation, a powerful helper sent from its abode in the temple:

> Yahweh will answer you in the day of distress.
> The name of the God of Jacob will set you on high.
> He will send your help from the sanctuary,
> and from Zion he will sustain you   (20.2f., cf. vv. 6, 8).

Thus the name joins the personified graces of the covenant in aiding God's king:

> And my faithfulness and fidelity will be beside him,
> and through my name his horn shall be high   (89.25).

By the aid of this name, as though with the supreme weapon, he cuts down the swarming enemies:

> All nations surrounded me –
> with the name of Yahweh how I cut them down!
> They surrounded me, wholly surrounded me –
> with the name of Yahweh, how I cut them down!
> They surrounded me like bees,
> they attacked like fire among thorns –
> with the name of Yahweh, how I cut them down!   (118.10–12).

The king's triumphal return into the temple through the 'gates of righteousness' (v. 19) can thus be described as an entry achieved by the name of Yahweh:

> Blessed be he who enters by the name of Yahweh!
> We bless you from the house of Yahweh   (118.26, p. 62).

In Psalm 54 the king looks to God's name, power (*gᵉbūrā*) and truth to come to his aid; he vows to testify that Yahweh's name has saved him:

> O God, by thy name save me
> and by thy power give me justice.
> Let the evil return to my assailants.
> By thy truth destroy them!
> I will confess thy name Yahweh, that it is good,
> that it has delivered me from all distress . . .   (54.3, 7f.).

Such praising of God's name by the king is a prominent feature: he proclaims (*qr'*) the name in ceremonies at the altar (116.13, 17), confesses it (*ydh* 138.2; 54.8), hymns it (*zmr*, 7.18; 61.9; 9.3; 92.2), recounts it (*spr*, 22.23), waits upon it (?, *qwh*, 52.11),[45] glorifies it (86.12). Indeed, God enjoys the king's praise of his name more than the sacrifice of animals:

> I will praise the name of God with a song,
> and I will magnify it with testimony,
> and this will please Yahweh more than an ox,
> more than a bull perfect in horn and hoof![46]   (69.31f.; cf. 7.18)

The association of the king with Yahweh's name means also that it would be bad for Yahweh's name if the king were abandoned to his enemies (p. 37). He can therefore look for help 'for the sake of thy name' (23.3; 143.11).

Sometimes in the king's psalms his loyal people, who join with him in worship, are designated by reference to Yahweh's name: they are those who rejoice in it (89.17, parallel to the covenant grace of 'righteousness'), love it (5.12; 69.37), know it (9.11; cf. 89.16), confess it (140.14), acknowledge its nearness (75.2), call for its universal recognition (66.2, 4).

11. *The king aided by God's spirit*

The gift of the 'spirit' is linked to the royal anointing in the stories of Saul (I Sam. 10) and David (I Sam. 16.13), and has a similar association in Isaiah 11.2; 42.1; 61.1f. By such a gift of the spirit Moses had carried the burden of supreme authority (Num. 11.17) and Joshua likewise (Num. 27.17f.; Deut. 34.9). By the spirit the ruler-judges saved their people (Judg. 6.34; 11.29). When Yahweh works a king's downfall, the good royal spirit may be replaced by an injurious one, as in the case of Saul (I Sam. 16.14; cf. Ahab, I Kings 22.21f., and Sennacherib, II Kings 19.7).

In the psalms also, among the emissaries that extend help to the king from Yahweh's person we may count his spirit. While the king may be conducted on the way to safety and happiness by Yahweh himself[47] or by emissaries such as his light or truth,[48] in 143.10 the guide is Yahweh's spirit: 'May thy good spirit lead me into a land of equity.' The theme of the spirit features prominently in 51.12–14. Having prayed for the creative renewal of his inner being (his heart and spirit), the king asks that he may continue in God's presence, which is with him in the form of 'the spirit of thy holiness' or 'thy holy spirit' (p. 71); moreover he prays to be strengthened and supported by that royal or princely spirit (p. 71) with which God equips rulers:

> A clean heart create for me O God,
> a firm spirit renew inside me.
> Cast me not from thy presence,
> and take not thy holy spirit from me.
> Restore to me the joy of thy salvation,
> and may the royal spirit uphold me.

12. *God's assurances to his king*

God's favour and goodwill to his king are expressed in various assurances and promises. Having chosen the dynastic father David (89.4, 20f.), God renews his favour and delight (*ḥpṣ*) upon successive kings (p. 146), extending to them the original promises. God grasps the king by his hand (73.23; 139.10)[49] or supports him with his right hand (18.36; 63.9; cf. 41.13).[50] The king is 'the man of God's right hand', the man upon whom God's right hand rests to make him strong in God's work (80.18; 89.22). God undertakes to be at his side amid all dangers:

> The Lord upon your right hand
> crushes kings on the day of his anger   (110.5).

> Yahweh is your guard,
> Yahweh is your shade on your right hand   (121.5).

God guards his king by night and day (91.5; 121.6) and especially when asleep, at his most vulnerable (3.6; 4.9). That God feasts him in the sight of his enemies (23.5) probably means that God has publicly indicated that he has taken the king into a protective covenant; those who would harm him must reckon with the covenant-lord (p. 37). God is like a shield about his king to ward off the enemies' weapons (3.4; 5.13; 18.31, 36; 28.7; 91.4; 144.2; cf. 119.114).

He raises him on high, thereby both singling him out for glory and lifting him clear of perils:

> I have raised a chosen one high above the people   (89.20).

> The name of the God of Jacob shall set you on high   (20.2).

> I will set him on high because he knows my name   (91.14).

> Thou art my glory and dost raise my head   (3.4).

> Now shall my head be high above my enemies   (27.6).

> Thou shalt set me on high
> above those who exalt themselves against me   (59.2).

> Thy salvation, O God, shall set me on high   (69.30).

Exaltation and victory are promised in the metaphor of the raised horn,[51] suggesting the triumphant bull which from ancient times had symbolized the might of gods and heroes:

> By my name shall his horn be high   (89.25).

> And thou hast raised high my horn like the wild bull's   (92.11).

> The horns of the righteous one shall be exalted   (75.11).

> And he shall give power to his king
> and raise high the horn of his anointed   (I Sam. 2.10; cf. Ps. 132.17).

As representative of God's cause, he can be promised victory over all his foes:

> The enemy shall not strike at him
> nor the evil man overcome him,
> and I shall crush his foes before him,
> and his adversaries I will conquer   (89.23f.).

> Upon asp and cobra you shall tread,
> On lion and dragon trample   (91.13).

Other examples are 18.48f.; 110.2; 132.18.

The old (perhaps Davidic) oracle proclaiming Yahweh's mastery of Canaan is invoked as an assurance of the king's victory (108). On a vaster scale are the promises of world-wide rule, amazing promises that arise from the festal ideology. As God's unique representative, he is to be 'head of the nations' (18.44) and 'the most high above the kings of the earth' (89.28). The nations are to be his 'inheritance' and the furthest bounds of earth his 'possession' (2.8); other kings and rulers of the earth must submit (2.10). In 72.8 it is likely that the 'river' is an ideological concept as in 46.5, the paradisal fountain beneath the sacred mountain Zion:

> And he shall rule from sea to sea
> and from the river to the bounds of the earth . . .
> And all kings shall bow down before him,
> and nations shall serve him   (72.8, 11).

Such world-wide rule is also granted in 89.26, where the king is pictured in a posture like that of the cosmic King-Creator, resting the hand of authority upon the subjugated water-foes (p. 144).

Another element in God's assurances to his king is the continuance of the dynasty. The clearest statement is in 89.5, 30–38. God has sworn in his covenant with David that the dynastic line shall continue for ever. Erring kings will be chastised, but the promise of eternal continuance will not be rescinded. The same doctrine is found in the oracle of Nathan in II Samuel 7. We find an echo of it in the ancient psalm 18.51: 'Yahweh practising fidelity to his anointed, to David and to his seed for eternity'. A more guarded statement occurs in 132.11f: Yahweh has sworn unconditionally that David's offspring will succeed him; the succession of remoter generations is qualified ('if they keep my covenant . . .'), but the stress still falls on the prospect of eternal continuance. Various passages concerning the continuance of the king's life and name can be related to the promise of dynastic succession and will be discussed in the next section, where the subject, the gift of life, is the culmination of all the promises. A further section will treat of the people's share in these royal blessings, the prosperity in nature and society.

To what extent do God's promises to his king have an eschatological character? The promises of world-wide rule and ideal
conditions in particular seem remote from realistic expectations,
short of some drastic transformation of history. Were such promises related only to some future dispensation, some new creation
beyond the present order? Foreign texts show how a present reign
could be viewed idealistically in terms of perfect conditions.[52] So
also in the promises to the Davidic king, the *basic* notions seem to
have been firmly related to the present reign: the divine election
and favour, protection, blessing, continuance (p. 134). As for the
theme of explicit world dominion, this is of a piece with the basic
theology of the Davidic role in the service of the supreme deity
as it was presented dramatically in the enthronement rites. The
context of festal celebration, where the ideal of God's kingdom
was actualized (chapter III) could accommodate statements of
Davidic greatness which might have caused difficulty elsewhere.

The interpretation of Psalm 89 (pp. 121f.) has considerable bearing on this question. Its lament takes its force from an understanding that the great promises of Davidic world empire should
already have been actualized. If this were a lament reflecting a
historical defeat, it would show how such promises were indeed
given a concrete reference. But no other lament appeals so to these
promises. This adds to the arguments that Psalm 89 depicts a
ritual humiliation. It will then be appealing to promises that come
alive only in the context of cultic drama. The lack of such appeals
in historical crises suggests that, especially in the later period of
reduced Davidic sovereignty, the theme of world-wide rule was in
practice removed further into the realm of eschatological hope.
Faced with political or personal dangers, the kings were content
in their prayers to appeal to God's general promises of favour,
protection and victory over enemies.

13. *God gives his king abundant life*

God's gifts to his king culminate in the granting of 'life', involving deliverance from death and in some sense the eternal enjoy-
ment of God's blessings. A prominent theme in the royal rituals
concerned the king being threatened by death, appealing to God,
and so being delivered (p. 133). In his subsequent enthroning it
was stressed that his prayer for life had been granted; the glory

which God now gave to his king involved eternal and blessed life:

> Yahweh, in thy power the king rejoices
> and in thy salvation how exceedingly joyful he is!
> The desire of his heart thou hast given him,
> and the request of his lips thou hast not refused.
> Truly thou didst meet him with blessings of good;
> Thou didst place on his head the crown of fine gold.
> Life he asked of thee, thou hast given it him,
> length of days for ever and ever.[53]
> Great is his glory in thy salvation,
> splendour and majesty thou hast placed upon him.
> Truly thou hast appointed him blessings for ever.
> Thou hast gladdened him with joy in thy presence   (21.2–7).

God has blessed him for ever (45.3), given him a throne for ever (45.7) and made him priest for ever (110.4). So it can be said that he will prolong days with the sun and before the moon for generations of generations (72.5, G).

> Thou addest days upon the days of the king,
> his years are like eternity.
> He sits for ever before God . . .   (61.7f.).

> Yahweh will guard your going out and entering
> from now until eternity   (121.8).

In 91.16 'length of days' is probably meant absolutely as in 21.5, and we may render:

> With years unnumbered I will satisfy him,
> and give him enjoyment of my salvation   (91.16).

To a considerable extent the idea of the king's eternal life is understood as the continuance of the dynasty. The life of David and his successors continues so long as his throne is occupied by one of his seed and name. For a life of this kind, God's promise of eternity has indeed been given:

> For ever I will establish your seed,
> and I will build your throne generation after generation   (89.5).

> For ever I will keep for him my fidelity,
> and my covenant is made sure for him   (vv. 29f.).

> And I will appoint for ever his seed,
> and his throne like the sun before me . . . (v. 37).

As already mentioned (p. 159), this promise of eternity appears in a more conditional form in Psalm 132. In 132.17f. the worshippers presumably thought of David as represented in his successors, a centre of strength and light throughout the generations:

> There I shall cause a horn to sprout for David;
> I will tend a lamp for my anointed;
> his enemies I will clothe in shame,
> but on himself his crown shall shine.

Both Psalms 45 and 72, which have just been quoted for the theme of eternal reign, include the thought of continuance through the father's name:

> In place of your fathers shall arise your sons . . .
> I will prolong mention of your name for all generations,
> therefore peoples will praise you for ever and ever (45.17f.).

> May his name endure for ever.
> While the sun endures, may his name be propagated (72.17).

The life of David and his seed is virtually one life, appearing in the reigning king:

> (Yahweh) works great salvation for his king,
> and shows fidelity to his anointed,
> to David and to his seed for ever (18.51).

> (Yahweh) that gives salvation to the kings,
> that delivers David his servant (144.10).

We may compare the conception in Isaiah 11.1 of the dynastic father as a tree, renewing itself in new growth (cf. Zech. 3.8).

From such passages it seems that the idea of the ancestor's continuing life in his 'seed' has a particularly strong form in the case of the royal family.[54] Furthermore, a tendency to see the king's destiny as eternal fellowship with God would result from the conceptions of the king in God's aura (p. 143) and as the unique Son (p. 146). God would surely not suffer one to whom he had extended such covenant privileges, his *ḥāsîd*, to see the Pit (16.10). To some extent, then, the kings seem to have been thought of as raised above a wholly negative fate in Sheol. Evidence of special privilege in this respect may be found in the siting of the royal

burial chambers within Jerusalem and eventually, it seems, adjacent to the temple.[55] As for the psalms, there appear to be a few
where the king claims 'life' not only as happiness in his present
existence and in the continuance of his children, but also as a
blissful communion with God that he himself will enjoy for ever.
Even though such psalms may be evoked by a danger to his present existence, his prayer for 'life' broadens out to the eternal
prospect. It may be that a threat to his present life was also felt as
a threat to his 'life hereafter', since a violent overthrow would
jeopardize the dynastic continuance and his own peaceful burial
in Zion and hence the conditions for his eternal happiness; if he
left this life already in a state of rejection, his claim to a special
destiny might be lost. (Kümmel, p. 92, finds a similar situation in
Hittite ideas: when a threat to the king's life is presaged, he steps
aside and installs a substitute-king to divert the danger; if, however, the real king should die during this temporary abdication,
he forfeits his royal privilege of divinization in the hereafter.)

Psalm 16 can well be understood as a text where the king's
prayer and hope seem to embrace both his present safety and his
personal eternity:

> Keep me, God, for I shelter in thee,
> I say, Thou art my Lord, Yahweh;
> only with thee is my good.

He rejects the spirits of the 'earth', that is, probably, the underworld,[56] by which some sought help:

> As for the deities which are in the dust
> and the lords which others worship[57] –
> may their troubles multiply who apostatize to such.
> Their libations of blood I will not pour out,
> and I will not take up their names upon my lips.
> Yahweh is my portion and my cup.
> Thou makest broad my lot,
> the lines have fallen out for me in a place of delights;
> truly my inheritance shines fair upon me.
> I will bless Yahweh who counsels me;
> for in the nights my reins instruct me.
> I set Yahweh before me continually,
> and from his[58] right hand I shall not be cast down.
> So my heart rejoices and my glory is glad,
> Yea, my flesh abides in safety.

For thou wilt not abandon my soul to Sheol.
Thou wilt not make thy covenanted one see the Pit.
Thou wilt cause me to know the path of life,
fullness of joys in thy presence,
pleasures in thy right hand for evermore.

Another example of such a prospect of personal eternity may be found in Psalm 73, which in the relevant passage draws markedly on royal phraseology. While the oppressors at last will come to a sudden end and fade like the images of a dream (vv. 19f.), the king will be strengthened and guided by God in this life and afterwards be taken for ever into God's glory:

And now I am continually beside thee.
Thou holdest my right hand.
By thy counsel thou wilt guide me,
and afterward in glory thou wilt take me.
Whom else do I need in heaven?
And beside thee I desire none on earth.
When my flesh and my heart fail,
God will remain the rock of my heart
and my portion for ever.
Those far from thee shall indeed perish;
Thou wilt destroy all who go after other gods.
But for me, drawing near to God is best.
In my Lord Yahweh I make my shelter,
to recount all thy works.

In both Psalms 16 and 73, the hope of eternal life is combined with emphatic rejection of other cults, – such as probably were connected with the nether world (Isa. 28.18 etc.).

In the ancient Near East generally, the emphasis on the continuance and force of royal life likewise led to various conceptions of glory after death. The fullest expression is in Egypt, where the dead king, identified with Osiris, passed into eternal life beyond.[59] The Hittite king's death is regularly spoken of as his 'becoming a god' (p. 101); the funerary ritual lasted at least thirteen days, the cremated bones being treated with great honour, and sacrifices offered to nourish the soul of the deceased (Gurney, *Hittites*, pp. 164f.). The Hurrians expected the return of ancient kings, an idea comparable to the expectation of 'David' in Ezekiel 34.23f. etc. (Cazelles). In Mesopotamia offerings were made before the statues of dead as well as of living rulers, perpetuating their relationship of favour with the gods (Labat, p. 371); kings were buried with rich ceremony which some scholars have compared with Tammuz worship (Labat, pp. 118f.); some rulers were divinized even in their lifetime (Labat, p. 372; Dhorme, p. 20). An eighth century Aramean king, Panammuwas I of Samal, expected his heir to offer sacrifice to his god Hadad, making remembrance of Panammuwas' name and praying that his soul would eat and drink with Hadad (Donner, Nr. 214). Ugaritic texts reflect the practice of erecting a stele and providing offerings for a dead king, and names of dead kings are listed with the divine determinative (J. Gray in *Ugaritica* 6). The combination of Ezekiel 28 and archaeological evidence suggests that the kings of Tyre aspired to a paradisal immortality (Barnett, p. 13). Canaanite influence has been found in the use of the winged sun-disk and scarab (associated in Egypt with eternal royal life) as royal symbols in Judah, appearing as stamps on jars (Cross, 'Judean stamps').

The form of conception and degree of importance given to the 'hereafter' aspect of the Davidic king's life no doubt varied, and its deposit in the traditions was rather ambivalent. But whatever aspect of royal life is primary in particular texts – whether the quality of present experience, or dynastic continuance or personal eternity, the psalms do agree on the importance of the basic gift itself. God is the one who raises his king from the gates of death (9.14), who takes him from the watery maw of Sheol and of Belial[60] (18; 40; 69; 116), who raises him from the dust of death to life in the temple and to the prospect of descendants (22, p. 167). He brings him through the valley of the shadow of death and restores his soul to enjoy countless years in God's house (23, cf. p. 38) where he feeds on all goodness and looks on God's beauty (27). He revives him when sick and sets him up before his face for ever (41). He delivers him from death to walk to and fro in God's house, to trust and praise God for eternity (52.10f.; cf. 92.13; 75.10) and acknowledge him as 'God of my life' (42.9), 'the living God' (18.47; 42.3).

14. *The king's life benefits the people*

God's gift of life to his king brings life also to his people. Their saying 'may the king live!' (I Kings 1.31 etc.)[61] was more than a pleasantry; their interest was involved. Under his shade they lived; he was their breath of life (Lam. 4.20). So his life was the sincere object of their prayers (61.6f., p. 48; 72.15). In Psalm 72 the theme of the eternal life of the righteous king (vv. 5, 17, p. 162) intertwines with that of the fertility of his land and people (vv. 3, 7, 16); he is like the life-bringing rain (v. 6). In Psalm 132 God's grace to David includes abundant food for Zion (v. 15). Psalm 144 shows how the deliverance of the king from the forces of death will result in health and fertility for all his society (p. 127):

> Save and deliver me from the hands of the alien hosts,
> whose mouth speaks wickedness
> and whose right hand deals falsely,
> so that our sons may be like plants well-grown when still young,
> o ir daughters columns carved for the building of a palace,
> our barns full of provisions of every kind,
> our flocks increasing by thousands and ten thousands in our fields,
> our cattle heavy with young,
> bearing without mishap in due time,
> and no cry of pain in our courts   (144.11–14).

In the related Psalm 18 the association of the people with the king in his sufferings and restoration appears in the generalizing testimony of vv. 27–32; the symbolic salvation of the king brings an assurance for all who share in the humble faith that has been signified in the royal ritual, – 'Thou savest a humble people . . . he is a shield to all who shelter in him . . . who is the Rock except our God?' The triumphant cry of v. 47 (p. 116) points to the power of God for life which now streams forth after the deliverance of his king:

> Yahweh lives, and blessed be my Rock
> and high is the God of my salvation!

In Psalm 118 the deliverance of the king means that Yahweh has given the light of life to his people (v. 27, cf. 18.29); the king, established in life, binds together his whole society in living order (v. 22). Later tradition suggests a further link between the king's deliverance and society's welfare, in that the 'Hosanna' of v. 25 was used as a prayer for rain (p. 62). Further, the 'royal grace' and 'dew' with which the king glistens at his enthronement (110.3, p. 147) represent powers that give life to the earth.[62]

In Psalm 22 the passing of the king from death to life is clearly taken as significant for the life of the universal community, and not only for the immediate circle of worshippers who share the sacramental meal and receive from the king his life-mediating blessing (v. 27); God's work for his king, prolonged through testimony and recurring ritual, will bring life also to succeeding generations and even affect the dead:

> Let all the ends of the earth commemorate this
> and return to Yahweh,
> and all the families of the nations
> worship before thee.
> For to Yahweh belongs the kingship
> and he rules now among the nations.
> The living on earth
> eat together as they worship.
> Those gone down to the nether world
> bow before him.[63]
> For he has made my soul live again to him.[64]
> (My)[65] seed shall serve him.
> Testimony shall be made to the Lord
> by (my)[66] generations!
> they shall make solemn entry
> and announce his righteous work,
> to a people yet to be born (they shall say),
> He has done it   (22.28–32).

In Psalm 69 also, the king's deliverance from the waters of death is followed by a meal of communion, where the pledge of life is extended to the society of worshippers, as the king pronounces on them the benediction 'May your heart live for ever!' (v. 33). Again, the joyful prospect extends to the whole world, but especially Zion, and stretches through generations to come.

Nor is the hope of enduring life in Psalm 73 without implications for the society. The blissful assurance is relevant to God's work with Israel (v. 1) and to a covenant with the sacred community (v. 15) and gives rise to testimony (v. 28).

In praying for his salvation, the king in Psalm 36 draws all mankind into the royal privileges, seeing them as sheltering under God's wings, feasting richly on the abundant gifts of God's house, and as blessed with the light of life (vv. 9f.). For them also he prays for the continuance of divine fidelity through the generations (vv. 8a, 11).

Psalm 92 also illustrates the linking of the people with the royal

vitality. With the assertion of God's own kingship comes the salvation of his king, who is pictured triumphant (horn raised) and
glistening with the vital oil of his anointing. He is 'the righteous
one', a lively and lofty tree. But the image of the tree passes to a
plural reference, comparing the righteous community to the trees
that flourish for ever in the temple.

In the neighbouring kingships there was likewise a strong belief
in the importance of the king for the vitality of his society (e.g.
Labat, pp. 277f.; Frankfort, ch. 4; Gray in *Ugaritica* 6). The Assyrian
kingship is compared to the legendary plant which conferred
immortality (Labat, p. 282).

15. *God's gifts balanced by demands on his king*

It would be wholly misleading to characterize the grace of the
royal covenant as unconditional. It is true that a fundamental element in that grace, the promise of dynastic continuance, is said to
be irrevocable in Psalm 89 and II Samuel 7, though in Psalm 132
God's position in event of apostasy is more reserved (p. 159). But
even in Psalm 89 remedial punishment is envisaged, and it cannot
be said that the balance is so different from that in the classical
prophets. They too had to reckon with the invincibility of God's
covenant love and match punishment with the fulfilment of the
ancient promise and purpose.

But the grace of God to his king included much beside the question of dynastic succession, and it is quite clear in the psalms that
the king acknowledged great obligations towards God which he
could not ignore if he were to remain in God's favour. We have
already seen how the king stood under God's laws and that his
role was to give effect to God's will in the community (p. 141).
He had to be humble and put his trust in Yahweh, not in other
gods or in human strength; he must deal fairly with all and
especially exert himself on behalf of the weak. These obligations
are woven into the texts from the great ritual occasions in such a
way that they are inseparable from the prospect of triumph and
blessing.[67]

In his prayers from particular crises, the king's appeals likewise
take Yahweh's requirements into account. Sometimes he confesses that he falls short of Yahweh's ideal (40.13; 41.5; 143.2;
cf. 51 and 73.21f.), or he may protest that in a particular case he

believes he is innocent (7; 16; 17; 35; 59; 69 etc.). In depicting his foes as treacherous, cruel, godless etc., he is again acknowledging that the issue turns upon Yahweh's standards for human conduct. When he is saved, he knows that Yahweh did not find iniquity in his heart (66.18).

The matching of divine requirements and gifts in the psalms is thus similar to the view in the histories, where David is a figure pre-eminent both in privilege (II Sam. 7) and in his devotion (I Kings 9.4; 11.4, 6; 14.8; cf. Ps. 78.70–2).

16. *The king's warm response to God's grace*

Posener (p. 30) has pointed out that expressions of warm and trusting piety are not the preserve of 'little people' in Egypt; the Pharaohs take the lead in such devotions. In Mesopotamia the rulers considered themselves pre-eminent in the tenderness of their relationship with their deity (Labat, pp. 111–16, 57–69). Likewise for Israel, there should be no reluctance to accept that the most ardent expressions of love, gratitude and trust towards God are appropriately found on the lips of his king. This follows naturally from the position of the king as already outlined.

The tone is well set by Psalm 18:

> I love thee (*'erḥāmᵉkā*), Yahweh my strength (18.2).

Similarly Psalm 116:

> I am filled with love (*'āhabtī*)
> for Yahweh hears the voice of my supplications (116.1).

God will deliver his king 'because he loves me ardently', *bī ḥāšaq* (91.14); this expression, like that quoted from Psalm 18, occurs nowhere else of man's love of God.

The king has great joy in the divine splendour which embraces him:

> Yahweh, in thy power the king is joyful,
> and in thy salvation how greatly he rejoices! (21.2; cf. 63.12).

He expresses his satisfaction in almost ecstatic language:

> Thy faithful love (*ḥesed*) is better than life itself . . .
> My soul will be satisfied as with the richest fare . . .
> My soul clings to thee . . . (63.4f.).

For him the unique good is to dwell in nearness to God, where he may hope to see him in visions and be guided in oracular signs:

> One thing have I asked of Yahweh;
> that alone I seek:
> that I should sit in the house of Yahweh
> all the days of my life,
> to behold the beauty of Yahweh
> and to divine in his temple   (27.4).

Such contact with God is appreciated also in 73.28 and 5.4. Even in the midst of dearth and general hostility, his heart warms with joy because of Yahweh, Yahweh alone, who keeps him in safety (4.8f.). The same tone sounds in Psalm 23; restoration to the house of Yahweh means rich satisfaction, like lush pastures and refreshing streams for flocks, or like ample fare at a banquet. When anxieties multiply, God's consolations come to enrapture his soul (94.19). He commits his spirit into the hand of God (31.6).

Correspondingly, when the king feels removed from God's saving presence, he expresses his deprivation with passionate yearning:

> O God, my God art thou.
> I seek thee earnestly.
> My soul thirsts for thee,
> My flesh pines for thee
> in a parched and weary land without water   (63.2).

> As a deer pants for channels of water,
> so my soul pants for thee, O God.
> My soul thirsts for God, the living God.
> When shall I enter and see the face of God?   (42.2f.).

17. *The king's designations for God as his personal saviour*

The warm piety just described is expressed also in the king's abundant designations of God as in gracious and individual relationship to him. Most comprehensively he says 'my God' (*'elōhay*, *'ēlī*).[68] Here he expresses his personal covenant with God, just as the national covenant gives rise to the phrase 'our God'. The king's use of 'my God' is often bound up with more particularizing expressions of God's relation to his king (18.3; 40.18; 91.2;

94.22 etc.). That 'my God' is a strong expression of privileged relationship is apparent in 89.27; God grants the king to use the expression and in the same breath declares his unique exaltation:

> He for his part shall cry to me,
> 'My father art thou,
> my God (*'ēlī*) and the rock of my salvation';
> I for my part will make him first-born,
> the most high over the kings of the earth.

A similar association of the divine paternity and the use of 'my God' (*'ēlī*) is found in 22.11 (see p. 147), a psalm which has already begun with an emphatic threefold 'my God (*'ēlī, 'ēlī* . . . *'elōhay*).

Frequent also in royal prayers is 'my Lord' (*'adōnāy*), if indeed the suffix is pronominal.[69] In addressing God as 'my King' (*malkī*, 5.3; 44.5; cf. 68.25; 84.4; 74.12, p. 61) the Davidic king can point to the source of his own kingship. A similar acknowledgment can be found in his designation of God as 'my shepherd' (23.1; cf. 28.9b), since the human king too is shepherd (78.70f.; II Sam. 5.2; cf. Isa. 44.28; Ezek. 34.23; Micah 5.3); or as 'my light' (27.1) since he too is light (II Sam. 21.17; 23.4; Pss. 18.29; 132.17); or as his 'shade' (121.5) since he too is shade (Lam. 4.20; Isa. 32.2); or as 'my shield' (7.11?; 18.3; 28.7; 144.2) since this was a common designation of rulers (47.10; Hos. 4.18). The king also acknowledges the source of his own royal glory in addressing God as 'my glory', 'my power' etc., thus:

> Thou Yahweh art a shield about me,
> my glory and he who lifts my head on high   (3.4).

> The High God[70] is my salvation and my glory,
> the Rock of my power; my shelter is in God   (62.8).

> Yahweh is my power and my shield   (28.7).

> I say to Yahweh, My God art thou . . .
> Yahweh my lord is the power of my salvation   (140.7f.).

'Salvation' is indeed another characteristic theme of royal texts, and the king emphatically recognizes God as its source. God is called 'the stronghold of the salvations of his anointed' (28.8), 'the rock of my salvation' (89.27), 'the horn of my salvation' (18.3), 'God of my salvation' (18.47; 51.16), 'the salvation of my face' (42.12), or simply 'my salvation' (22.2; 27.1); somewhat similar is 'God of my righteousness' (4.2).

His personal covenant with God is especially apparent when he calls God 'God of my fidelity (*ḥasdī* 59.11, 18) or just 'my fidelity' (144.2). Even more so when he designates God as 'he who severed me from my mother's womb' (71.6), 'he who raises me from the gates of death' (9.14), 'God of my life' (42.3), and 'the God who accomplishes my cause' (57.3).

Many of the designations acknowledge God as the king's rescuer and place of refuge or security, apparently reflecting his prevailing need for aid against militant foes: 'my stronghold', *mᵉṣūdātī* (18.3; 71.3; 144.2); 'my rock', *ṣūrī* (28.1; 18.3, 47; 62.2, 7; 92.16; 144.1); 'my crag', *salʿī* (18.3; 42.10; 71.3); 'my high fortress', *miśgabbī* (18.3; 59.10, 17f.; 62.3, 7; 144.2; cf. 94.22); 'my refuge', *mᵉʿōzī* (?) (43.2; 31.5); 'my shelter', *maḥsī* (71.7; 73.28; 91.2, 9; cf. 61.4; 94.22; 142.6); 'my strength', *ḥizqī* (18.2); 'my help', *ʿezrātī* (40.18; cf. 54.6); 'my rescuer', *mᵉpallᵉṭī* (18.3, 49; 40.18; 144.2).

The king likes to accumulate such designations of God, whether in thanksgiving or appeal. This is appropriately done in the grandest manner in 18.2f. and hardly less in 144.1f. Some other examples of such accumulations can be found in 3.4, 8; 28.1, 7; 22.2f.; 27.1; 31.3–5; 40.18; 42.3; 54.6; 62.2f., 7f.; 71.3, 5–7; 91.2; 94.22.

Just as 89.27 singles out the king as the one privileged to call on Yahweh with such abundant personal titles ('my father, my God and rock of my salvation'), so 91.2 characterizes the king as him 'who says to Yahweh, My shelter, and my stronghold, my God in whom I trust' (cf. 16.1; 142.6).

18. *The king as God's chief cultic minister*

The significance of the cult in ancient societies must entail that the man whom God had made nearest to himself and invested with his authority should also be the leader in things cultic; and such is the position generally in the ancient Near East. In principle the Israelite king too had a pre-eminence as one brought near to God and imbued with his 'holiness', which afforded communion (pp. 142–5). His ordination involved his sanctification, God pouring over him the 'oil of his holiness' (p. 144). In a psalm from such ceremonies God names him 'priest for ever' (110.4), and the context includes the themes of his sitting beside God and his rebirth in divine graces. His office being in the succession of the ancient Melchizedek's, he is priest-king of the supreme God, the Creator (Gen. 14.19).

In the essence of priesthood none could compare with him. For the essential is to be able to come near to God, to commune with him, to see his face and hear his voice. The king, God's son and servant, was granted not only to approach, but to sit and abide perpetually in God's presence. With such grace of intimacy and his consequent authority, the king must in principle be the leader in the ordering of God's house, a ruling steward-servant who appointed and controlled lesser servants, who ordered the furnishings, the programme of service, the supplies and repairs. In principle he should present sacrifices, make petitions, see visions, receive omens and oracles, convey to the people admonitions, benedictions and judgments. In actual practice the picture of the king's priestly pre-eminence might be blurred by the physical necessity to delegate his functions, by the survival of privileged groups from before the monarchy, by vagaries of inspirational gifts, especially prophecy. It is not surprising therefore that the historical books sometimes acknowledge the king's cultic leadership,[71] but sometimes tend to diminish it.[72] By their nature, however, the psalms reflect the king's position in principle and often show him in his cultic role.[73]

Psalm 132 indicates that David's successors re-enacted the first conducting of the ark to Zion, and hence led the ceremony in priestly fashion (p. 125). As depicted in the histories, the king will thus have worn the ephod, danced, played, sung, sacrificed, pronounced benedictions, and generally directed the whole proceedings. Such activities appear again in various psalms. He may be robed for rites of splendour (cf. 21.6; 132.18b; 45.3) or humiliation (35.13; 42-3, p. 70; 102.18). He leads dancing processions around the altar (118.27). He sings and plays to God, and indeed, with his command of the temple's resources and in view of the eternity of his office (p. 160), he can offer superlative praises: the finest instruments (144.9; 92.4), a 'new song' (40.4; 144.9), an unending round – daily, day and night, for ever (61.9; 92.3), heard by peoples, kings and gods (57.10; 138.1, 4). His words of benediction at a sacrificial meal may be heard in 22.27 and 69.33.

He sacrifices abundantly (cf. I Kings 3.4):

> Fat burnt-offerings I offer to thee
> with the smoke of rams;
> I make ready cattle
> together with goats   (66.15; cf. 54.8).

The people hope that Yahweh will remember all the king's *minḥā* and *'ōlā* offerings and so send salvation from Zion (20.4). The king exhorts all men to a piety which includes 'sacrifices of righteousness' (4.6). He raises the 'cup of salvation' (116.13), but libations for other gods he will not pour (16.4). Associated with his offerings, we find his solemn entry and proskynesis (5.4, 8); allusions to such temple entries[74] may be fairly frequent (cf. 40.8; 42.3; 66.13; 71.16; 73.17; 118.19; 138.2). In addition to obvious processional movements such as in Psalm 118, the king's processions may be alluded to elsewhere:

> Yahweh, lead me in thy righteousness
> in view of my adversaries,
> make level before me thy way   (5.9).

> He leads me in the highway of righteousness[75]
> for the sake of his name   (23.3).

> Send out thy light and thy truth
> that they may lead me;
> let them bring me to thy holy mountain
> and to thy sacred dwelling   (43.3).

> My soul sticks close behind thee
> for thy right hand has grasped me   (63.9).

The histories' picture of the dancing priest-king David seems to live again in 42.5:

> I passed into the sacred dwelling (*sāk*),
> I led the dancing procession[76] up to the house of God;
> with the sound of praise and thanksgiving,
> a multitude in sacred dance   (42.5).

The king is prominent in leading prayers. Evening, morning and noon, presumably the main set times, he prays hard in time of danger (55.18). Standing perhaps on some prominent place,[77] he raises outspread hands in a gesture of supplication (28.2; 77.3; 143.6) or praise (63.5).[78] He invokes the epiphany of God in phrases like those used by the priests of the ark: 'Arise, O Yahweh', 'Awake!', 'Be lifted up!', 'Shine forth!' (7.7; 17.13; 35.2; 57.6; 59.5f.; 94.1f.; cf. Isa. 51.9; Hab. 2.19; Num. 10.35). He invokes doom on his foes in a manner suggestive of ritual usage, setting up a verbal image of the enemy and then shattering it (7; 10; 36; 52; 53 etc.).

Various other priestly traits may be detected. In 55.16 the fate of the king's enemies is to be like that which befell the men who challenged the priestly prerogatives of Moses and Aaron (Num. 16.30f.). His 'walking about before God' (116.9; 56.14) may be compared with the priesthood represented by Eli (I Sam. 2.30). His zeal for God's temple (69.10) and his love for it (26.8) are presumably manifest in concrete proofs which he can use to support his prayers; such would be his maintenance of the fabric, his ensuring of adequate provisions, his dedication of gifts, his ordering of services.[79]

The intimacy with God which is the king's privilege makes it appropriate that prophetic experience should also be his. He may expect personally to receive guidance through visions of God, dreams and signs.[80] Residing for ever in Yahweh's presence, he will be gladdened by visions of Yahweh's beauty and by the communications he receives from Yahweh in the processes of cultic enquiry (27.4, see p. 170). He seeks such encounters (p. 131). God comes to him by night to advise him in his royal duties:

I bless Yahweh who counsels me,
for in the nights my kidneys instruct me   (16.7).

By thy counsel thou dost guide me   (73.24).

So in the sanctuary I would behold thee
to be satisfied with thy power and thy glory   (63.3; p. 50).

Oh when shall I enter and see the face of God?   (42.3).

I make remembrance of thee upon my couch,
in the watches of the night
I recite concerning thee   (63.7).

And by night he sends his vision to be with me   (42.9; p. 153).

Such visitations of God are a sign of favour (cf. 86.17); God has tested and proved him and confirmed his righteousness:

Thou triest my heart,
when thou visitest in the night;
thou refinest me
till thou findest nothing amiss   (17.3).

Confirmed in righteousness, I shall behold thy face;
I shall be richly satisfied with thy form on awakening   (17.15).

The king himself hears God speak.[81] If in practice he was dependent on prophetic specialists, these fall from view in the ideal picture of the psalms. The king announces: 'He has said to me ...' (2.7). 'Yahweh swore to David' (132.11); 'thou didst speak in a vision to thy covenanted one' (?) (89.20). God 'digs open' his ear, enabling him to hear the divine voice (40.7). The revelations are recurring experiences:

> Once God spoke,
> twice I heard this,
> that power is of God
> and to thee, my Lord, pertains fidelity   (62.12).

God will speak to his soul saying 'I am thy salvation' (35.3). In the morning, a favoured hour of revelation (Isa. 50.4), he may thus be caused to hear God's *ḥesed*, and caused to know the course of action he should follow (143.8). The grace of hearing combines with that of seeing:

> From[82] thee my heart conveys the message
> 'Seek my face'.
> Thy face, Yahweh, I seek   (27.8).

His very psalms stem from inspiration, as when he castigates the wicked:

> An oracle about the sin of the wicked
> is in the midst of my heart   (36.2).

Having heard God's voice, he conveys the divine pronouncements (2.5f.; 75.3f.); kings of the earth thus hear them and are converted (138.4). Thus inspired, he may be said to have lips flowing with grace (45.3). His psalms often contain visionary portrayals of God (2.4; 11.4; 75.9; 102.20). He sees deep into the ways of evil, recognizing the spectres that haunt the city (55.10), perceiving the final fate of the wicked (73.17). The special relation of the king to the divine word and spirit (pp. 154, 156) also contributes to his privilege in such prophetic ministries. This view of kingship persists in New Testament times, when David is counted a prophet (Acts 2.30) and the eschatological prophet should be made king (John 6.14f.).

The king's judicial role can also be seen as part of his function. Judgment was ultimately of God and it seemed therefore best delivered by those most familiar with the holy sphere, his priestly servants. As chief of these servants, the king is the supreme judge, conveying God's justice (72.1f.; 75; 101; p. 141). Pilgrims to Jerusalem honour it as the scene of festal worship and of judgment given by the house of David (122.5). Because of his capacity to 'hear' the divine counsel, as just described, he is all the more fitted to decide difficult cases (I Kings 3.9; cf. John 5.30).

19. *The king's work of atonement*

In post-exilic times annual rites of atonement were carried out by the chief priest at Jerusalem, who with sacrifice and other ceremonies made expiation for anything amiss in himself and his family, in the sanctuary, and in the whole people.[83] A similar atoning role is envisaged for the ruler in Ezekiel 45.17. We can confidently assume that ideas and rites of this kind will have existed also in the time of the monarchy and that the king, in view of his priestly role as just described, will have taken an important part in the proceedings. It has often been pointed out that the accoutrements of the post-exilic chief priest have been taken over from the earlier kings, implying also a transference of functions.[84] It is particularly interesting that one of the most important items which the chief priest inherited from the kings, the golden flower attached to the front of the turban, is said to have atoning significance (Ex. 28.36–8).[85] Wearing this emblem, which is inscribed 'Holy to Yahweh' (*qōdeš lyhwh*), the chief priest will 'bear the iniquity', i.e. make atonement, for anything displeasing to God in the people's gifts; 'perpetually' or 'regularly' (*tāmīd*) on his forehead, it will serve to make the people acceptable (*lᵉrāṣōn*) before Yahweh. While the form of this interpretation may indeed be post-exilic, there is no need to assume that the association of ideas was a wholly new invention. It is probable that it builds upon an earlier link between the emblem of the royal office and a royal work of atonement. The character of the emblem, a flower, points to a relation between such atonement and the king's special gift of life and life-giving power.[86]

It is notable that Solomon's great prayer at the autumn festival and consecration of the temple (I Kings 8) founds a way of reconciliation: 'and when thou hearest, forgive'. In a similar festal context, the remembrance of David's voluntary suffering served to secure God's favour on the dynasty and society (Ps. 132.1).

It is possible that in Psalm 56 we have a prayer of the king recited at a ceremony of expiation quite similar to that of the scapegoat, for the most plausible explanation of the superscription is
that a dove was released into the desert towards the 'distant gods',
the powers of Sheol, just as the goat was sent to Azazel; thus guilt
was dispatched to oblivion (cf. Zech. 5.5–11; p. 75). The further
heading *miktām* ('covering'?) may also point to an aim of atonement (p. 47); all its occurrences are over psalms claimed as royal
in chapter II (Pss. 16; 56; 57; 59; 60), except Psalm 58 which is at
least national in reference. Psalm 102 may disclose to us, even if
indirectly, the custom of the king, afflicted in penitential rites of
fasting and weeping in sackcloth and ashes, pleading for the good
of Zion. His own person here is the focus of the needs of all his
people, so that the bearing of his prayer turns now upon himself,
now upon the community, without any sense of transition. The
restoration of Zion in a time of grace, when the appointment
(*mō'ēd*) is kept (v. 14), reflects the liturgical tradition of atonement
and restoration in the new year (p. 80).

In Psalm 22 the king's own person, degraded in symbolic death,
becomes a turning point; from his humiliation there opens the
prospect of new life and joy for all; the sacrificial meal betokens
unhindered communion between God and man; the kingship of
God is experienced with new force and his life-giving power
touches even the denizens of Sheol. The symbolic royal 'death'
could thus be said to be availing on behalf of God's community,
although we should probably not translate 116.15 to this effect
(p. 82). A similar pattern can be traced in Psalm 144, where
God's rescue of his king from the powers of evil gives prospect of
healthy fertility among the crops, animals and people of his realm.
In such securing of God's grace and removal of the threat to life,
there is implicit the royal work of atonement.

Even though, at the end of the day, it is essential that the king
be found 'righteous' or acceptable to God (cf. 101; 18.21 etc.;
cf. p. 168), it seems that in the great annual ceremonies he had to
make radical confession of his sins, taking upon himself also the
burden of all his people (Ps. 51); such self-depreciation is part of
the righteousness which pleases God. He prays for purification in
words which hint that, as in the case of the Babylonian king, his
annual affliction included receiving blows. After his ordeals he can
say:

> I shall not die but live
> and recount the works of Yah.
> Sorely did Yah scourge me
> but he did not give me over to death　(118.17f.).

A hint of such blows is found also in Psalm 51, where the 'washing' from sin may resemble the process of beating and stamping the dirt out of clothes (*kbs*):

> Thoroughly pound me clean of my iniquity . . .　(v. 4).

> Thou shalt pound me clean
> and I shall be whiter than snow　(v. 9).

God's chastisement can even be said to have broken his bones (v. 10). Perhaps there is a reminiscence of the blows suffered by the righteous king also in the language of 73.13f.:

> But in vain I cleansed my heart
> and washed my hands in purity,
> for I was stricken all the day
> and chastised every morning.

Other cleansing ceremonies in the annual rite will have included sprinkling, sometimes from a hyssop shrub,[87] with holy water or sacrificial blood:

> With hyssop thou shalt rid me of sin
> and I shall be clean　(51.9). .

All this indicates how in the ceremonies of atonement the king's own person had a central significance, outweighing the value of the animal sacrifices of expiation which were also part of the ceremonies. One may speculate whether the expiatory bull was originally in substitution for the king. Various practices of substitution for the king and others in special circumstances are known in neighbouring countries,[88] while the principle of substituting an animal for a human sacrifice was well established in Israel;[89] the notion of efficacious sacrifice of a leader may occasionally be glimpsed in Israelite narratives (Num. 25.4; Ex. 32.32; II Sam. 21; II Kings 3.27; cf. Deut. 3.26; 4.21). However this may be, it seems that there was a tendency to make comparison between the king's self-offering in the rites of humiliation and the sacrifice of the animals, a comparison which taught that it was the former which was the essential. In his elevated position as confidant of God and master of the temple ceremonies, he can declare with remarkable boldness God's view of the matter:

> Sacrifice and offering thou didst not relish,
> so thou didst reveal to my hearing;
> burnt offering and sin offering thou didst not ask.
> Then I responded, Behold I enter
> as written of me in the roll of the protocol.
> To do thy will, O my God, I am ready;
> truly thy law is within my inner parts[90] (40.7–9; p. 43).

In another context he can hope that his prayer with raised palms may be as availing as the incense and evening offerings (141.2; p. 85).

In his appeal to God at the festival, the afflicted king represents the utmost human weakness and suffering; as '*ānī*, the poor and needy one (22.25; cf. p. 180), he both shows his humility, depending on God alone, and appeals to the heavenly King who undertakes the rescue of the poor. So the ordeal shows him in a pathetic condition: a worm (22.7), a rejected stone (118.22), one who is mocked, hunted, smitten into the dust (22; 89). The king's prayers from real crises take up the same theme: here is one afflicted and helpless (35.10; 40.18; 69.30; 140.13 etc.), who even suffers for God's sake (69.8–10; 44.23 with his people).

The afflictions which the king undergoes in his ritual ordeals also express the profoundest penitence on behalf of all the community, the crushing of all evil self-will. The king gives expression to such penitence in his prayer and declares that this his 'broken heart' is the sacrifice which God wants above all else:

> For thou dost not relish sacrifice,
> though I gladly give it;
> burnt offering is not thy pleasure.
> God's favourite sacrifices are a broken spirit,
> the broken and crushed heart, O God,
> thou dost not scorn   (51.18f.).

On this basis the king can confidently make intercession for Zion, that God will deal well with her in his good favour, *rāṣōn* (v. 20). It was this good favour, *rāṣōn*, which, as we have seen, the king's gold headpiece signified, gaining the people acceptance before Yahweh. When Jerusalem's walls are accordingly blessed and 'built up',[91] the king concludes, Yahweh will enjoy the offering of sacrifices of communion and (presumably) glad testimony (v. 21).

20. *The king as admonisher of mankind*

As ruler of men on God's behalf, the king cannot be solely concerned with subjugating them by military and administrative power. No less than any other upholder of divine law or any cultic leader, priest or prophet, he must stand before the people and address them with teachings and exhortations, now warning them, now encouraging them. But whereas a Moses or a Samuel directs his admonition to the representative gathering of Israel, it is appropriate for the king, with his world-wide commission, to address all mankind or their rulers.

The importance of this part of the king's duties is shown by the prominence it is given in the central rites of his office. Thus in Psalm 2 the king devotes himself to such admonition of the rulers of the peoples of the world; he warns them against rebellion, exhorts them to worship Yahweh with awe and submission, and testifies that this is the true way of happiness:

> Now therefore, O kings, act wisely,
> be admonished, O rulers of the earth.
> Worship Yahweh with fear,
> sing praises with awe.
> Kiss in submission,[92]
> lest he angers and you perish from the way,
> for his anger will blaze suddenly.
> Happy are all who shelter in him (2.10f.).

This admonition is linked with his conveyance of an oracle (vv. 5 and 7). A similar admonition in Psalm 75 is linked with prophetic and judicial powers; the king conveys an oracle in vv. 3f. and from v. 5 he amplifies God's message with an address to the rebellious:

> I declare to the boasters, Boast not,
> and to the wicked, Raise not your horn,
> raise not your horn so high,
> speak not with arrogant neck.
> For not from east or west
> nor from the wilderness comes exaltation,
> but God rules,
> abasing one, exalting another (75.5–8).

Somewhat similar is the rebuke of the arrogant in I Samuel 2.3f.,
originally a royal psalm (v. 10).

An admonition in Psalm 4 resumes the themes of Psalm 2, for
the king warns men not to despise his high office and summons
them to loyalty and true religion:

> O sons of men, how long must my glory be derided,
> how long will you prefer futility
> and seek a false god?
> But know that Yahweh has honoured his covenant partner,
> Yahweh hears when I call upon him.
> Stand in awe and do not rebel.
> Contemplate on your couch and be silent.
> Sacrifice communion-sacrifices
> and trust in Yahweh   (4.3–6).

The tone of the warning address is sometimes sharper:

> Why do you glory in evil, O mighty man . . .?
> God shall surely uproot you for ever . . .   (52.3f.).

> How long will you raise your shouts against a man,
> how long will you all attack
> as against a leaning wall, a crumbling defence?   (62.4)

> Understand, most stupid of people!
> You fools, when will you learn wisdom?
> . . . Will not the teacher of nations chastise?   (94.8f.)

To others his tone is more one of encouragement:

> Trust in him at all times, O people,
> pour out your heart before him . . .
> Trust not in wrong-doing . . .   (62.9f.).

> How can you say to my soul,
> 'flee, birds, to your mountains'?
> Yahweh is in his holy temple,
> his eyes see,
> his gaze examines the sons of men   (11.1f.).

21. *The king as God's witness to the world*

In the passages just treated there is apparent an element of testimony, as the king avers that Yahweh alone is worthy of men's
trust and that his way alone is the way of happiness. This brings us

to one of the chief works to which the king is called, his work of religious witness.[93] From the uniquely rich experience that the king has of God, he must bear witness for him before the congregation and in principle before all the world. It is likely that this is the royal task denoted by the Davidic title in Isaiah 55.4, 'witness for the peoples'; a similar sense of '*ēd*, 'witness' is found in Isaiah 43.10f. and 44.8f., where the Israelites are called to testify to other nations about the marvels of Yahweh's salvation and his superiority to other gods.

With a wonderful story to tell of his own salvation, the king undertakes to testify of Yahweh's work before all peoples:

> Therefore I will confess thee among the nations, Yahweh,
> and thy name will I celebrate   (18.50).

> Confirmed is my heart, O God,
> confirmed my heart;
> I will sing and celebrate.
> Awake, my glory!
> Awake, lute and harp!
> I will awaken the angel of dawn.
> I will confess thee among the peoples, Lord,
> I will celebrate thee among the peoples.
> For high as the heavens is thy fidelity,
> and thy truth as the skies   (57.8–11).

Enthroned before God for ever, replenished with life, the rescued king will carry on this work perpetually:

> So shall I celebrate thy name for ever,
> fulfilling my vows day after day   (61.9).

> Truly thy faithful love is better than life;
> my lips glorify thee.
> Surely I will bless thee through all my life;
> proclaiming thy name, I will raise my hands.
> My soul shall be feasted with rich fare,
> and with singing lips my mouth shall give praise   (63.4–6).

> Open to me the gates of righteousness!
> I will enter them and confess Yah   (118.19).

> O God, a new song I will sing in thy praise,
> with a ten-stringed lute I will celebrate thee
> as giver of salvation to the kings,
> as deliverer of David thy servant   (144.9f.).

I will confess Yahweh with all my heart,
I will recount all thy miracles.
I will rejoice and exult in thy praise,
I will celebrate thy name, O Most High   (9.2f.).

Thus, with his own mouth, the king will cause men to know of
Yahweh's work in promise and fulfilment, which he, in the
Davidic covenant, has pre-eminently experienced:

Yahweh's acts of fidelity I will sing for ever,
to all generations I will make known
thy faithfulness with my mouth   (89.2).

Indeed, the royal role of witness is a theme of basic importance in
this great psalm (p. 186), and it would be appropriate if the term
'*ēd* in v. 38 in fact denoted the king;[94] the point would be the contrast between the ideal of the king seated on the divine throne on
the cloud-capped holy mountain and the humiliated king, flung
down and desecrated in the dust:

His seed shall continue for ever,
and his throne in my presence like the sun;
like the moon he is confirmed eternally,
and he is established to be witness in the clouds   (89.37f.).

That the king, on his exalted throne, can send out his witness
through the celestial regions is a conception taken up in Psalm
138.1:

I will confess thee with all my heart,
in the presence of the gods I will celebrate thee   (cf. 57.9).

The outreach of the royal testimony can also be illustrated from
22.23f. In the first place it is heard by the festal assembly, the
brotherly fellowship of 'fearers of Yahweh':

I will tell of thy name to my brethren,
in the midst of the congregation I will praise thee . . .
Of thee is my praise in the great congregation,
my vows I will fulfil before his fearers.

But it soon appears that all nations are affected (vv. 28f.), even the
dead, and since the dynastic continuance has been confirmed, the
Davidic witness will continue to make its impact on generations
yet unborn (vv. 31f., p. 167).

In Mesopotamia also there is stress on the king's task as pro-
claimer of his deity's glory to all peoples, among the gods, and for
ever.[95] The Hittite king Hattusilis III presents his justification for
his seizure of power in the form of a testimony to his goddess:
'I tell the divine power of Ishtar; let all men hear it . . .', and he
begins and ends by ordering the devotion of all future kings of his
'seed' to her (Gurney, *Hittites*, pp. 175f.).

22. *The role of witness as a plea in royal prayers*

Because of his special role of witness, the king is able to strengthen
his prayers by pointing to the new force which his testimony will
gain when he is delivered. He will sing a 'new song' (144.9; cf.
40.4), accompanied by instruments of rare worth (144.9; 43.4;
71.22f.; cf. 92.4), by costly sacrifices (66.13–15; 54.8; 56.13;
116.16f.), confessing God when he presides over the vast assembly
of Israel (35.18; cf. 22.26; 40.10f.; 52.10f.; 116.12f.), witnessing to
all the world (57.8–11), maintaining his testifying praises in the
daily cult (61.9; 92.2f.; cf. 35.28; 71.22f.) and through the unending succession of the dynasty (52.10f.; 61.9; 75.10; cf. 89.2).

He can also sharpen his appeals by indicating how incongruous
it would be if God were to forsake one so prominent in testifying
to his faithfulness. Thus in Psalm 40, before praying for God's
love, fidelity and truth (vv. 12f.) he stresses how he has borne witness in the festal assembly to God's faithful power.

> I proclaimed the victory of righteousness
> in the great congregation.
> Behold, my lips I did not restrain,
> Yahweh, thou thyself knowest it.
> Thy righteous work I did not hide
> in the midst of my heart,
> thy faithfulness and salvation I announced.
> I did not conceal thy fidelity and truth
> from the great congregation   (40.10f.).

Earlier in the psalm, the better to establish his point, he has
actually delivered in compact form a typical piece of royal testimony (vv. 2–6). The same intention may be found in Psalms 42–43,
for before praying for the covenant-graces, he recalls how he used
to lead the procession and the praising testimonies (see p. 174).
Certainly in Psalm 89 the king strengthens his great prayer of

lament both by pointing to himself as God's principal witness
(vv. 2f., 38, p. 184) and by giving a specimen of his habitual testimony to the power and fidelity of God (vv. 6–19). Towards one
so prominent in telling of his fidelity, how can Yahweh deal so
unfaithfully as to violate the Davidic covenant? In Psalms 9–10 he
points to himself as recounter of God's deeds (9.2f.) and promises
so to continue (9.15), while also actually delivering specimens of
his praising witness (9.4–13, 16–19; 10.16); and all this in support
of his lamenting prayer (9.14, 20f.; 10.1–15). Yet another example
is Psalm 27. Before the king begins his supplication in v. 7, he
testifies to Yahweh's grace (broadly vv. 1–6) and speaks of his
celebrating Yahweh with festal sacrifices and music (v. 6, a vow
here?). Psalm 86 is another striking example, the sorrowful prayer
being supported by praise using the great themes of royal witness
– Yahweh's uniqueness, the conversion of the nations, his miracles,
his fidelity to his king whom he delivers from Sheol etc. (vv. 8f.).
Psalms 108 and 36 also precede the call for help with a fine demonstration of testifying praise.

In Psalm 71, where the king makes ample use of his calling to be
God's witness to strengthen his prayer, it is not easy to be sure
where he is vowing future thanksgiving and where he is pointing
to witness that he has faithfully accomplished. The latter alterna-
tive may be right in vv. 7f.:

> I have stood as a sign to the multitudes,
> whilst thou wast my shelter of power;
> my mouth has been filled with thy praise,
> all day long telling thy glory.

The king has thus appeared as a living proof of God's salvation
standing out before the vast assembly, for he has uniquely experienced God's grace and then declared it to the concourse of worshippers. How could he now be cast aside in the time of old age
(v. 9)? Again, in v. 17, he points to his past witness:

> O God, thou hast taught me from my childhood
> and to the present time I have declared thy miracles.

But then he uses the plea of his future witness:

> As for me, continually I shall hope
> and I shall add to all thy praise.
> My mouth shall recount thy righteousness,

all the day thy salvation . . .
I will enter with (proclamation of)
the mighty acts of the Lord Yahweh,
I will commemorate thy righteousness, thine alone.
Forsake me not,
till I declare the deeds of thine arm
to (rising) generations,
and thy might to all who shall come[96] . . .   (71.14–24).

23. *The king's witness is inspired*

In 71.17 the parallelism suggests that the king's ability to give eloquent testimony of God's work arises from God's tuition:

> O God, thou hast taught me from my childhood,
> and to the present time I have declared thy miracles.

In 51.14–17 also, there is a suggestion that God inspires the king's edifying witness. His prayer for the holy spirit and royal spirit (pp. 71, 157) leads to his undertaking to teach sinners God's ways (v. 15), and he hopes that God will open his lips in testimony:

> Deliver me from every stain, O God,
> the God of my salvation,
> and my lips shall sing of thy righteous work.
> O my lord, thou shalt open my lips
> and my mouth shall declare thy praise   (51.16f.).

It is Yahweh who puts in the king's mouth his song of good tidings in the festal drama (40.4, p. 42), in accordance with the fact that his appointment so to witness is from Yahweh (Isa. 55.4, p. 183). Indeed, the work of God to which the king testifies is a profound mystery which is hidden from the godless; but God has shown it to his king, enabling him to sing with joy the gospel of God's triumph over evil (92.1–7). We may compare the emphasis in II Samuel 23.1f. that the following utterance of the king concerning just rule is inspired:

> The spirit of Yahweh speaks through me,
> and his word is upon my tongue . . .

24. *Sacrifice in relation to the king's witness*

There was a close link between sacrifice and testimony, since the experience of God's help was often marked by sacrifice for the purpose of thanksgiving. The act itself and the words of testimony that accompanied it, often in fulfilment of a vow made in the time of distress, together served as *tōdā*, public confession of Yahweh the only Saviour. Since the king was already prominent both as God's witness and as the chief provider of sacrifices, the two elements will have featured prominently in royal acts of thanksgiving (66.15f.; 27.6). A good illustration occurs in Psalm 116, where the king is offering votive sacrifices and libations as he stands at the altar in the presence of the people of God and proclaims the name and attributes of Yahweh.

We have already seen how in the matter of atonement the parts played by the king's own person and the sacrifices themselves gave rise to a comparison being drawn: it was the king's own self-offering which had greatest value in Yahweh's sight (p. 179). It might be expected that in the matter of testimony also, comparison might be made between the value of the sacrifices and that of the king's praising witness, to the advantage of the latter. Such seems to be the case in 69.31f.:

> I will praise the name of God with a song,
> and I will magnify it with confession,
> and this shall please Yahweh more than an ox,
> more than a bull perfect in horn and hoof.

25. *The subject of the king's witness*

To a great extent the king's testimony in praise of Yahweh centres on what Yahweh has done for him personally. Sometimes there is a story of deliverance to tell, in form at least referring to a particular occasion. He was in mortal danger, he cried to Yahweh, was heard and saved:

> Lamenting (p. 114), I called upon Yahweh
> and from my enemies I was saved.
> The cords of death bound me about,
> the torrents of Belial overwhelmed me,
> the cords of Sheol encircled me,
> the traps of death assailed me.
> In my distress I called upon Yahweh
> and to my God I shouted for help.
> In his temple he heard my voice,
> and my crying to him reached his ears ...   (18.4f., cf. 116.2f.).

I waited long for Yahweh (*or* cried loudly to Y.)[97]
and he inclined to me and heard my cry,
and he brought me up from the roaring pit,
from the miry bog,
and he set my feet upon the rock,
securing my steps   (40.2–3).

The 'particular occasion' seems sometimes to have been the symbolic enactment of deliverance in the annual sacraments (see chapter III), and so leads all the more readily to a description of continuing grace rather than of an event:

Truly thou dost light my lamp, Yahweh;
my God illumines my darkness.
By thee I run at a troop,
and by my God I can leap a wall   (18.29f.).

Yahweh is my light . . .
When the evil ones advance on me to devour my flesh
they stumble and fall,
when a camp is pitched against me
my heart fears not,
when an army rises against me,
I trust in this   (27.1–3).

The testimony of Psalm 23 can be understood as pointing both to the rite of deliverance and also to a continuing privilege:

Yahweh is my shepherd . . .
He restores my soul,
he leads me in the highway of righteousness   (p. 174)
for the sake of his name.
Though I walk through the chasm of the death-shadow,
I fear no evil . . .

Indeed, testimony to the enduring grace of Yahweh towards him appears as a favourite motif in the king's psalms, whether it is part of a psalm of thanksgiving (18.2f., 29–31; 118.14 etc.) or used to strengthen a supplication (3.4; 54.6 etc.). Particularly eloquent are epithets of God which express his grace to his king (p. 170):

Yahweh is my crag and my stronghold and my rescuer,
my God, my rock in which I shelter,
my shield and the horn of my salvation,
my high fortress   (18.3).

> Blessed be Yahweh my rock
> who trains my hands for battle,
> my fingers for war;
> my fidelity and my stronghold,
> my high fortress and my rescuer,
> my shield and he in whom I shelter,
> he who subdues my people under me   (144.1f.).

The importance of such personal testimony for the general audience is not always stated explicitly. They are expected to know that the relationship he tells of is significant in itself (cf. 2.6), – their king enjoying God's favour. An example is Psalm 23, which strikingly lacks any application of the testimony for the benefit of an audience. In other cases, however, the relevance of the attested relationship is suggested or even clearly spelt out. He is backed by Yahweh and must be obeyed (Pss. 2; 4; 18; 62). Since God's favour to his king results in blessing for the people, such royal testimony is the signal for rejoicing (22.24f.; 35.27; 40.17f.; 69.7; 118.24; 140.13f.; cf. 20.6).

But the king's exaltation is not a separation from the people. He is their representative, the one in whom all have a part. It is appropriate, therefore, that often the king's personal testimony is applied as an example for all. What God has done for him displays the principles of God's dealings with mankind as a whole. The personal story is thus extended to a universal application:

> Yahweh dealt with me according to my righteousness,
> according to the cleanness of my hands he rewarded me . . .
> With the true covenant-partner thou dealest truly,
> with the loyal thou art loyal,
> with the pure thou art pure,
> but the crooked thou wilt entangle.
> Thou indeed dost save a humble people,
> but haughty looks thou dost bring low   (18.21–28).

> Happy is the man who has made Yahweh his confidence,
> and turned not to idols and false gods   (40.5).

In 66.18f. the lesson to be drawn from his case is suggested less directly, but still clearly enough:

> If I had tolerated evil in my heart,
> the Lord would not have heard me.
> But God did hear me,
> he attended to the sound of my prayer.

The king's witness to what God does for him is often closely bound up with his witness to God's mighty works as Creator and Ruler of all. Indeed, these two forms of witness are sometimes so perfectly united as to indicate that the salvation of the world is indeed bound up with the salvation of the king.

The two subjects of testimony are linked in Psalm 89. In witnessing to Yahweh's covenant love, the king is chiefly thinking of God's relation to the dynasty, but this is aligned with God's triumphant ascendancy over the sea, Rahab, his enemies and all heavenly beings (vv. 6f.), his creation of the world and his life-giving rule.

The integration of the two subjects (salvation of king and world) is more thorough in Psalms 9–10. The king testifies and rejoices that his enemies have fled before Yahweh. The statement that Yahweh has thus vindicated him is parallel to one that Yahweh is enthroned as righteous ruler (9.5). This enthronement is the theme of what follows. Yahweh has 'roared' at the rebellious nations, banished the armies of chaos and established himself as universal ruler and saviour of the poor (9.6f.). These achievements (*ᵃlilōt*) of Yahweh are to be further declared among all nations. At this point the king breaks off his witness and pleads for himself in some present distress:

> Be gracious to me, Yahweh;
> See the affliction I suffer from my enemies,
> thou that raisest me up from the gates of death (9.14).

A similar integration is evident in Psalm 92. The king, given special insight, bears witness to Yahweh's work, deeds and plans which achieve the overthrow of Yahweh's enemies. Immediately (v. 11) he refers to his own exaltation by Yahweh, Yahweh's gift to him of vital power, and the defeat of his enemies.

The conclusion of Psalm 22 shows a similar association. Praising Yahweh for his deliverance, the king proclaims Yahweh's universal kingship (v. 29) and envisages the ever-widening circle of his worshippers (cf. 69.31–37).

In the light of such passages, it becomes easier to draw together the elements in Psalm 40. The king testifies to his own salvation, but understands it to have a far-reaching significance. 'Multitudes' will be affected (v. 4). It is aligned with the mighty works and miracles which Yahweh does for his people (v. 6). All is a unity of

salvation for which the king responds in self-offering (vv. 7–9).
So his testimony is not just a story of an individual's delivery, but
a gospel, an announcement of a great victory of God for the salvation of all the society (v. 10). He has a 'new song' to sing (v. 4),
and elsewhere such a new song is clearly associated with the
proclamation of God's victorious kingship (p. 43).

Apart from such cases of the linking of the salvation of king and
world, it is not surprising that the king's work as witness should
include the reciting or 'remembering' of the traditions of primeval
or ancestral salvation. Since this was the core of Israelite worship,
the king as cult-leader inherited the task. In Psalm 77 he counters
the prevailing suffering with such a recitation. He sings the
memorial (*zkr*), intones (*hgh*), recites or chants (*syh*) the tradition
of Yahweh's deeds (*ma'alālīm, pele', pō'al, 'alīlōt*, 77.12f.). Likewise
in 143.5:

> I make remembrance of the days of the ancient time,
> I intone the tradition of thy work,
> I chant the action of thy hands . . .

In 71.14f. he speaks of recounting Yahweh's righteous work and
salvation which surpass all telling; he enters the temple to tell of
Yahweh's mighty works, to make remembrance of his righteous
work; all his life he has been presenting the story of his miracles
(p. 186).

26. *Characteristic elements of the king's witness*

Several recurring items in the royal testimony are worth notice by
way of summary.

Frequent are the *exhortations to trust in Yahweh* rather than in any
other powers or human prowess:

> It is better to shelter in Yahweh
> than to trust in man,
> better to shelter in Yahweh
> than to trust in princes   (118.8f.; cf. 20.8; 44.7; 108.13).

Rather similar is Ishtar's oracle to the Assyrian king Esarhaddon,
'Fear not . . . trust not in men, turn your eyes to me, look always
to me'; and also Ashurbanipal's statement, 'It is not by the power
of my bow, but by the force of my gods . . . that I vanquish my
enemies' (Labat, pp. 258, 261).

The Israelite king must oppose the temptation to gain strength through other cults:

> Happy the man who has made Yahweh his confidence
> and has not turned to idols and false gods!   (40.5)

Such 'vanity' and 'lies' must be put away, and all trust placed in Yahweh (4.2–6). Human strength also is vapour and lies; only Yahweh is powerful and reliable (62.9–13). The theme can be made into a plea from human frailty:

> Yahweh, what is man that thou shouldest know him,
> the son of man that thou shouldest think of him?
> Man is like vapour,
> his days like a passing shadow   (144.3f.).

Another favourite item is *Yahweh's incomparability*:

> Who is god except Yahweh
> and who is rock but our God?   (18.32)

> Who in the clouds compares with Yahweh,
> who is like Yahweh among the sons of the gods?   (89.7)

> Such great things thou hast done –
> O God, who is like thee?   (71.19; cf. 86.10; I Sam. 2.2)

The comparison turns on the mighty acts also in 40.6:

> Thou hast multiplied thy miracles, Yahweh my God,
> and in thy purposes for us thou art beyond compare.
> If I declare and proclaim them,
> they surpass all telling.

Similarly 77.14:

> O God, thy way is in holy power.
> What deity is as great as God?

It is characteristic of the king's praise *to 'bless' Yahweh*:

> Yahweh lives and blessed be my rock
> and exalted be the God of my salvation!   (18.47f.)

> Blessed be Yahweh for he has heard
> the sound of my supplications,
> Yahweh my power and my shield . . .   (28.6f.).

> Blessed be Yahweh my rock!   (144.1)

> Blessed be God who has not turned back my prayer
> nor his fidelity from me   (66.20).

> Blessed be Yahweh
> for he marvellously showed his fidelity for me
> in a besieged city   (31.22).

Such blessing he promises to utter:

> So I will bless thee all my life,
> proclaiming thy name I will raise my hands   (63.5).

> I will bless Yahweh who has counselled me   (16.7).

Another recurring item is the commendation of faith by *use of 'aš^erē, 'happy is he who'*:

> Happy are all who shelter in him!   (2.12)

> Happy is the people in such a state!
> Happy the people that has Yahweh for its God!   (144.15)

> Happy the man that has made Yahweh his confidence!   (40.5)

In this last example, the formula is useful in turning the king's experience into a lesson of general application (p. 190). A similar tendency may be found in 94.12, in view of what has been said above about Yahweh's instruction and chastisement of the king (pp. 147f., 179):

> Happy is the man whom Yah scourges
> and from thy instruction thou teachest him!

In 41.2, however, the generalization seems to contain a reference to royal duty and to be quoted here specifically in favour of the praying king: Happy is such a man and God will heal him when sick . . . and am I not such a man and will not God heal me now? Such seems to be the implied thought.

Another common feature is *the king's accumulation of epithets for God in relation to himself*, as already discussed (p. 172). Characteristic also is *his praise of God's covenant-love* (fidelity, truth, etc., p. 153); also *his praise of God's word* (p. 154) and *his celebration of the name of Yahweh* (p. 156).

Finally mention may be made of *the theme of answered prayer*. This has special significance in the king's psalms, since it corresponds to an aspect of his privilege (p. 195). Emphatic use of this theme occurs in the testimony of 18.4, 7 quoted above (p. 188). So also 116.1f. (p. 169); 28.6 (p. 41); 66.17 (p. 51) and 40.2 (p. 189). Another example is 118.5:

> Hemmed in by danger I called upon Yah,
> Yah answered me and gave me liberty.

Or again, 138.3:

> On the day when I called,
> thou didst answer me;
> thou didst make me exult,
> my soul being filled with power.

27. *The king's grace of answered prayer*

'Everything proceeding from the lips of his Majesty', it was said of the Pharaoh, 'his father (the god) Amon causes to be realized there and then.' The sun god 'rises in the horizon each day to hear all his prayer'; Re says each day 'what is there in your heart that I may accomplish for you?' (Posener, pp. 42f.). Of the Assyrian king it is said that, when he makes his daily sacrifices, 'his prayer will be well received by the god' (Labat, p. 136); again, 'on the order of the great gods he attained the object of the desires of his heart' (Seux, p. 143); sometimes his only weapon was prayer, in response to which his gods destroyed the coalitions of his foes (Labat, p. 264). The Hittite king had the prerogative of *evocatio*, whereby he could call on the deities of a hostile city to come over to him with the enemy's goods (Dussaud, p. 351).

A decisive moment in the classical story of King David's tribulations concerns a prayer of the king: may Yahweh bring to folly the counsel which Ahitophel will give to the forces of the usurper Absalom! Against all worldly probabilities the king's prayer is signally answered; at once Hushai presents himself and the counter-measures proceed successfully, to the doom of Ahitophel and his master (II Sam. 15.31f.).[98] On another occasion it is clear that a subject might have faith in the special efficacy of the king's prayers on his behalf (II Sam. 14.11). Again, the weight of the king's execration was such that it could be deemed sufficient to replace judicial retribution (II Sam. 3).

The psalms also indicate that the king is privileged in prayer. It belongs to his position as the one most favoured by God in intimacy and access. It is not fortuitous, therefore, that, as already noted, his testimonies so often include the theme of his prayers being answered (p. 194).

Sometimes he points to his privilege in prayer when warning his adversaries; they had better submit, lest he pray against them with deadly effect:

> O sons of men, how long must my glory be despised . . .
> Yahweh hears when I cry to him . . .   (4.3f., p. 182).

This is similar in effect to Psalm 2:

> Why do the nations rage . . .
> I will recount the statute of Yahweh,
> He declares to me: You are my son,
> Ask of me and I will make the nations your inheritance . . .
> Wherefore, O kings, act wisely . . .

This immense 'ask of me' may be compared with I Kings 3.5 (Solomon) and Psalm 89.27. In the latter God makes David supreme, his first-born son; and the implication is that his victories will be won chiefly by the weapon of prayer:

> He for his part will call to me,
> My father art thou, my God and the rock of my salvation.
> I for my part will make him first-born,
> most high over the kings of the earth.

In 91.15 the climax of Yahweh's promises to his king is that Yahweh will answer his prayers, deliver and glorify him. No wonder that in danger he can support his prayers with a declaration of trust in Yahweh who gives him supremacy through the answering of his prayers:

> But thou, Yahweh, art a shield about me,
> my glory and the lifter up of my head;
> with my voice I cry to Yahweh,
> and he answers me from his holy mountain   (3.4f.).

> When I cry to God Most High,
> to the God who accomplishes my cause,
> he sends from heaven to save me . . .   (57.3f.).

In 140.7 the privilege is claimed in a way that seems to echo the promise in 89.27:

> I declare to Yahweh, My God art thou,
> Give ear, Yahweh, to the sound of my petitions.

Indeed in a large number of passages where the king calls attention to the earnestness of his prayers and asks to be heard, we should remember this background of his privilege in prayer.[99] In the same connection we can also mention the boldness of expression which he often uses ('Arise', 'Awake' etc., p. 174).

In two royal psalms where the speaker is other than the king, there is also reference to the king's prayers as clearly of prime importance:

> May Yahweh answer thee in the day of distress . . .
> may he grant thee according to thy heart,
> may he fulfil all thy petitions . . .
> He will answer him from his holy heavens . . .   (Ps. 20).

> The desire of his heart thou hast given him,
> the request of his lips hast thou not refused.
> Life he asked of thee,
> thou hast given it him . . .   (Ps. 21.3, 5).

This prayer for life summarizes the most characteristic content of the king's prayers (cf. p. 160).

Another aspect emerges when, as he himself gives warning (p. 182), he invokes doom on his foes, the wicked, the oppressors of the community.[100] In a manner comparable with the Pharaoh's use of earthenware images, he sets up a verbal representation of the wicked and then, as it were, demolishes it with his powerful imprecation (7.12f.; 52 etc.). Here we can see the king inheriting duties from the old amphictyonic ministers whose curses purged and protected the society, not only against foreign enemies, but also against sinners, especially secret ones, within Israel.

The king's advantages in prayer, however, do not spare him agony. In the great royal rites he appealed to God in pathetic dirge-like style (Ps. 101, p. 123) and indeed prayed from the extremities of human weakness; in the same manner he prayed in times of war or sickness (p. 180). The meaning of the 'ask and I will give you' had to be worked out in accordance with the reason for the king's existence – that God's will be done.

V

CONCLUSION

Let us now draw together the main conclusions.

In chapter I general arguments were presented to show that, as Birkeland and Mowinckel had thought, far more of the psalms were composed for the use of Davidic kings than the ten which Gunkel and his many followers allow. Here was a treasure-house of material to help solve important problems in the study of kingship. The argument first showed the inadequacy of non-royal interpretations and then collected twelve *a priori* considerations favouring a royal interpretation of the Psalms of the Individual.

In chapter II each of the disputed psalms was examined in turn. Thirty-one were found to contain clearly royal elements and to fit well in detail and as a whole with a royal interpretation. A further twenty-three were less obvious cases, but in the wake of the preceding studies they could with probability be recognized as utterances of the king. The various situations in which the king offered these psalms were reviewed on pp. 130f. Some were located in regular rituals, but most seemed to have been composed in a crisis, often the threat of war; other misfortunes include the insecurity of an ageing king, sickness, dearth, and foreign domination. Some psalms are connected with royal incubation or other ways of seeking guidance by oracle or augury.

To clarify the functions of the royal psalmody further, chapter III examined rites of new year and enthronement first in Mesopotamia, Egypt, and the Hittite and Canaanite states, and then in Israel. The great royal psalms of Gunkel's group were studied individually and found to be mostly from rites renewing the royal office in the autumn festival. To this problematic but extremely important area of study the additional psalms claimed as royal made a useful contribution, both those from the heart of the rituals and those that only reflect them. From all the evidence gathered, the presentation of the king's office in the autumn festival appeared to have been a lively drama of humiliation and glorification. It was a sacrament which both touched the current ruler and also conveyed an ideal prophetic vision.

Chapter IV displayed the main elements of the royal ideal of the psalms. In many cases it was possible to base the treatment on the generally recognized royal psalms and then develop it in more detail from the large group added in chapter II. In a few cases this additional group provided the main evidence, some check being furnished by data outside the psalms, as in the case of atonement. The additional psalms also helped us to grasp the significance of items represented in Gunkel's group but easily overlooked, such as the king's work as admonisher and witness for Yahweh before all peoples and his privilege in prayer. A summary of the elements of the royal ideal presented in this chapter is provided by the Contents, where the twenty-seven headings are listed. Especially noteworthy are the king's close and tender relationship with God, his protection by the angelic graces, his part in God's world-wide dominion, his deliverance from death into abundant life, his leadership in worship, which comprises functions of atonement, intercession, revelation, and evangelical witness.

The subject which has thus opened before us gives much food for thought. For one thing, there is much to ponder in the relation of the Davidic kingship to that of other ancient peoples. At many points in our discussion we have seen resemblances with holy monarchies of the Egyptians, Sumerians, Babylonians, Assyrians, Hittites and others. Each has in the end to be grasped in its wholeness and its own context; the great gaps in our knowledge must not be filled by gratuitous transfers of items from other cultures and epochs, still less by synthetic items which existed nowhere. Nevertheless, we have seen links between the divine/royal ideas and practices of the surrounding cultures on the one hand and the Israelite royal festivals and prayers on the other. No one who has discerned the sincerity, beauty, pathos and beneficence which could exist in the non-Israelite royal institutions would regret these links. It seems rather a strength of the biblical tradition that great things common to humanity from remote epochs entered it, to issue again as a new creation in the gospel, able to evoke response from all, as deep calls to deep.

Another matter for thought is the contrast between the high theory of the Davidic kingship and the poor light in which the kings often appeared. I have stressed that the royal portrait in the psalms is an ideal, though intersecting with actual experience (pp. 133f., ct. 120, 160, 199). Particular kings might be adjudged evil men (Jer. 22.13–19; II Kings 21); some circles even disapproved of the office itself (Judg. 8.23; I Sam. 8). For the most part, however, the Israelite was ready to ascribe high value to the leader he considered to have been selected by God. Such high valuation was accordingly found not only in the king's psalms. I have adduced passages from many other books of the OT to illustrate the royal ideals. From beginning and end of the Davidic dynasty this high valuation is attested (II Sam. 21.17; Lam. 4.20).

The prophetic literature likewise sees the Davidic dynasty as chosen by God but sometimes places the fulfilment of the royal ideal *in the future* (Isa. 11; 32; Jer. 23; Ezek. 37 etc.). This turning to the future was no doubt accentuated by the removal of the dynasty in the exile, and in an earlier age by despair over current rulers (Isa. 7). But it would be rash to ascribe the origin of the future hope wholly to such circumstances. In some form it is likely to be as old as kingship itself. We have noted the Hurrian belief in pre-Davidic times that ancient kings would return (p. 164); and the theme of future royal progeny, announced in visions and oracles, was no doubt an ancient concern, as in the Ugaritic text Keret. We have seen too that prophets had a considerable part in the royal rites, mediating promises of God and conveying his grace to the kings; no doubt they helped greatly to raise the drama to its level of intense imagination and rapture. And while we found that the rites were sacraments to benefit the king and society of that day, they also had prophetic quality in that they disclosed the perfect and ultimate in cosmic and social relations.

In the end, then, we see prophecy and the royal institution intertwined. While some modern interpreters persist in setting prophecy over against kingship, for the people of the OT both were complementary appointments of God, though both could be abused. The balance of my conclusions, with their positive appraisal of the royal office, is thus in accord with the ancient outlook. The Orthodox ikon tradition of the Madonna Hodegetria and Prophets speaks for me in this respect. The painters depict the child Messiah and his mother; on each side is a border of seven prophetic figures from the OT holding scrolls of oracles, and first among them are David on the one side and Solomon on the other.

NOTES

I HOW MANY PSALMS ARE ROYAL?
GENERAL ARGUMENTS

1. In *Einl.*, p. 172, he lists these as Pss. 3; 5; 6; 7; 13; 17; 22; 25; 26; 27.7–14; 28; 31; 35; 38; 39; 42; 43; 51; 54; 55; 56; 57; 59; 61; 63; 64; 69; 70; 71; 86; 88; 102; 109; 120; 130; 140–3. Attached to these are the 'psalms of confidence': 4; 11; 16; 23; 27.1–6; 62; 131; also parts of composite psalms such as 19; 36; 77; 94; 118; 119; 121; 123; 139; and a freer composition, 52. Johnson 'The Psalms' gives a good account of Gunkel's classification.

2. Delekat, p. 8; Beyerlin, pp. 15f.

3. Beyerlin, p. 16.

4. Cf. Hertzberg, p. 26.

5. G. W. Anderson, pp. 28f., describes Birkeland's work as illuminating but suffering from a lack of flexibility.

6. *KM*, p. 25, but p. 108 n. 84 is more cautious.

7. The article 'The Psalter' is translated in his *Critical Essays*.

8. The most balanced approach to psalm headings is, I consider, that of Mowinckel (*PIW* II, ch. 23), who finds here some data of great antiquity and not without value for research into the early use of the psalms. Recent contributions include those of Sawyer and Childs.

9. So Engnell, *SBU* II, cols. 672f.

10. For this extension cf. I Kings 12.16 and Ps. 144.10.

11. For these various possibilities cf. Mowinckel, *Ps. st.* VI, pp. 72f., and *PIW* II, pp. 98f.; Bentzen, *DSK*, pp. 49f.; Kraus, pp. xxixf.; Engnell, *SBU* II, cols. 627f.

12. It is found in the midrashic notes in some psalm headings (Pss. 3; 7; 18; 34; 51; 52; 54; 56; 57; 59; 60; 63; 142; Briggs I, p. lxiii). Cf. also the biblical tradition of David's skill in poetry and music: I Sam. 16.15f.; II Sam. 1.17f.; 3.33; 6.5; 23.1; I Chron. 23.5; Neh. 12.36; Amos 6.5.

13. E.g. the thanksgiving of Neb-re (*ANET*, p. 380), which specifies the circumstances; also the neo-Sumerian letter-prayers, specific and in prose, even if they contribute to the tradition of psalmody, as Hallo thinks.

14. Cf. Mowinckel, *PIW* II, pp. 111–25.

II   PARTICULAR PSALMS

1. A sketch of royal elements in the 'psalms of the individual' is attempted by Bernhardt, pp. 262–79. This work (as also de Fraine's) is right to attack some of the wilder contributions of the 'ritual pattern' school. But there is a lack of discrimination. Johnson has to complain that the distortion of his views by Bernhardt amounts to 'a farrago of misrepresentation' (*Book List* of the Society for OT Study, 1962, p. 42).

2. Mowinckel, *Ps. st.* I, p. 156, and *GT*; Birkeland, p. 175; Widengren, *Accadian Psalms*, p. 291. On the eve of consecrating the new temple, the Sumerian ruler Gudea spends the night in the old temple to be purified and inspired (Labat, pp. 255f.).

3. *Ps. st.* IV, p. 7; *PIW* II, p. 209; Engnell, *SBU* II, col. 633. Sumerian pieces of this type are studied by Dalglish, pp. 21f.

4. For 'secrets' denoting liturgy cf. *PIW* II, p. 216.

5. The essence of royal duty is expressed as the care of the weak in Jer. 21.12; 22.16; Ps. 72.12–14 and Ugaritic *Keret*.

6. *Ps. st.* I, p. 155; in *GT* related to a king. Birkeland, p. 355.

7. Cf. Gen. 27; Isa. 40.16; Ps. 50.10–12. Contrast Deut. 12.15. *PIW* II, p. 214.

8. Read *kārū*? Cf. Kraus. Tammuz in the underworld is attacked by demons who bind his hands and arms, *CR*, pp. 55f.

9. Lipiński (*Royauté*, pp. 326f.) compares Egyptian texts about the joy of the departed when the sun-god enters the netherworld. Cf. also the praise of Sethos I connected with his establishment of his mortuary temple: 'Mayest thou lead all the living, (thou being) at the head of the spirits upon the throne of Horus. Lo, thou art king upon the throne of Re . . . the underworld is hidden and joyful through thy counsels, thou awakenest those who are slumbering. Thou givest light to those who are in darkness . . . the cavern-dwellers lift up their faces' (David, p. 212.)

10. Snaith (*VT* Sup. 14, pp. 151f.) stresses that *nḥm* is 'comfort *out of* (not *in*) sorrow' and discusses the connection with the Syriac sense 'quicken the dead', 'resurrection'.

11. *ANEP*, no. 400, shows the Pharaoh and his queen sitting before a table of offerings under symbols of the sun-god. No. 859 shows a dignitary sitting with a cup before an offering table. Labat, fig. 3, shows Gudea given a cup by the gods. See Labat, p. 137, for the Assyrian king's participation in meals with the gods. Mesopotamian representations of two figures dining or drinking together have been connected with the king's role in the new-year festival (king/god with goddess) by van Buren, pp. 10–13, and Moortgat (*CR*, pp. 18–41).

12. For this and the following see further my article in *The Bible Translator* 16. Merrill independently comes to similar conclusions and connects the psalm with enthronement rites.

13. Gunkel, *Einl.*, p. 148; Bentzen, *DSK*, p. 83, comparing Ezek. 16.5f. and the Sargon legend (*ANET*, p. 119); Birkeland, p. 182. Cf. Gudea to his goddess: 'I have no mother, you are my mother; I have no father, you are my father' (Labat, p. 57).

14. Gunkel compares their aim 'to eat my flesh' with King Kila-muwa's description of the attacks of enemy kings, but the sense of the phrase in the inscription is not certain (Donner, Nr. 24; *ANET*, p. 500; Birkeland, p. 187).

15. Cf. such leading in Pss. 5 and 23; indeed *l^ema^can* in 27.11 may have a sense like *neged* in 23.5, 'over against'. Cf. also *l^ema'an* in 5.9; 8.3; 69.19. Buttenwieser, p. 180, is also sensitive to the nuance in these passages, but his derivation of the word (as an infinitive 'to refute') seems unnecessary.

16. Deut. 31.7, 23; Josh. 1.6f., 9, 18. Cf. Noth, *Joshua*, pp. 28f.

17. Or, with some Mss, 'Y. is the power of his people/army'.

18. For such encouraging words, cf. the 'Fear not' sayings in the holy war (von Rad, *Der Heilige Krieg*, p. 10). But the actual designation of God as 'my/thy salvation' is rare, and always, in my view, with reference to the king, Zion, or Israel: 27.1; 35.3; 62.3 (cf. 89.27); Isa. 12.2; 62.11.

19. For *yigdal yhwh* cf. Num. 14.16f.; II Sam. 7.26; Mal. 1.5; for *ḥpṣ* cf. p. 146; for 'servant', p. 149.

20. 'The King's Self-sacrifice'. Cf. also my *Psalms* and my article 'The King as God's Witness', pp. 32–5.

21. Its unity is respected by Bentzen, also by Crüsemann, pp. 258–63, and Ridderbos, BZAW 117, pp. 289f.

22. Cf. 2.7; II Kings 11.12. Von Rad gives an account of the coronation document in 'Das judäische Königsritual'. Widengren (*SK*, pp. 29, 64) thinks the document was more comprehensive, the whole law being handed to the king. See further Johnson, *SKAI*, p. 24 n. 2, and Jones.

23. The similarity is noted by Delitzsch. See the examples in Seux, pp. 36, 81, 223, 240, 402. Deities are also represented with large ears to indicate their divine wisdom, e.g. Porada, nos. 976E, 977, 990, and cf. *ANET*, p. 62 line 97.

24. *maśkīl* well expresses the strong exercise of royal skill, cf. Jer. 3.15; 10.21; 23.5, and further Josh. 1.8; I Sam. 18.5, 30; I Kings 2.3; II Kings 18.7; I Chron. 22.12; II Chron. 2.11; Pss. 2.10; 101.2 (p. 123) and Isa. 52.13. For *'el* 'in regard to', 'for the sake of', see BDB, pp. 40f.

25. *Ps. st.* IV, pp. 46–9; *GT*; *PIW* II, p. 214; similarly Engnell, *SBU* II, col. 633.

26. After Akkadian *katāmu* 'to cover', *Ps. st.* IV, pp. 4f.; *PIW* II, p. 209; *SBU*, col. 633.

27. *Ps. st.* IV, pp. 16f.; *PIW* II, p. 213.

28. This possibility is exploited, perhaps too one-sidedly, by Willesen.

29. The (divinized) king's helmet is thus distinguished on the stele of Naram Sin (*ANEP*, no. 309). The horns were originally a sign of divinity (Dhorme, pp. 13f.) and are worn, for example, by Baal (*ANEP*, no. 490) and by the Hittite god of war (see Akurgal, pp. 103f.).

30. *'ōmar* should perhaps be *'ōmēr*, participle, cf. G, S, J; others prefer *'^emōr*, imperative. In v. 9 the conjecture *kī 'āmartā* is attractive;

otherwise this thought may in fact be understood: 'For thou – (thou sayest) 'Y. is my shelter'.

31. For *bll* as intransitive cf. Lane I, pp. 242f.; also Delitzsch and likewise Gray (*Legacy*, p. 271) who adds a Ugaritic cognate.

32. Cf. the depiction of the Assyrian king being touched with cones, ch. IV no. 39.

33. *bōᵃrîm bāʿām* seem at first sight to be Israelites, and if the oppressors in the rest of the psalm are a foreign power, it is those weak in faith in Israel who are addressed here. Perhaps, however, the phrase means 'O most stupid of people'; for *ʿam* of 'people' in general see BDB, p. 766b no. 4, similarly *GT*, making reference to Isa. 42.5. Dahood proposes that *ʿam* here means 'sagacity'.

34. This strikes me as the best explanation of this 'we' style, even though some of the 'national laments' are relatively late; the form is rare in the ancient world. Contrast Mowinckel, *PIW* I, p. 194.

35. In *Kongesalmerne* he construes v. 10: 'Look down, our shield Yahweh, look on thine anointed's face' and says that the king himself speaks here. In *GT* he contrues as I have done, but still supposes the king to be the speaker.

36. Cf. Mowinckel, *PIW* I, p. 31.

37. In addition, *'ēlî* may be intended in v. 1, since the final *y* is omitted in vv. 2, 6.

38. A king of Alalakh is termed the 'special possession' of his goddess, the term resembling that describing Israel in Ex. 19.5 (Wiseman, p. 130; Greenberg).

39. The yearning for the temple invites comparison with the Assyrian lament noted on ch. IV n. 19; so Lipiński, p. 155.

40. E.g. Ezek. 6.9; 18.31; 33.11; 36.25f.; Isa. 1.18; 43.25f.; 57.15f.; 59.2, 12; 63.9–14; 64.5f.; 66.2 (Lam. 3.4). Cf. the parallels listed by Dalglish, pp. 224f.

41. *ndb* refers to princely rank more often than to 'willingness' etc., and is notable in royal names, such as Abinadab son of Saul, Nadab son of Jeroboam, Nadabya son of Jehoiachin. In Prov. 25.6f. *nādîb* and *melek* are parallel. Bentzen concludes: 'He prays here: Support me with a truly royal soul (en rigtig kongesjæl), so that I can be what the king ought to be in the chosen people.' *ndbt* in Ps. 110.3 becomes *archē* 'dominion' in G; cf. p. 166 and de Savignac, pp. 118–20.

42. Dalglish, p. 158; Westermann.

43. Cf. Prov. 8.14; Isa. 11.2; 9.5. De Boer ('The Counsellor') surveys 'counsel' and 'counsellor' and concludes that as a class the counsellors are all attached to the king's household or concerned with government; it is particularly the king who needs counsellors at his court.

44. Cf. G, V, and Dahood with reference to Ugaritic.

45. Von Rad (*OT Theology* II, pp. 218f.) explains this passage of the king's free access to Yahweh's secret counsels; Mowinckel (*HTC*, pp. 179f., 238) of the king's priestly access.

46. He makes a new suggestion in *Evildoers*, pp. 36f., allowing for sinners in Israel and turning against a 'life after death' interpretation;

he relates v. 17 to illegitimate sanctuaries whose devastation evidenced Yahweh's judgment.

47. Donner, Nr. 202; *ANET*, p. 501. Note '*ānī* in Zech. 9.9, below, pp. 80, 180.

48. Engnell, *SBU* II, col. 641; Porter, 'Succession of Joshua', p. 116.

49. *SBU* II, col. 635. Cf. also Widengren, 'Konungens vistelse'.

III THE ROYAL RITES

1. For the details summarized in this and the next paragraph, see especially Falkenstein, 'Akīti-Fest', pp. 147–82.

2. Falkenstein and von Soden, *SAGH*, pp. 374, 137f.

3. I know of this unpublished text from W. G. Lambert. Cf. Legrain, p. 40.

4. Cf. Lambert, *JSS* 1968, p. 112.

5. The question is usefully surveyed by Nakata.

6. This distinction is the main theme of Posener; similarly Bonnet, pp. 385f.

7. Cf. the meagre results of the surveys by Hooke (*MR*, pp. 68f.), Engnell (*Studies*, pp. 71f.), Ringgren, *HR*.

8. Cf. the doubts of de Langhe in *MRK*, pp. 122–48. A more positive view is presented by J. Gray, *Legacy*, and in *Ugaritica VI*.

9. Wellhausen, ch. 3; Volz, pp. 7f.; Snaith, *JNYF*, chs. 1–2; Kraus, *Worship*, pp. 62f.

10. Mishna, *Rosh hash.* 1, first speaks of four kinds of new-year's day but then uses 'the beginning of the year' only to mean 1 Tishri.

11. G. B. Gray, pp. 300f.; Mowinckel, *Zum isr. Neujahr*, p. 12; Kraus, *Worship*, p. 62.

12. Snaith, *JNYF*, pp. 58f.; Kutsch.

13. Kraus, *Worship*, pp. 67f.

14. Mowinckel, *Zum isr. Neujahr*, pp. 27f.; Zimmerli, *Ezekiel*, p. 995.

15. Auerbach argues that the change was in 604 BC.

16. *Ps. st.* II, p. 88, following Benzinger; Snaith, *JYNF*, p. 96. Yet another approach, with not dissimilar results, is that of Morgenstern in numerous studies since 1924, summarized in his 'Cultic setting', pp. 5f.

17. Kraus (*Worship*, pp. 67f.) traces 1 Tishri to a pre-exilic new-moon day.

18. While it is the Zion-kingship theme which is followed in our present discussion, it is not intended to deny that the festival also resumed pre-monarchy worship, in which the Sinai covenant was renewed. This latter aspect, emphasized by Kraus and above all by Weiser, is clearly recognized by Mowinckel (*PIW* I, pp. 155–61) and is attested by such psalms as 81; 95; 99 and 50.

19. The female arch-enemy in Nahum seems to combine Nineveh, Ishtar, and the chaos-foe; cf. my *Obadiah*, pp. 60f. For Belial as embodiment of death or Sheol see Thomas, 'Belial'.

20. My 'Hab. 3' and *Obadiah*.

21. Cf. 'oracle of the King whose name is Yahweh Sebaoth', Jer. 46.18; 48.15; 51.57.

22. My commentary on Zeph. 2.5–15 in *Obadiah*. Cf. Bentzen, 'Ritual Background', on a similarly aimed series in Amos 1–2.

23. Bentzen, 'Ritual Background'.

24. Likewise Ginsberg. Support for the priority of the psalms comes also from the novel approach of Culley, pp. 108, 113, from Lipiński, and from Ringgren, 'D.-jes. och k.'. The objections of Westermann (*Praise*, pp. 146f.) were of little weight, whereas his later commentary on Isa. 40–66 rightly stresses the prophet's dependence on temple psalmody. For Kraus' withdrawal of similar objections see below, pp. 110f.

25. *Ps. st.* II, pp. 202f.; *PIW* I, pp. 130f.; Johnson, *SKAI*, pp. 33f.; Kraus, pp. 197f.; Porter, *JTS* 1954. Roberts argues that the biblical Zion tradition is Davidic-Solomonic but not directly taken as a whole from the Canaanites, since he considers the functions of El and Baal to be here confused.

26. Lipiński re-examines the question in detail and concludes in favour of the inchoative sense 'has become king', originally a proclamation of accession which can be echoed in antiphons.

27. On Rev. 11.15–17 see *PIW* II, p. 223; Lipiński, p. 455.

28. A useful recent portrayal of the dramatic liturgy of Yahweh's victory and royal ascension at the autumn festival is made by Lipiński, pp. 432–51.

29. Egyptian representation of enemies in figurines, lists and other portrayals was partly to ensure the submission of foreign peoples in general. Details in Noth, 'Thebes', pp. 21f.

30. In 'The Role', p. 107, he wrote: 'We see the kings of the earth held captive after their defeat in the ritual combat, and compelled to acquiesce in the triumphant enthronement of the Davidic king.'

31. Likewise Morgenstern, 'Cultic setting', pp. 15f., but supposing that the new-year festival was in spring until Solomon's reign.

32. Bright, p. 169; Bentzen, *KM*, p. 16; *PIW* I, p. 128; *Ps. st.* II, pp. 7f. See above, p. 96.

33. I Sam. 11.14 is evidence that the notion of 'making new the kingship' at a cultic centre was known in Israel.

34. Mowinckel (*PIW* I, pp. 71f.) compares the Pharaoh's thanksgiving for his deliverance at the battle of Kadesh; but that would only show how clearly a historical battle should have been reflected! Moreover, Pharaoh does not describe the deity's intervention as an epiphany but as help such as might be experienced by anyone (Posener, pp. 77f.).

35. Porter (*JTS* 1954) argues from II Sam. 6–7 for a modified sacred marriage in David's festival. Ringgren ('Hieros Gamos') suggests that sacred marriage centred in Mesopotamia on the renewal of the land's fertility, but in Egypt on the continuance of the dynasty, while in Canaan and Israel the two aspects were combined.

36. Lipiński, *Poème*; Dumortier (who rightly describes as fragile Lipiński's deductions from a Qumran fragment).

37. The ark is feminine in I Sam. 4.17 and II Chron. 8.11 and there is little to be gained by pronouncing the suffixes as masculine, referring (says Gunkel) to Yahweh and his shrine. The fem. suffixes have been thought to refer to the preceding story of David's vow; thus Johnson explains that the psalm attests the discovery of this tradition near Bethlehem (*SKAI*, p. 21).

38. Gunkel thinks the call is for obeisance at the station of Kiriath Jearim.

39. But according to *SKAI*, p. 20, the ark is here lifted into its place.

40. For reassessment of 'Aramaisms' cf. Honeyman, p. 278; Wagner, pp. 150f.

41. Whereas Ps. 144 is often despised as derivative from Ps. 18, Culley, p. 109, questions the assumption of dependence.

IV THE IDEAL OF THE KING'S OFFICE
IN THE PSALMS

1. Taking the *lāmed* before *yhwh* and *qdwš* as only emphatic, with Thomas, *TRP*; Dahood; Johnson, *SKAI*, p. 109.

2. Jer. 21.12; 22.16; Ps. 72.12–14; *ANET*, pp. 149a, 178a.

3. Cf. Eaton, *JTS* 1968, p. 608.

4. Expressions for enemies are set out by Gunkel, *Einl.*, pp. 196f., and by Keel, pp. 94–8 (nearly 100 expressions).

5. Transferring the preceding *m* with G.

6. Psalms 3; 4; 5; 7; 35; 36; 40; 52; 54; 55; 57; 69; 109; 120; 143.

7. 7.2; 42.9; 43.3; 54.7; 71.3 etc.

8. 18.6; 7.16; 9.16; 35.7; 57.7; 91.3; 116.3; 140.6.

9. 2.1; 63.12; 144.8; 3.3 etc.

10. 5.5–10; 10; 11.2; 27.12; 35.15f., 19f.; 41.9; 55.5; 59.13; 63.12; 91.3–6; 140.4, 12.

11. 3.8; 7.2f.; 10; 17.12; 22.13, 17, 21f.; 27.2; 57.5; 91.13.

12. 59.7. The implication is present in many of the passages cited for this paragraph.

13. 9.14; 18.5f.; 22.17; 23.4; 40.3; 41.9; 144.7.

14. Cf. Eaton, *JTS* 1968, pp. 604f.

15. *tōrā* may be used of Davidic rule in II Sam. 7.19; so Cazelles, 'Shiloh', p. 250.

16. Likewise RSV 'your divine throne endures . . .'. The problem is discussed by Emerton and Mulder.

17. Many other occurrences of *ḥsh* are perhaps to be associated with this sheltering of the king: 7.2; 11.1; 16.1 (cf. 17.7); 118.8 etc.

18. 5.9; 16.8; 17.5; 18.36; 23.3; 27.11; 73.23–4; 121.5; 139.10; 143.10; and see p. 174.

19. In Mesopotamia the king is called 'the glance of the eyes' of the god, or is said to be chosen by the glance of his eyes, Labat, p. 45, Seux, p. 207.

20. For such 'correspondence' in Assyria see Albrektson, p. 49; in Persia, l'Orange, p. 489.

21. The Hittite king was entitled 'anointed', but whether anointing was a rite of the other great kings is not entirely clear. Cf. pp. 95, 101.

22. If *r'h* = *rwh*; so Driver, BZAW 103, p. 97; Thomas, *TRP*, p. 23.

23. For *'l* = 'from' cf. Driver, *JSS* 1964, p. 349.

24. Cf. *bḥr* in I Sam. 10.24; 16.8f. (more generally: II Sam. 6.21; 16.18; Ps. 78.70; Deut. 17.15; I Kings 8.16; I Chron. 28.4, 5; II Chron. 6.1).

25. Pronouncing *'immᵉkā* and *ḥilekā. hdrt* means 'apparition' in Ugaritic; here the plural would be formed as a masc. and used with *beth essentiae*, GK 119i. Alternatively, the reading '(thy birth) on the mountains of holiness' would be quite apt. For *nᵉdābōt* cf. ch. II n. 41.

26. Joseph's descendants were 'born on his knees' (Gen. 50.23). Divine assistance at the birth of the royal child is vividly represented in polytheistic style in Egypt (references in Bonnet, p. 383b). The Mesopotamian royal child was accepted and suckled by his goddess (Labat, p.64).

27. Cooke, p. 216, comparing Ruth 4.16. See also above, ch. II n. 13.

28. Cf. II Kings 13.16. Egyptian and other parallels are noted by Gunkel on Psalm 18.

29. *yᵉhāb*, found only here, appears in the Vss. as 'anxiety' (G, S), 'hope' (T) and 'love' (J); 'burden' is proposed in the Talmud (Delitzsch).

30. Zimmerli, *The Servant of God*, pp. 9f.

31. So Nebuchadnezzar in Jer. 27.6; Moses in Num. 12.7f. and Ex. 14.31, where he is 'the vizier, the true steward of Yahweh' (Zimmerli, op. cit., p. 19). Mesopotamian kings use a similar designation, Seux, pp. 362f.

32. The collocation may be pathetic: he is persecuted though he bore the burden. *rabbīm* can precede its noun (Delitzsch), and the thought is well known (*ANET*, p. 178a; Num. 11.12); Nebuchadnezzar, among others, is entitled 'shepherd of great peoples (*niši rabātim*)', Seux, pp. 248f., esp. n. 79.

33. 2.6; 'his king' in 18.51 and I Sam. 2.10.

34. 132.17; 'his anointed' in 2.2; 18.51; I Sam. 2.10.

35. 89.4; cf. 106.23 of Moses.

36. Literally 'Y. has made wonderful (/has distinguished) a covenant-fellow for himself.'

37. Cf. II Sam. 23.3; Zech. 9.9; von Rad, *OT Theology* I, p. 322.

38. Literally 'As (with) a shield thou crownest him with grace', a compression of metaphors.

39. Cf. Kraus, pp. 321, 593, 621; Dahood on Pss. 23, 42, 61. In an Assyrian example, *ANEP* no. 617, a being with human body and eagle's head and wings touches the king with a cone to convey vitality (cf. Gadd, pp. 49, 91f.).

40. See Dahood, after Gaster.

41. *rdp* of closely following a leader, as Judg. 3.28.

42. Von Rad, *OT Theology* I, p. 341, says the word to David 'passed down through the ages like a guardian angel'.

43. 89.4, 20, 35f., 50; 132.11; 110.1, 4; 2.5–7.

44. Assuming a transitive usage; otherwise, 'Awake to my help, for thou hast commanded judgment'.

45. Or 'proclaim', Dahood after J. Barth.

46. An animal fully qualified for sacrifice, cf. Delitzsch.

47. 23.3; 31.4; 61.3; 73.24; pp. 143f., 174.

48. 43.3; cf. 139.10, God's hand.

49. Cf. Isa. 41.10, 13; 42.6; 45.1; also the Hittite king, pp. 143f.

50. Cf. Pss.; 20.3; 3.6; 51.14; 71.6; 94.18.

51. Sorg, pp. 51f., and above, ch. II n. 29.

52. Engnell, *Studies*, pp. 39–45, has gathered Mesopotamian texts; for Egypt see *ANET*, pp. 378f.; for the Caliphate see Ringgren, 'Religious aspects', p. 743.

53. A comparable Ugaritic sentence, cited by Dahood, specifies 'immortality' (*blmt*), *ANET*, p. 151b.

54. The Hittite king can be referred to by the name of the dynastic founder, T/Labarnas, whose spirit thus lives on in his line (Gurney, *MRK*, pp. 114f.).

55. Albright ('The High Place') thinks Ezekiel objects to memorial stelae of dead kings who were buried fairly near; similarly Zimmerli, *Ezechiel*, p. 1082.

56. For *'ereṣ* = underworld see Dahood on 18.8; he does not claim this meaning in Ps. 16.

57. Dubious; I surmise that we have a set phrase reflecting the words of their worshippers; thus, 'and the lords (of whom men say) "all my delight is in them" '. Cf. Isa. 44.9 *ḥᵃmūdēhem*, 'those in whom they have pleasure' = 'their idols'.

58. This natural sense can be reached by a slight emendation or by Dahood's theory of a third person suffix -*y* like Phoenician.

59. Fairman, *MRK*, p. 98; Frankfort, ch. 2; Posener, p. 19.

60. Perhaps 'the Swallower', death; so Thomas, 'Belial'.

61. But de Boer argues that the sense is indicative, 'The king lives'.

62. De Savignac, pp. 117f., comparing 68.10, Isa. 26.19 and the sun-glory in Egypt.

63. Cf. ch. II n. 8.

64. 'my soul . . . to him' with some Mss. and Vss. Otherwise: 'and he who kept not his soul alive', attached to the previous sentence.

65. -*y* may have been deliberately omitted before the following *y*-.

66. As previous note. Otherwise '(to the Lord) for ever'.

67. 18.20f.; 40.5f.; 45.5; 72.1f.; 89.31f.; 91.2, 14; 101; 118.8f.; 132.12.

68. *'ēlī* is not as widely used as *'ᵉlōhay*, occurring only in 18.3; 22.2, 11; 63.2; 68.25; 89.27; 102.25; 118.28; 140.7.

69. 'My lord' (-*āy*) seems to have been assimilated to 'the Lord' (-*āy*, emphatic afformative); see *TWAT*.

70. If '*al* is a divine name (cf. Dahood); otherwise 'undertaken by God'.

71. II Sam. 6; 8.18; I Kings 8; II Kings 16 etc. Cf. Gunkel on Ps. 110.

72. I Sam. 13.8f.; II Chron. 26.16f.

73. Cf. Ugaritic sources: the 'idealizing' texts, *Keret* and *Aqhat*, have priestly functions discharged by Kings Keret and Dan'el and by no other, but the 'practical' administrative texts bring orders of priests into the picture (Gray, pp. 209f.).

74. This sense of *bw'* is noted in BDB, p. 97 1b.

75. Cf. 'gates of righteousness' in 118.19 and my article 'Problems'.

76. The piel is perhaps preferable, cf. BDB.

77. Cf. II Chron. 6.13; II Kings 11.14.

78. For such postures and gestures cf. Gunkel on Ps. 28.2 and Gray, *Kings*, p. 219.

79. Mesopotamian kings were especially pious in building and caring for temples, Labat, pp. 177, 255f.; Seux, pp. 372f. In an Assyrian lament, which in part resembles a text of Ashurbanipal, it is said of the temple: 'I constantly thought of its fine things; the fire of Ezida has burnt my heart' (Lambert, *RA* 1959, p. 131).

80. Cf. I Kings 3.4f.; 9.2f. Likewise in Egypt (Posener, pp. 85f.), Mesopotamia (Labat, p. 180), and Ugarit (Gray, *Legacy*, p. 210). Gadd, p. 26, points out that visionary experience may help to legitimize a king.

81. Cf. II Sam. 23 and foreign kings in Gen. 20.3f. and II Kings 18.25; also previous note.

82. A common meaning in Ugaritic; otherwise 'concerning thee', the inspiration taken for granted.

83. Lev. 16; 23.26–32; Num. 29.7–11.

84. For example Noth, *Laws*, pp. 235f.

85. See Noth, *ibid*.

86. Cf. de Buck. Judean royal symbols on jar stamps include rosettes as well as the winged sun-disk and scarab (above, p. 165).

87. Cf. Ezek. 36.25; Ex. 12.22; Lev. 14.4f.; Num. 19.6, 18.

88. Labat, pp. 352f.; Dhorme, pp. 229f, 253; J. Gray, *PEQ* 1955; Kümmel. Kümmel stresses the distinction between magical substitutes, rites of carrying away evil, and offerings; nevertheless, the sacrifice of a bull is part of the substitution rituals to deflect presaged evil from the Hittite king.

89. Gen. 22; Ex. 13.11–15; 34.19–20.

90. Possibly this also makes comparison with animal sacrifices, since the divine will was read in the entrails of sacrificed beasts. More generally, Dalglish, pp. 200f., notes the juxtaposition of the presentation of sacrifice with self-presentation in an Akkadian text.

91. Cf. Zorell, p. 118: *bnh* of restoring happiness or making prosper. Note also the niphal (BDB, p. 125) 'be established, built up'. Cf. the Babylonian festal prayer on p. 94.

92. 'Kiss *his feet*' is good as emendations go. *Br* can be explained as 'the ground', or 'sincerely', or as 'the Son' (to avoid the assonance *ben pen*).

93. Eaton, *ASTI* 7.

94. *Ibid.*, pp. 35f.

95. *ANET*, p. 387a; Seux, pp. 227, 272, 66, 326, etc.; Stummer, pp. 103f.

96. We could render: 'while I declare the deeds of thine arm to the congregation, and thy might to all who enter (the temple)'; cf. Dahood.

97. See Dahood.

98. Cf. von Rad, *OT Theology* I, p. 315.

99. 4.2; 5.2–4; 17.1; 22.2f.; 27.7; 28.1f.; 54.4; 55.2f., 17; 61.2f.; 69.4, 14, 17f.; 71.2; 77.2–4; 102.1; 143.1.

100. 3.8; 5.11; 11.6; 28.3–5; 35.4–8; 36.13; 40.15f.; 54.7; 63.10f.; 144.5f.

LIST OF WORKS CITED

(Works that have been referred to by author's name only are marked †
in the list if the author has more than one entry.)

Ahlström, G. W., *Psalm 89: eine Liturgie aus dem Ritual des leidenden Königs*, Lund 1959

Akurgal, E., 'Die Kunst der Hethiter', *Historia*, Einzelschr. 7, 1964, pp.74–118

Albrektson, B., *History and the Gods*, Lund 1967

Albright, W. F., *From the Stone Age to Christianity*, 2nd ed., Baltimore 1957

Anderson, G. W., 'Enemies and Evildoers in the Book of Psalms', *BRJL* 48, 1965, pp. 16–29

Auerbach, E., 'Der Wechsel des Jahres-Anfangs in Juda', *VT* 9, 1959, pp. 113–21

Baethgen, F., *Die Psalmen* (HKAT II.2), 3rd ed., 1904

Balla, E., *Das Ich der Psalmen* (FRLANT 16), 1912

Barnett, R. D., 'Ezekiel and Tyre', *EI* 9, 1969, pp. 6–13 and plates

Begrich, J., *Studien zu Deuterojesaja*, 1938, reissued Munich 1963

Bentzen, A., *Jahves Gæst*, Copenhagen 1926
  †*Salmer*, Copenhagen 1939
  Jesaja, Copenhagen 1944
  Det sakrale kongedømme (= *DSK*), Copenhagen 1945
  'The Cultic Use of the Story of the Ark in Samuel', *JBL* 67, 1948, pp. 37–53
  'The Ritual Background of Amos 1–2', *OTS* 8, 1950, pp. 85–99
  King and Messiah (= *KM*), ET Oxford 1955 and 1970

Bernhardt, K.-H., *Das Problem der altorientalischen Königsideologie* (*VT* Sup. 8), 1961

Berridge, J. M., *Prophet, People and the Word of Yahweh*, Zürich 1970

Beyerlin, W., *Die Rettung der Bedrängten in den Feindpsalmen der Einzelnen* (FRLANT 99), 1970

Bič, M., 'Das erste Buch des Psalters: eine Thronbesteigungsfestliturgie', *The Sacral Kingship* (*Numen* Sup. 4), 1959, pp. 316–32

Birkeland, H., †*Die Feinde des Individuums in der israelitischen Psalmenliteratur*, Oslo 1933
  The Evildoers in the Book of Psalms, Oslo 1955

Bleeker, C. J., †*Egyptian festivals* (*Numen* Sup. 12), 1967
  'The Religion of Ancient Egypt', *HR*, pp. 40–114

and Widengren, G. (eds), *Historia Religionum I: Religions of the Past* (= *HR*), Leiden 1969

de Boer, P., 'Vive le roi', *VT* 5, 1955, pp. 225–31

'The Counsellor', *Wisdom in Israel* (*VT* Sup. 3), 1955, pp. 47–71

Bonnet, H., *Reallexicon der ägyptischen Religionsgeschichte*, Berlin 1952

Botterweck, G. J. and Ringgren, H. (eds), *Theologisches Wörterbuch zum Alten Testament*, Stuttgart 1970ff.; ET, *Theological Dictionary of the Old Testament*, Grand Rapids, Michigan, 1974ff.

Briggs, C. A. and E. C., *Psalms* (International Critical Commentary), Edinburgh 1906–7

Bright, J., *Jeremiah* (Anchor Bible), New York 1965

Brown, Driver and Briggs, *Hebrew and English Lexicon of the OT* (= *BDB*), Oxford 1906

de Buck, A., 'La fleur au front du grand-prêtre', *OTS* 9, 1951, pp. 18–29

Budde, K., *Die schönsten Psalmen*, Leipzig 1915

van Buren, E. D., 'The Scorpion in Mesopotamian Art and Religion', *Archiv für Orientforschung* 12, 1937–9, pp. 1–28

Buttenwieser, M., *The Psalms Chronologically Treated, with a New Translation*, Chicago 1938

Cazelles, H., 'Shiloh, the Customary Laws and the Return of the Ancient Kings', *Proclamation and Presence: Essays in Honour of G. Henton Davies*, ed. J. I. Durham and J. R. Porter, London 1970, pp. 239–54

Chassinat, E., *Le mystère d'Osiris au mois de Khoiak*, Cairo 1966–8

Cheyne, T. K., *The Book of Psalms*, London 1888

Childs, B. S., 'Psalm Titles and Midrashic Exegesis', *JSS* 16, 1971, pp. 137–50

Compte rendu de la troisième rencontre assyriologique, Leiden 1954

Cooke, G., 'The Israelite King as Son of God', *ZAW* 73, 1961, pp. 202–25

Cross, F. M. and Freedman, D. N., 'A Royal Song of Thanksgiving: II Sam. 22 = Ps. 18', *JBL* 72, 1953, pp. 15–34

Cross, F. M., 'Judean Stamps', *EI* 9, 1969, pp. 20–7

Crüsemann, F., *Studien zur Formgeschichte von Hymnus und Danklied in Israel*, Neukirchen 1969

Culley, R. C., *Oral Formulaic Language in the Biblical Psalms*, Toronto 1967

Dahood, M., *Psalms* (Anchor Bible), New York 1966–70

Dalglish, E. R., *Psalm 51*, Leiden 1962

Danell, G. A., *Psalm 139*, UUÅ 1951

David, A. R., *Religious ritual at Abydos (c. 1300 BC)*, Warminster 1973

Delekat, L., *Asylie und Schutzorakel am Zionheiligtum*, Leiden 1967

Delitzsch, F., *Die Psalmen*, 5th ed., Leipzig 1894

Dhorme, E., *Les religions de Babylonie et d'Assyrie* (Mana: Introduction à l'histoire des religions I.2), Paris 1949

Donner, H., and Röllig, W., *Kanaanäische und aramäische Inschriften*, Wiesbaden 1962–4

Driver, G. R., Review of Chicago Assyrian Dictionary vol. ṣ, in *JSS* 9, 1964, pp. 346–50

'Isaiah 52.13–53.12: the Servant of the Lord', *In Memoriam Paul Kahle* (BZAW 103), 1968, pp. 90–105

Duhm, B., *Die Psalmen* (Kurzer Hand-Commentar zum AT 14), 2nd ed., Tübingen 1922

Dumortier, J.-B., 'Un rituel d'inthronisation: le Ps. 89.2–38', *VT* 22, 1972, pp. 176–96

Dussaud, R., *Les religions des Hittites et des Hourrites, des Phéniciens et des Syriens* (Mana: Introduction à l'histoire des religions I.2), Paris 1949

Eaton, J. H., *Obadiah, Nahum, Habakkuk and Zephaniah* (TBC), London 1961

'Hard Sayings X: Ps. 4.6–7', *Theology* 67, 1964, pp. 355–7

'The Origin and Meaning of Hab. 3', *ZAW* 76, 1964, pp. 144–71

'Problems of Translation in Ps. 23.3f.', *The Bible Translator* 16, 1965, pp. 171–6

'The King's Self-sacrifice: a Re-interpretation of Ps. 40', *Alta* (Univ. of Birmingham review) 3, 1967, pp. 141–5

Psalms (TBC), London 1967

'Some Questions of Philology and Exegesis in the Psalms', *JTS* n.s. 19, 1968, pp. 603–9

'The King as God's Witness', *ASTI* 7, Leiden 1970, pp. 25–40

Emerton, J. A., 'The Syntactical Problem of Ps. 45.7', *JSS* 13, 1968, pp. 58–63

Engnell, I., *Studies in Divine Kingship in the Ancient Near East* (=*Studies*), Uppsala 1943, reprinted Oxford 1967

(ed.), *Svenskt Bibliskt Uppslagsverk* I–II (= *SBU*), 2nd ed., Stockholm, 1962–3. English translations of some articles by Engnell appear in his *Critical Essays on the OT*, London 1970

Erman, A., *Aegypten und aegyptischen Leben im Altertum*, revised by H. Ranke, Tübingen 1923

Fairman, H. W., 'Worship and Festivals in an Egyptian Temple', *BJRL* 37, 1954–5, pp. 165–203

'The Kingship Rituals of Egypt', *MRK*, pp. 74–104

Falkenstein, A. and von Soden, W., *Sumerische und akkadische Hymnen und Gebete* (= *SAHG*), Zürich 1953

Falkenstein, A., 'Akīti-Fest und akīti-Festhaus', *Festschrift J. Friedrich* (ed. R. von Kienle), Heidelberg 1959, pp. 14–182

de Fraine, R., *L'aspect religieux de la royauté israélite*, Rome 1954

Frankfort, H., *Kingship and the Gods*, Chicago 1948

Frazer, J. G., *The Golden Bough*, London 1923–7

Gadd, C. J., 'Babylonian Myth and Ritual', *MR*, pp. 40–67

Ideas of Divine Rule in the Ancient East, London 1948

Gesenius, W. and Kautzsch, E., *Hebrew Grammar*, Oxford 1910

Ginsberg, H. L., 'A Strand in the Cord of Hebraic Hymnody', *EI* 9, 1969, pp. 45–50

Goedicke, H., *Die Stellung des Königs im Alten Reich* (Ägyptologische Abhandlungen 2), Wiesbaden 1960

Gray, G. B., *Sacrifice in the Old Testament*, Oxford 1925

Gray, J., †*The Legacy of Canaan* (*VT* Sup. 5), 2nd ed., 1965
  I & II Kings (OTL), 2nd ed., London 1970
  'Royal Substitution in the Ancient Near East', *PEQ* 1955, pp. 180–2
  'Sacral Kingship in Ugarit', *Ugaritica* 6, Paris 1969, pp. 289–302
Greenberg, M., 'Hebrew s^egullā: Akkadian *sikiltu*', *JAOS* 71, 1951,
  pp. 172–4
Gunkel, H., 'Die Königspsalmen', *Preussische Jahrbücher* 158, 1914,
  pp. 42–68
  †*Die Psalmen* (HKAT II.2), 1926
  Einleitung in die Psalmen (= *Einl.*), completed by J. Begrich (HKAT
  II Erganzungsband), 1933
Gurney, O. R., *The Hittites*, Penguin Books, 2nd ed., 1954
  'Hittite Kingship', *MRK*, pp. 105–21
Güterbock, H. G., 'Religion und Kultus der Hethiter', *Historia*,
  Einzelschr. 7, 1964, pp. 54–73
Hallo, W. W., 'Individual Prayer in Sumerian', *JAOS* 88, 1968, pp.
  71–89
Hertzberg, H. H., *I and II Samuel*, ET (OTL), 1964
Holman, J., 'The Structure of Ps. 139', *VT* 21, 1971, pp. 298–310
Honeyman, A. M., 'Semitic Epigraphy and Hebrew Philology', *OTMS*,
  pp. 264–82
Hooke, S. H. (ed.), *Myth and Ritual*, Oxford 1933
  (ed.), *Myth, Ritual and Kingship*, Oxford 1958
Hvidberg, F., *Weeping and Laughter in the Old Testament*, Copenhagen
  1962
Johnson, A. R., 'The Role of the King in the Jerusalem Cultus', *The
  Labyrinth* (ed. S. H. Hooke), London 1935, pp. 71–111
  'The Psalms', *OTMS*, pp. 162–209
  Sacral Kingship in Ancient Israel (= *SKAI*), (1955), 2nd ed., Cardiff
  1967
Jones, G. H., 'The Decree of Yahweh', *VT* 15, 1965, pp. 336–44
Josephus, *Jewish Antiquities*, Loeb Classical Library, London 1934
Kaiser, O., *Der königliche Knecht* (FRLANT 70), 1959
  'Erwägungen zu Ps. 101', *ZAW* 74, 1962, pp. 195–205
Kapelrud, A. S., *The Ras Shamra Discoveries and the Old Testament*,
  Oxford 1965
Keel, O., *Feinde und Gottesleugner . . . in den Individuelpsalmen*, Stuttgart
  1969
Kirkpatrick, A. F., *The Book of Psalms* (Cambridge Bible), 1902
Kittel, R., *Die Psalmen* (KAT 13), 5th–6th ed., 1929
Knudtzon, J. A., *Die El-Amarna Tafeln*, Leipzig 1915
Koole, J. L., 'Ps. 15 – eine königliche Einzugsliturgie?', *OTS* 13, 1963,
  pp. 98–111
Kraus, H.-J., *Die Königsherrschaft Gottes im Alten Testament*, Tübingen
  1951
  †*Psalmen* (BKAT XV), 1960
  Worship in Israel, ET Oxford 1966
Kümmel, H. M., *Ersatzrituale für den hethitischen König*, Wiesbaden 1967

Kutsch, E., ' "Am Ende des Jahres" . . . in Ex. 23.16', *ZAW* 83, 1971, pp. 15–21
Labat, R., *Le caractère religieux de la royauté assyro-babylonienne*, Paris 1939
Lambert, W. G., 'The Sultantepe Tablets', *RA* 53, 1959, pp. 119–38
'The Great Battle . . . in the Akītu-house', *Iraq* 25, 1963, pp. 189f.
'Myth and Ritual as Conceived by the Babylonians', *JSS* 13, 1968, pp. 104–24
Lane, E. W., *An Arabic-English Lexicon*, London 1863f.
de Langhe, R., 'Myth, Ritual and Kingship in the Ras Shamra Tablets', *MRK*, pp. 122–48
Legrain, L., *Royal Inscriptions and Fragments from Nippur and Babylon*, Philadelphia 1926
Lipiński, E., †*La royauté de Yahwé*, Brussels 1965
Le poème royal du Ps. 89.1–5, 20–38, Paris 1967
Merrill, A. L., 'Ps. 23 and the Jerusalem Tradition', *VT* 15, 1965, pp. 354–60
Moortgat, M. A., 'Der Bilderzyklus des Tammuz', *CR*, pp. 18–41
Moret, A., *Du caractère religieux de la royauté pharaonique*, Paris 1902
Morgenstern, J., 'A Chapter in the History of the High-priesthood', *American Journal of Semitic Languages and Literatures* 55, 1938, pp. 1–24, 183–97, 360–77
'The Cultic Setting of the Enthronement Psalms', *Hebrew Union College Annual* 35, 1964, pp. 1–42
Mowinckel, S., *Kongesalmerne i det Gamle Testament,* Kristiania 1916
Psalmenstudien (= Ps. st.) I–VI, Kristiania, 1921–4; reprint Amsterdam 1961
Zum israelitischen Neujahr und zur Deutung der Thronbesteigungspsalmen, ANVO 1952
Det Gamle Testamente IV.1, Salmeboken (= GT), Oslo 1955
He that Cometh (= HTC), Oxford 1956
The Psalms in Israel's Worship (= PSI), Oxford 1962
Mulder, J., *Studies on Ps. 45*, Karmel, Almelo, Netherlands 1972
Müller, K. F., *Das assyrische Ritual* I, Leipzig 1937
Nakata, I., 'Problems of the Babylonian Akītu Festival', *Journal of the Ancient Near Eastern Society of Columbia University* 1, 1968, pp. 41–9
Noth, M., *Das Buch Joshua* (HAT 7), 2nd ed. 1953
The Laws in the Pentateuch and Other Studies, ET Edinburgh 1966
'Thebes', *Archaeology & OT Study*, ed. D. W. Thomas, Oxford 1967, pp. 21–35
l'Orange, H. P., 'Expressions of Cosmic Kingship in the Ancient World', *The Sacral Kingship* (Numen Sup. 4), 1959, pp. 481–92
Pallis, S. A., *The Babylonian Akītu Festival*, Copenhagen 1926
Parker, R. A., *The Calendars of Ancient Egypt*, Chicago 1950
Petuchowski, J., '*Hōshī‘āh nā* in Ps. 118.25: a Prayer for Rain', *VT* 5, 1955, pp. 266–71
Plutarch, *De Iside et Osiride* (ed. J. G. Griffiths), Cardiff 1970
Porada, E. (ed.), *Corpus of Ancient Near Eastern Seals in North American Collections* I, Washington 1948

Porter, J. R., 'The Interpretation of II Sam. 6 and Ps. 132', *JTS* n.s. 5, 1954, pp. 161–73
'The Succession of Joshua', *Proclamation and Presence: Essays in Honour of G. Henton Davies*, ed. J. I. Durham and J. R. Porter, pp. 102–32
Posener, G., *De la divinité du Pharaon*, Paris 1960
Pritchard, J. B. (ed.), *Ancient Near Eastern Texts*, 2nd ed., Princeton 1955
The Ancient Near East in Pictures, Princeton 1954
The Ancient Near East: supplementary texts and pictures, Princeton 1969
von Rad, G., 'Das judäische Königsritual', *Theologische Literaturzeitung*, 1947, pp. 211–16. Translated as ch. 10 of his *The Problem of the Hexateuch*
Old Testament Theology I–II, ET Edinburgh 1962–5
Der heilige Krieg im alten Israel, 4th ed., Göttingen 1965
The Problem of the Hexateuch and Other Essays, ET Edinburgh 1966
Ridderbos, N., †'The Structure of Ps. 40', *OTS* 14, 1965, pp. 296–304
Die Psalmen, BZAW 117, 1972
Ringgren, H., 'Einige Bemerkungen zum 73 Psalm', *VT* 3, 1953, pp. 265–72
The Messiah in the OT, ET (SBT 18), 1956
'Some Religious Aspects of the Caliphate' (*Numen* Sup. 4), 1959, pp. 737–48
'Hieros gamos i Egypten, Sumer och Israel', *Religion och Bibel* 18, 1959, pp. 23–51
'Deuterojesaja och kultspråket', *Teologinen Aikakauskirja* 72, 1967, pp. 166–76
'The Religion of Ancient Syria', *HR*, pp. 195–222. See also under Botterweck
Roberts, J. M., 'The Davidic Origin of the Zion Tradition', *JBL* 92, 1973, pp. 329–44
Rowley, H. (ed.), *The OT and Modern Study*, Oxford 1951
Sanders, J. A., *The Psalms Scroll of Qumran Cave 11*, Oxford 1965
†*The Dead Sea Psalms Scroll*, New York 1967
de Savignac, J., 'Essai d'interprétation du Ps. 110 à l'aide de la littérature égyptienne', *OTS* 9, 1951, pp. 107–35
Sawyer, J. F., 'An Analysis of the Context and Meaning of the Psalm-headings', *Transactions of the Glasgow University Oriental Society* 22, 1967–8, pp. 26–38
Schmidt, H., *Das Gebet der Angeklagten im Alten Testament* (BZAW 49), 1928
Die Thronfahrt Jahwes, Tübingen 1927
†*Die Psalmen* (HAT 15), 1934
Seux, M.-J., *Épithètes royales akkadiennes et sumériennes*, Paris 1967
Smend, R., 'Ueber das Ich der Psalmen', *ZAW* 8, 1888, pp. 49–147
Snaith, N. H., *The Jewish New Year Festival* (= *JNYF*), London 1948
Isaiah 40–66, in *VT* Sup. 14, 1967, pp. 135–262
von Soden, W., 'Gibt es ein Zeugnis dafür, dass die Babylonier an die

Wiederauferstehung Marduks geglaubt haben?', *ZA* n.f. 17, 1955, pp. 130–66

Soggin, J. A., *Das Königtum in Israel* (BZAW 104), 1967

Sorg, R., *Habakkuk 3 and Selah*, Fifield, Wisconsin, 1968

Stummer, F., *Sumerisch-akkadische Parallelen zum Aufbau alttestamentlicher Psalmen*, Paderborn 1922

Thomas, D. Winton, '*ṣlmwt* in the OT', *JSS* 7, 1962, pp. 191–200
'Belial in the OT', *Biblical and Patristic Studies in memory of R. P. Casey*, ed. J. N. Birdsall and R. W. Thomson, Freiburg 1963, pp. 11–19
The Text of the Revised Psalter, London 1963

de Vaux, R., *Ancient Israel*, ET London 1961

te Velde, H., *Seth, God of Confusion*, Leiden 1967

Volz, P., †*Das Neujahrsfest Jahwes*, Tübingen 1912
Jesaia II (KAT 9.2), 1932

Wagner, M., *Die lexikalischen und grammatikalischen Aramäismen* (BZAW 96), 1966

Weiser, A., *Die Psalmen* (ATD 14–15), 7th ed., 1966; ET of 5th ed. of 1959, *The Psalms* (OTL), 1962

Weissbach, F. H., *Die Keilinschriften der Achämeniden*, Leipzig 1911, reprint 1968

Wellhausen, J., *Prolegomena to the History of Israel*, ET Edinburgh 1885

Westermann, C., *The Praise of God in the Psalms*, ET London 1966
†*Isaiah 40–66*, ET (OTL) 1969

Widengren, G., *The Accadian and Hebrew Psalms of Lamentation*, Stockholm 1937
'Konungens vistelse in dödsriket: Ps. 88', *SEÅ* 10, 1945, pp. 66–81
Muhammed, the Apostle of God and his Ascension, UUÅ 1955
Sakrales Königtum im Alten Testament und im Judentum (= *SK*), Stuttgart 1955
'Early Hebrew Myths', *MRK*, pp. 149–203
see also under Bleeker

Willesen, F., 'The Cultic Situation of Ps. 74', *VT* 2, 1952, pp. 289–306

Wiseman, D. J., 'Alalakh', *Archaeology and OT Study*, ed. D. Winton Thomas, Oxford 1967, pp. 118–35

Würthwein, E., 'Erwägungen zu Ps. 73', in *Festschrift fur A. Bertholet*, Tübingen 1950, pp. 532–49

Zimmerli, W. and Jeremias, J., *The Servant of God*, ET (SBT 21), 1957

Zimmerli, W., *Ezechiel* (BKAT XIII), 1969

Zimmern, H., *Zum babylonischen Neujahrsfest* I–II, in *Berichte . . . der sächsischen Gesellschaft der Wissenschaft*, Berlin, vol. 58, 1906, pp. 126f.; vol. 70/5, 1918

Zorell, F., *Lexicon Hebraicum*, Rome 1966

SELECT INDEXES

Actualize, 127
ʿānī, 8of., 180
Anoint, 59, 95, 98, 112, 118f., 139, 144, 151, 156f., 168
Aramaism, 82, 208 n.40
Ark, 125f.
ʾašērē, 193

Balla, E., 13
Bentzen, A., 17
Bernhardt, K.-H., 203 n.1
Beyerlin, W., 8
Bič, M., 19
Birkeland, H., 12f., 24
bll, 205 n.31
Burial, 162f.

Calendar, 97, 104f.
Chosen, 146, 149, 151
Correspondence of heavenly and earthly, 144, 153f., 171
Counsel, 43, 67, 205 n.43
Crown, 117, 121, 146, 149, 153, 177, 206 n.38

Dahood, M., 19
Day of Atonement, 104f., 177f.
Delekat, L., 7
Deutero-Isaiah, 107
Democratization, 15, 24, 29, 41
Dynasty (continuance), 159, 161f., 165, 184f.

Eaton, J. H., 19f.
Engnell, I., 17f.

Enthronement in autumn festival, God, 105f., 108; man, 112
Enthronement Psalms, 104f.
Eschatology, 108, 110, 134, 160

Glory, 145f., 161, 164
Gunkel, H., 2f., 23f., 25, 105, 108

Hand (grasping etc.), 5, 63, 77, 143, 157f.
ḥāsīd, 67, 151
headings of psalms, 18, 20f., 29, 32, 35, 47, 49, 53, 58–60, 65, 67, 71, 75, 79, 80f., 83, 115, 119, 124f., 149, 178
ḥesed, 152f.

Incomparability of God, 193
Incubation, 28, 30, 33, 66, 67, 78, 131, 175f.
Intercession, 78f.

Johnson, A. R., 109f., 133f.
Judge (king as), 176f.

Kraus, H.-J., 9, 110f.

lemaʿan, p.204 n.15
Lipiński, E., 207

Marriage, 118f.
Morgenstern, J., 206 n.16
Mowinckel, S., 11f., 16, 23, 102f., 133

ndb, 205 n.41
New song, 43, 127, 185, 192

Personify, 153-5
Pleasure (God's in king), 140, 146, 157
Plutarch, 109
Portion, 66, 85, 152, 164
Predestination, 148
Prostration, 146

Ringgren, H., 19
Roberts, J. M., 207 n.25

Sacrifice, 42, 44, 72, 82, 85, 92, 94, 156, 164-7, 173f., 179, 185, 187f.
ṣaddiq, 151f.
Sanders, J. A., 21

Schmidt, H., 6, 109
Shadow, 5, 38, 57, 143f., 165
Shepherd, 40, 136, 149f., 206 n.32
Smend, R., 13
Symbolic actions, 62, 69, 78, 89f., 98f., 101, 106, 108f., 110f., 174

Thanksgiving (sacrifice of), 187f.
Throne, 142-4, 162
tōrā, 142
Tree, 59, 73, 152, 168

Volz, P., 103f., 106f.

Weiser, A., 10
Westermann, C., 207 n.24
Widengren, G., 30, 119

Zimmern, H., 94f.

In the section on the Psalms, bold type indicates the basic treatment

Exodus
28.36f. 177
32.32 179

Numbers
25.4 179

Judges
8.23 200

I Samuel
1–2 10
8 200
11.14 207 n.33

II Samuel
3 195
7 159
14.11 195
15.31f. 195
21 179
21.17 200
23.1f. 187, 142

I Kings
3.5 196
3.9 177
8 177
10.9 146

II Kings
3.27 179
21 200

I Chronicles 21f.
28.5 142
29.23 142

Psalms
2 **111f.**, 196
2.6 145
2.10f. 181
3 4f., 9f., **27f.**
3.3 140
4 **29f.**
4.3f. 182, 196
4.4 151
4.8f. 170
5 **65**
5.9 174
5.11 138
7 10, **30f.**
7.7 154
7.12f. 197
9–10 **32f.**, 133, 184, 186, 191
11 **65f.**
11.1f. 182
11.3 152
16 **66f.**, 163f.
16.7 175
16.10 151
17 **33f.**
17.3 175
17.4 154
17.7 138
17.8 144

17.15 175
18 **113f.**, 188f.
18.2 169
18.20 146
18.21f. 141, 166, 189f.
18.31 154
18.32 193
18.47f. 166, 193
18.50 183
18.51 153, 162
20 **116f.**, 155, 197
21 **117**
21.2–7 145, 153, 161, 169, 197
21.8–13 139
22 7, 18, 19, 22, **34f.**, 132, 178, 191
22.9 140
22.10f. 147
22.23f. 184
22.27f. 166f.
23 **36f.**, 189f.
23.3 174
23.6 153
27 **39f.**, 186
27.1–3 189
27.4 170
27.8 176
28 **40f.**
28.9 136

Psalms (*cont.*)
31 **67f.**, 194
35 **41f.**
35.27 150
36 **69,** 167
36.2 176
40 **42f.**, 133, 191
40.2–6 185, 189,
                190, 193
40.7f. 180, 185
40.12 153
41 **44f.**, 194
41.4 148
41.13 143
42–43 **69f.**, 185
42.2f. 170, 174f.
42.5 174
42.9 153, 175
43.3 153, 174
44 **61**
44.5f. 139
45 **118f.**, 139, 142
45.7 142f.
45.8 144
45.17f. 162
48 108f.
49 38
51 **71f.**, 178f.
51.8 148
51.12–14 157
51.16f. 187
51.18f. 180f.
52 **73,** 197
52.3f. 182
54 **73f.**, 138, 156
54.7 153
55 **74f.**
55.23 148
56 **75,** 178
56.5f. 154
57 **46f.**
57.4 153
57.8–11 183
59 **47**
59.11 153
59.14 136
60 **61**
61 38, **47**

61.5 143
61.7f. 161
61.8 153
61.9 183
62 **49f.**
62.4 182
62.8 145, 171
62.9f. 176, 182
63 5, **50f.**, 143
63.2 170
63.3 145, 175
63.4f. 153, 169f.,
            183, 194
63.9 174
65 8
66 **51**
66.18f. 190, 194
69 7, **51f.**, 156, 167
69.10 138
69.31f. 188
70 **53f.**
71 **54f.**, 133
71.3 154
71.5 147
71.7–24 140, 186f.,
                192
72 **120**
72.1f. 141
72.8, 11 159
72.17 162
73 **75f.**
73.13f. 179
73.19f. 164, 175
74 61
75 **55f.**, 151
75.5f. 181
77 **79,** 192
77.9 155
77.14 193
78.70–72 149
80 61
83 61
84 61
86 **79f.**, 186
89 **56f.**, **181f.**, 144–
        96 *passim*
89.37f. 184
91 **57f.**

91.1f. 143
91.4 153
91.8 139
91.11f. 144
91.13 159
91.14 155, 169
91.16 161
92 **58f.**, 168, 191
92.1–7 187
92.13 152
94 **59f.**, 135f.
94.8f. 182
94.12 192
101 **122f.**, 141, 197
102 **80f.**, 178
108 **60f.**
109 **81**
110 **124f.**
110.1 139f.
110.3 147, 166
110.5 157
116 81f., 188
116.1 169
116.16 150
117 82
118 8, **61f.**, **131f.**,
            139
118.1–4 153
118.5 195
118.8f. 192
118.10f. 155f.
118.17f. 147, 179
118.19 183
118.22, 27 166
118.29 153
120 **82f.**
121 **83**
121.5 158
132 **125**
132.17f. 162
138 **63**
138.1 184
138.2 154
139 **23f.**
140 **63f.**
141 **24f.**
141.2 180
142 **85**

Psalms (cont.)
143 **64**
144 **127f.**
144.1, 3f. 193
144.9f. 183
144.10 162
144.11f. 166

Isaiah 107, 200
11.1 162
42.1 146
52.7f. 107
55.4 183

Jeremiah
8.19 106f.

22.28 68
22–23 200
26.1 113

Lamentations
1.6 71
2.9 142
4.20 140, 166, 200

Ezekiel
34.23f. 164
37 200

Amos 107

Nahum 106

Habakkuk 32, 106

Zephaniah 106

Zechariah
9.9 206 n.47
14.16f. 106

Mark
1.11 146

John
5.30 177